THE PRACTICAL BOOK OF CHINAWARE

PLATE 1

WORCESTER PLATTER

Scale blue border, exotic multi-coloured birds, butterflies and insects in shaped reserved white panels edged with gilt Rococo scrolls. Centre white, with birds

Courtesy of the British Museum

The Practical Book of
CHINAWARE

BY

HAROLD DONALDSON EBERLEIN

AND

ROGER WEARNE RAMSDELL

*With 205 Reproductions and Diagrams
Including 12 in Full Color*

HALCYON HOUSE

NEW YORK

COPYRIGHT, 1925, BY J. B. LIPPINCOTT COMPANY

HALCYON HOUSE EDITION, JULY, 1936
Reprinted, October, 1936
Reprinted, May, 1937
Reprinted, October, 1938

HALCYON HOUSE *editions are published and distributed by Blue Ribbon Books, Inc., 386 Fourth Avenue, New York City.*

PRINTED IN THE UNITED STATES OF AMERICA
BY THE CORNWALL PRESS, INC., CORNWALL, N. Y.

TO THE MASTER AND MISTRESS OF HAR-
INGTON HOUSE, BOURTON-ON-THE-WATER,
GLOUCESTERSHIRE, THIS VOLUME IS DED-
ICATED WITH SINCERE FRIENDSHIP AND
REGARDS

FOREWORD

THIS is the only work in one volume that covers the chinaware of all countries. It is a complete compendium for the collector and all in search of information, fully setting forth the essential facts, systematically arranged for easy and ready consultation, and with many cross references and comparisons.

The novice, who delights in the beauties and possession of old china, but knows little about the means of identifying the various kinds he admires or seeks, will find herein the key and a trusty guide for his quest.

The collector of long experience, who is familiar with the characteristics of many different makes of china and is usually able to identify them from personal knowledge without other assistance, will nevertheless find in this volume the necessary data for reference or comparison which few can hope to carry wholly in their heads and for which it is convenient to turn to an handbook. The book has been schemed throughout to make it especially convenient for just this sort of ready consultation. The comparative tables and cross references will be found particularly helpful for this purpose.

"Of making many books there is no end," might well be said of books about chinaware and porcelain in general. The subject has always been peculiarly alluring, and to glance at a bibliography of the books that have been written, dealing with one phase or another of the ceramic art, is positively appalling. In the face of such a multitude of volumes, it may be asked why the authors venture to put forth another. The answer is simple. It is, just because there are so many other books and because none of them covers the ground in the same way.

Many of these books deal with only some one particular kind of china, or with some particular phase of its manufacture. Many others are so highly specialised on the purely technical side of manufacture as to be of little direct value to the average person. Many more are so loosely arranged and so diffuse in generalities that they are almost useless for casual reference; extended search and perusal are necessary in order to get at any specific facts. Many are in foreign languages. Many are out of print. To have even a third of them for consultation would mean a fair-sized library on chinaware alone.

In the present volume it has been the aim of the authors so to marshal the facts and condense the statements that convenience of use may be assured and waste of time through searching in the wrong place avoided. They have endeavoured, so to speak, to reduce the subject to its lowest terms and to present the essential facts in such order and arrangement that all the aspects and interrelations may be quickly grasped. In other words, they have tried to make a usable book, and its usability is its justification.

It has seemed not only advisable but absolutely necessary to set limits of date beyond which the different sorts of china cannot be considered. These limits extend from the beginnings of manufacture to 1840, and they are set for the following reasons. First of all, china, like everything else, suffered from the nineteenth century collapse that befell good design and good taste, a collapse that had become general by 1840. Thereafter, for a long time, there was little made that was worth recording. Second, the fashion for one factory to copy the works of another, though always practised to some extent, had grown so common by this date that individuality was at a discount.

FOREWORD

Third, were all the modern varieties of china to be included, the bulk of the volume would be unmanageable and much of the matter contained would not interest the majority of readers. Fourth, the characteristics of modern china are sufficiently well known and the different sorts bear enough identification to make notice herein unnecessary.

This book deals only with such china as the person of average means can expect to have, either by way of inherited ownership or by purchase. What are distinctly "museum" rarities are omitted; space devoted to them would little avail most readers. The rarer kinds of Oriental porcelain, therefore, are not considered; besides, they are very fully treated in books exclusively devoted to them. For the same reason—unlikelihood or impossibility of acquisition—various European porcelains are mentioned only in general historical notices and without the detailed discussion bestowed on the varieties of china made more extensively and over a longer period. Such, for example, are the sixteenth century Medici porcelain, made in Florence, and the seventeenth century porcelain made at Rouen. In cases like these the manufacture lasted for only a very short time and comparatively few pieces were made. To-day there are less than fifty authentic specimens of the Medici china known, and the Rouen china is likewise about equally rare. Needless to say, all the known examples of either have been jealously cherished for years past in either museums or well-known private collections, so that there is not the least chance of the china-lover or collector lighting upon anything of the sort by way of a "find."

Following the general introductory matter, the arrangement of this volume goes by countries. First comes the china of China along with the Japanese porcelain; in this division are treated those sorts of Oriental china that exercised a profound influence on early European design and those sorts that found their way to the West in large enough quantities to make them well known features of domestic plenishing in England and America in previous generations. Amongst these last will be found the so-called Lowestoft that never saw the town of Lowestoft. Next follow the china products of the different European countries. Then comes the chinaware of England and America, appearing last so that the reader may see straightway how far foreign influences have or have not affected the art in the forms most familiar to the majority of us.

There are five factors to consider in judging a piece of chinaware—the body or "paste," the glaze, the makers' marks, the manner of decoration and the character of the colours. These are all dealt with in their appropriate places.

In conclusion the authors wish to thank all who have contributed to the making of this volume, but especially William Burton, Esquire, for his many kindnesses in criticism and his courteous permission to quote several passages from his writings; the authorities of the British Museum and of the Victoria and Albert Museum, especially W. W. Winkworth, Esquire, A. G. Cook, Esquire, Eric Maclagan, Esquire, Bernard Rackham, Esquire, and William King, Esquire; Doctor Samuel W. Woodhouse, Jr., Esquire, of the Pennsylvania Museum in Philadelphia, Henry Batsford, Esquire, and the directors of the Museums at Worcester and Doccia; and Messrs. Reeves and Turner for the gracious permission to use a number of the marks from Chaffers.

HAROLD DONALDSON EBERLEIN
ROGER WEARNE RAMSDELL

BROADWAY, WORCESTERSHIRE
April, 1925

CONTENTS

	PAGE
"China-Mania"	1
What Chinaware Is	14
The Making of Chinaware	22
General Advice to the Student of Chinaware	30
Oriental Chinaware and the West	38
Italian Chinaware	83
Medici	83
Ginori (Doccia)	84
Venice	92
Capo di Monte	95
Le Nove	100
Vinovo (Torino)	101
Rome	102
Este (Ferrara)	102
French Chinaware	103
Rouen	103
St. Cloud	105
Lille	110
Chantilly	111
Mennecy-Villeroy	115
Vincennes	119
Sceaux	127
Tournay	129
Orléans	132
Sèvres	133
Bourg-la-Reine	149
Arras	150
St. Amand	151
Paris	151
Vaux	158
Lauraguais	166
Strasburg	166
Niderviller	169
Marseilles	172
Limoges	172
Valenciennes	173
Caen	174
Spanish and Portuguese	176

CONTENTS

	PAGE
GERMAN CHINAWARE	178
DRESDEN (MEISSEN)—SAXONY	178
BERLIN—PRUSSIA	187
HÖCHST	190
NYMPHENBURG—BAVARIA	192
FÜRSTENBERG—BRUNSWICK	195
LUDWIGSBURG—WURTEMBURG	197
FRANKENTHAL—BADEN	198
ANSBACH—THURINGIA	200
AUSTRIAN CHINAWARE	201
VIENNA	201
HEREND (HUNGARY)	203
SWISS CHINAWARE	205
NYON	205
ZURICH	206
DUTCH AND BELGIAN CHINAWARE	207
WEESP	207
AMSTERDAM	207
LOOSDRECHT	208
OUDE AMSTEL	208
NIEUWE AMSTEL	208
THE HAGUE	210
BRUSSELS	211
SWEDISH AND DANISH CHINAWARE	213
MARIEBERG	213
COPENHAGEN	215
RUSSIAN AND POLISH CHINAWARE	218
ST. PETERSBURG	218
MOSCOW	219
KORZEC	219
ENGLISH CHINAWARE	220
BOW	220
CHELSEA	230
WORCESTER	240
DERBY	247
LONGTON HALL	251
LIVERPOOL	253
LOWESTOFT	254
PLYMOUTH	258
BRISTOL	260
NEW HALL	264
PINXTON AND TORKSEY	266

CONTENTS

ENGLISH CHINAWARE—*Continued*   PAGE
    CAUGHLEY 268
    CHURCH GRESLEY 268
    COALPORT 271
    SPODE 273
    MINTON 278
    DAVENPORT (LONGPORT) 278
    WEDGWOOD (ETRURIA) 279
    NANTGARW 280
    SWANSEA 282
    ROCKINGHAM 285
    WIRKSWORTH 287
    MADELEY 288
    LANE DELPH (MASON) 291
    CAULDON (RIDGWAY) 291

AMERICAN CHINAWARE 293
    NORTH CAMBRIDGE 294
    PHILADELPHIA (SOUTHWARK) 294
    BERGEN (NEW JERSEY) 296
    NEW YORK 297
    PHILADELPHIA (TUCKER) 297

BIBLIOGRAPHY 303
INDEX 311

ILLUSTRATIONS

Plate		Page
1	Worcester Platter................(Colour Plate) *Frontispiece*	
2	Table of Characteristic Contours........................	4
3	Characteristic Types of Decoration......................	4
4	Covered Blue and White Ming Jar......................	4
5	A. Blue and White Ming Bowl........................	4
	B. Blue and White Ming Platter......................	20
6	Sea-Green Celadon Vase.............................	20
7	A. "Rice Grain" Cup and Saucer.....................	20
	B. Blue and White Pierced Cup......................	20
	C. "White Ware" Prunus Blossom Cup................	20
8	Blue and White Prunus or "Hawthorn" Jar.............	20
9	"Batavian" Vase, "Dead-Leaf" Brown Glaze............	20
10	Chinese "Imari" Platter...................(Colour Plate)	24
11	A. Blue and White K'ang Hsi Bowl...................	36
	B. Blue and White Ming Plate.......................	36
12	Two Eighteenth Century Blue and White Plates..........	36
13	Eight-Sided K'ang Hsi Bowl.........................	36
14	Eighteenth Century Polychrome Tray...................	36
15	K'ang Hsi Bowl, Nankin Yellow Ground................	52
16	A. K'ang Hsi Polychrome Plate......................	52
	B. K'ang Hsi Plate *Jouee-Head* Border...............	52
17	A. *Famille Rose* Octagonal Plate............(Colour Plate)	56
	B. *Famille Verte* Plate....................(Colour Plate)	56
18	A. Plate with Red Bat Decoration....................	60
	B. Eighteenth Century Octagonal Plate................	60
19	A. Blue and Gold Cup and Saucer, Eighteenth Century...	60
	B. Seventeenth Century Cup and Saucer...............	60
20	A. K'ang Hsi Plate, "Mandarin" Figures..............	60
	B. Eighteenth Century "Jesuit" Plate.................	60
21	A. Eighteenth Century Plate with Waved Rim..........	60
	B. Chinese "Lowestoft" Mug........................	60
22	A. Chinese "Lowestoft" Beaker Vase.................	68
	B. Chinese "Lowestoft" Covered Jar.................	68
23	A. Small Chinese "Lowestoft" Bowl..................	68
	B. Chinese Green "Lowestoft" Sauce Boat.............	68
24	"Lowestoft" Helmet Cream Jug and Sugar Bason........	76
25	A. "Lowestoft" Cup, Black Decoration................	76
	B. "Lowestoft" Saucer, Transfer Imitation.............	76
26	A. Eighteenth Century "Lowestoft" Teapot............	76
	B. "Lowestoft" Teapot, Brown Monochrome...........	76

ILLUSTRATIONS

27	A. Apple-Green "Lowestoft" Platter	76
	B. "Lowestoft" Dish, Strawberry Decoration	76
28	Japanese Imari Platter (Colour Plate)	78
29	A. Eight-Sided Hizen Polychrome Bowl	84
	B. Kutani Pear-Shaped Polychrome Bottle	84
30	Bowl of Medici China	84
31	Ginori Platter, 1737	84
32	A. Ginori Ice Pail, "Dresden" Manner	84
	B. Ginori Soup Plate, Moulded Rim	84
33	A. Ginori Platter, Chinese Peony Decoration	92
	B. Ginori Covered Dish, Modelled Ornament	92
34	A. Ginori Plate, "Empire" Style	92
	B. Ginori Plate, Oriental Decoration	92
35	A. Ginori Neo-Classic Urn-Shaped Jar	92
	B. Ginori Neo-Classic Chocolate Pot	92
36	A. Ginori Sweetmeat Dish, with Medallion	92
	B. Ginori Tureen on Legs	92
37	Ginori Modelled Figures	100
38	A and B. Ginori Cups and Saucers, Monochrome	100
	C. Ginori Reproduction of Capo di Monte Figure	100
39	A. Sceaux Ice Pail (Colour Plate)	98
	B. Ginori Oval Platter (Colour Plate)	108
40	A. Capo di Monte Cup	108
	B. Naples "Pompeian" Tureen and Platter	108
41	Le Nove Jardinière	108
42	A. Venetian Cup and Saucer	108
	B. Venetian Tray with Shaped Rim	108
43	A. St. Cloud Moulded Flower Pot	108
	B. St. Cloud "Prunus" Blossom Teapot	108
44	A. St. Cloud Jar, Blue Baroque Decoration	116
	B. St. Cloud Jar, Polychrome Reliefs	116
45	Chantilly Gravy Boat, "Kakiyemon" Manner	116
46	A and B. Chantilly Flower Pot and Lobate Dish	116
	C. Chantilly Oval Pierced Fruit Dish	116
47	Mennecy-Villeroy Vase	116
48	A. Mennecy-Villeroy Covered Jar	124
	B. Mennecy-Villeroy Covered Dish	124
49	Three Vincennes Vases	124
50	A. Tournai Flower Pot	124
	B. Arras Flower Pot, Blue Decoration	124
51	A. Dresden Plate, "Kakiyemon" Manner (Colour Plate)	126
	B. Sèvres Green Covered Jar (Colour Plate)	126
52	A. Sèvres "Directoire" Cup and Saucer	132
	B. Sèvres Diapered Cup and Saucer	132
53	Sèvres "Vine and Trellis" Teapot	132

ILLUSTRATIONS

54	A. Sèvres Octagon Plate	132
	B. Sèvres Flare-Top Cup and Saucer	132
55	Sèvres Jug, Empire Shape	132
56	A. Sèvres Cup and Saucer, Empire Shape	140
	B. Sèvres Cup and Saucer	140
57	Blue and Gold Bowl and Ewer	140
58	A. Caen Jug, Empire Shape	140
	B. Empire Jug, All Gold Decoration	140
59	A. Niderviller Flower Pot	140
	B. Valenciennes Covered Sugar Bason	140
60	A. Dresden "Onion" Pattern Soup Plate	148
	B. Dresden Cup and Saucer, Typical Flowers	148
61	A. Early Dresden Chocolate Pot	148
	B. Early Dresden Jug	148
62	A. Dresden Figure of Lace Maker	148
	B. Dresden Jardinière	148
63	A. Nymphenburg Flower Pot	148
	B. Höchst Sauce Boat	148
64	A. Berlin Tea Caddy	156
	B. Ansbach Teapot	156
65	Ludwigsburg Tureen	156
66	A. Vienna Milk Jug, Empire Shape	156
	B. Nymphenburg Cup and Saucer	156
67	A. Herend Tray with Pierced Rim	156
	B. Copenhagen Soup Tureen	156
68	A. Bow Blue and White Plate, Chinese Manner	172
	B. Bow Blue and White Sauce Boat, Chinese Manner	172
	C. Bow Sauce Boat, Rococo Manner	172
	D. Bow Sauce Boat, "White Ware"	172
69	A. Bow Mug with Bulging Base	172
	B. Bow Globular Teapot	172
70	A. Bow Pierced Fruit Dish	172
	B. Bow Plate, Moulded Rim	172
71	A. Bow Vase in the White	172
	B. Bow Vase, Cobalt Ground	172
	C. Bow Candlestick, Modelled Figure	172
72	A. Bow Pierced Fruit-Dish and Stand	180
	B. Barrel-Shaped Chelsea Mug	180
73	Chelsea Oblong Octagonal Platter	180
74	A. Chelsea Fluted Chocolate Pot	180
	B. Chelsea Eight-Sided Vase	180
75	A. Chelsea Flower Holder	180
	B. Late Chelsea Covered Sugar Bason	180
76	A. Bristol Tray (Colour Plate)	222
	B. Lowestoft Cup and Saucer (Colour Plate)	222

ILLUSTRATIONS

77	A. Worcester "Imari" Teapot	228
	B. Worcester "Imari" Plate	228
78	Late Worcester Landscape Plate	228
79	A. Worcester Blue and White Bowl	228
	B. Worcester Plate, Shaped Reserved Panels	228
80	Worcester Chocolate Pot, "Mandarin" Figures	228
81	Worcester Vase, Late Period	236
82	Worcester Chocolate Pot, Domed Lid	236
83	Worcester Soup Plate, Green Monochrome	236
84	Early Worcester Apple Green Mug	236
85	A. Derby Oval Butter Dish	244
	B. Derby Vase, Blue Ground	244
86	A. Derby Plate, Flowered Border	244
	B. Derby Plate, "Imari" Manner	244
87	A. Derby Arabesque Cup and Saucer	244
	B. Derby Bowl	244
88	Plymouth Covered Jar, Chinese Shape	244
89	Plymouth Mug, Swelling Base	252
90	A. Plymouth Mug	252
	B. Plymouth Sauce Boat, Rococo Shape	252
91	Bristol Chocolate Pot, Domed Lid	252
92	A. Bristol Pear-Shaped Chocolate Pot	252
	B. Bristol Figure of *Autumn*	252
93	A. Bristol Plate with Birds and Butterflies	260
	B. Bristol Plate with Flowers and Ribbons	260
94	A. Eighteenth Century Chinese Powder-Blue Vase. (Colour Plate)	254
	B. Caughley Mug (Colour Plate)	254
95	A. Lowestoft Small Bowl	260
	B. Lowestoft Mug, Cornflower Decoration	260
96	A. Lowestoft Butter Boat	260
	B. Lowestoft Cream Jug	260
	C. Lowestoft Pierced Fruit Basket	260
97	A. Caughley Saucer, Blue and Gold Decoration	260
	B. Caughley Two-Handled, Covered Cup	260
98	A. Spode Oblong Sugar Bason	268
	B. Caughley Oval Sugar Bason	268
99	A. Spode Covered Butter Dish	268
	B. Spode Stone-China Plate	268
100	Spode Oval Dish, Transfer Printed	268
101	A and B. Spode Butter Dish and Tray	268
102	A. Spode Vase, "Imari" Decoration	276
	B and C. Spode Cup and Saucers, "Imari" Manner	276
103	A. New Hall Cup and Saucer	276
	B. New Hall Straight-Sided Teapot	276

ILLUSTRATIONS   xix

104	A. Swansea Vase, Modelled Flowers	276
	B. Pinxton Jardinière	276
105	A. Nantgarw Plate, Flower *Motifs*	276
	B. Nantgarw Plate, Reserved Panels	276
106	Nantgarw Plate, Bird *Motif*	284
107	A. Coalport Cup and Saucer	284
	B. Nantgarw Inkpot, Empire Shape	284
108	A. Coalport Butter Dish in Tray	284
	B. Coalport Cylindrical Vase	284
109	A. Rockingham Sugar Bason	284
	B. Rockingham Jug	284
110	A. Liverpool Cup and Saucer	292
	B. Longton Hall Vase	292
111	A. Tucker Shell-Shaped Dish	292
	B. Tucker Jug, Characteristic Shape	292
112	A. Tucker Sugar Bason, c. 1830	292
	B. Tucker Coffee Pot, c. 1830	292
113	Large Tucker Water Jug, Typical Shape	292
114	A. Small Tucker Plate	292
	B. Vase-Shaped Tucker Jug	292
115	A. Fragment of Southwark Porcelain	292
	B. Oriental Teapot and Cups, Seventeenth Century	292
116	A. Blue Staffordshire Plate	292
	B. Liverpool Jug, c. 1800	292

DIAGRAMS

Fig.		
1	Characteristic Chinese Porcelain Shapes	57
2	Characteristic Chinese Porcelain Shapes	58
3	Characteristic Diaper Patterns used in Chinese Porcelain	68
4	Characteristic Diaper Patterns used in Chinese Porcelain	69
5	Characteristic Diaper Patterns used in Chinese Porcelain	70
6	Typical Emblems used in Chinese Porcelain	72
7	Typical Emblems used in Chinese Porcelain	73

THE PRACTICAL BOOK OF CHINAWARE

"CHINA-MANIA"

"CHINA-MANIA" was an epidemic that once held the whole of Europe in polite and beneficent thrall. Its furore was as great as "tulip mania," but longer-lived; for the results of both we have cause to be thankful. Chinaware was the "new toy" of the Western world from the middle of the seventeenth century until the eighteenth was well advanced. During all that time the enthusiasm for Oriental chinaware maintained an intensity that we of to-day, accustomed as we are to the finest porcelains of East and West, find it hard to understand. However much we may sincerely delight in rare or beautiful chinaware, the keenness of our admiration for porcelain as porcelain—porcelain as the embodiment of certain physical properties—is somewhat blunted by constant association. We have been used to it from infancy. We take it as a matter of course; it is a familiar incident of everyday life. Even though we may treasure no especially noteworthy porcelain amongst our own household possessions, we know it well in the collections of museums. To our seventeenth century forebears, however, the wondrous quality of the porcelain substance was a revelation that provoked unmeasured delight. They straightway recognised porcelain as the most patrician product of the potter's art and paid homage to its worth.

But, over and above the charm of an hitherto almost unknown substance of exquisite delicacy and refinement, which extended trade with the Orient had placed within their reach, there were combined with it the marvels of glowing, brilliant colour, the engaging patterns of decoration, and a beguiling novelty in the diversity of shapes. It is no wonder that chinaware won an instant hold upon their affections. Personal whim and the behests of fashion doubtless played their parts at first in establishing the sway of chinaware, but its own intrinsic excellences made so strong an appeal to common-sense and good taste that the permanency of its place could never afterward be in question.

We are so used to chinaware as a part of the daily machinery of polite life that it is an effort to envision the way of things before china cups and saucers, plates, platters and dishes became commonly accepted table plenishings. The nobility and gentry had table services of silver or pewter, pewter of course being much the more abundant. At the same time, there was a certain amount of Delft pottery in use. Even amongst the less well to do there was usually a plentiful garnishing of pewter, while the hinds were content with simple and substantial earthenware that would come under the head of crockery.

The habit of drinking tea, coffee and chocolate, which came into vogue about the middle of the seventeenth century and gained headway with amazing rapidity, gave the initial impetus to a general introduction of chinaware and supplied the stimulus for its popular acquisition. So long as ale was a prevalent breakfast beverage, or meet for polite tween-meals refreshment in the afternoon, the most fastidious could be quite content with mugs and tankards of silver or pewter. But these new exotic drinks required something different. Imagine drinking tea out of a pewter tankard! The glamour would be gone and the flavour would be annihilated. Tea pre-eminently, and coffee and chocolate in scarcely less degree, demanded the association of porcelain both for the sake of the flavour and also on æsthetic grounds. It was natural that these foreign potables should be accompanied by vessels deemed appropriate to their serving in the countries of their origin. This was peculiarly true in the case of tea, the subtleties of whose taste and fragrance could so easily be destroyed by contact with a wrong substance. Fashion prescribed dainty cups of porcelain, later designated "China-ware" from the place of its provenance, although "Gombroon ware" was an earlier name to which we shall have occasion to allude hereafter.

Fashion having set the seal of its approval upon tea-drinking and the use of porcelain therefor, the chief devotees of fashion accordingly employed tea tackle of the choicest chinaware they could come by. The emulative instinct in humanity has ever been the same. What the leading devotees of fashion did, that other folk imitated as fast as they could. And thus the use of teacups and their related accompaniments became one of the foremost means of causing a general, popular and intimate acquaintance with the worth and desirability of chinaware. The old table services of pewter or silver were not summarily abandoned the instant china teacups came into the house, but once the possessors of porcelain tea equipage learned to appreciate the elegance and manifold fascination of chinaware—and this they did very soon—it was only a short time before other items of chinaware multiplied with amazing rapidity until its possession became a positive mania and complete table services of porcelain became the pride of their owners' hearts. Queen Mary was a sincere admirer and ardent collector of chinaware and her example had much to do with firmly fixing its hold upon popular esteem. China-mania and the Queen's precedent were responsible for evolving a new article of furniture —the hooded china cabinet with glass doors that made its appearance as a distinctive mobiliary item of the William and Mary period. This gave an opportunity to display, without undue ostentation, the choice pieces of porcelain that china-lovers delighted to acquire.

What was true in England was also true in the American Colonies. The Colonists were always alert to know exactly what was going on in the Mother Country, even to the minutest detail in the current fashions of clothing. Whatever elegancies of domestic appointment came into general favour in England were sure to appear a very little while afterward in the houses of affluent Americans in New England, the Middle Colonies and the South, for they were prospering and wealth was increasing apace as the result of their industry, initiative and commercial activity. Their circumstances, growing yearly easier, enabled them to gratify their tastes for the refinements of life and to order from London merchants whatever luxuries within reason they desired.

Before the seventeenth century came to a close, there was an appreciable amount of good china to be found in and round about Boston, Philadelphia and New York, and throughout the great plantations of the South. In the early years of the eighteenth century the quantity of china arriving at American ports waxed steadily more and more,

PLATE 2

BAROQUE ROCOCO NEO-CLASSIC NEO-GREC

Teapots

Cups

Various

TABLE OF CHARACTERISTIC CONTOURS
A. K'ang Hsi, Baroque; B. Worcester, Rococo; C. Derby, Neo-Classic; D. Derby, Neo-Grec;
E. Chinese, Baroque; F. Chelsea, Rococo; G. Sèvres, Neo-Classic; H. Sèvres, Neo-Grec;
I. St. Cloud, Baroque; J. Mennecy, Rococo; K. Spode, Neo-Classic; L. Vienna, Neo-Grec

PLATE 3

CHARACTERISTIC TYPES OF DECORATION

A. Moulded; B. Modelled; C. Baroque; D. Blue and White; E. Kakiyemon; F. Imari; G. "Mandarin"; H. Hizen; I. Dresden "scattered flower and insect"; J. "Pompeian'; K. Reserved panel; L. Chinese bird and flower; M. Arabesque; N. Cameo; O. Transfer printing; P. Heraldic; Q. "Lowestoft" flower; R. Raised gilding

PLATE 4

COVERED BLUE AND WHITE JAR OF MING PERIOD
Glaze of faint bluish tinge; flowing pattern in light blue and two shades of dark blue
Courtesy of the British Museum

PLATE 5

A. BLUE AND WHITE BOWL OF MING PERIOD, LATE 16TH CENTURY
Greenish blue tinge in glaze; figures in house, trees, scrolls and inner diaper border in light and dark blue

B. LARGE BLUE AND WHITE DEEP PLATTER OF MING PERIOD
Greenish tinge in glaze; decorations in many varying shades of blue with dark blue line work; shaped panels in border containing emblems and flowers; landscape in centre; Persian and Indian influence

Courtesy of the British Museum

and from the middle of the century onward the stream of both Oriental and British porcelain imported reached such volume as to justify in great measure the assertion that the "history of the production of English china can be traced as easily in New England as in old England." It would have been truer if the writer here quoted had said, "America" instead of "New England;" New England, though well supplied, had by no means a monopoly of the good things, for much of the best china, both Oriental and British, was to be found in Philadelphia, New York and the South. There was an especially large quantity in Philadelphia and its neighbourhood.

We must bear in mind, however, that the early distribution of chinaware in the American Colonies was by no means uniform. While the seaports and places within easy reach of them secured the coveted porcelain with little delay, and while the planters of the South and the manorial families of the Hudson lightly set aside the obstacles of distance and inconveniences of transportation to obtain any luxuries they wished, in the ordinary run of events the generality of people who lived in the less accessible portions of the country did not acquire very much chinaware until a somewhat later date than the more favoured folk who enjoyed ready communication with the shipping centres. For example, it was not until 1757 that "Maple Grove" was built at Marlborough in Ulster County, in the Province of New York. Madame du Bois, the mistress of "Maple Grove," is said to have used the first complete dinner service of china in that neighbourhood, "and curious housewives from the country round about came journeying thither to gaze with interest on this unwonted piece of luxury." The du Bois dinner service, nevertheless, could scarcely have been the first in the county for polite, wealthy, luxury-loving Kingston-on-Hudson must surely have cultivated and gratified the taste for porcelain long ere this. At the same time to instance the differences in date of porcelain penetration in the Colonies, there are the dainty handleless teacups of Chinese porcelain from which William Penn sipped his Oolong when he visited some of the substantial Friends of Philadelphia in the latter part of the seventeenth century. These little teacups are still treasured by the descendants of the original owners. Fine china, too, doubtless formed part of the equipment of Pennsbury, in Bucks, for the Proprietary, despite Quaker principles, had an exquisite taste and was not averse to a degree of dignified courtliness that permitted him to make his journeys between Pennsbury and the infant City of Brotherly Love in a stately barge with its due complement of rowers.

In France the popular vogue of porcelain as a utilitarian household accessory, apart from its presence in the form of rare *objets d'art*, received its initial impetus from the dictates of stern necessity. On two occasions, once after the ruinous war of 1691, and, again, after the famine of 1709, Louis XIV, and the nobles of France were obliged to send their silver plate to the Mint in order to obtain badly needed funds in a period of economic tension. To take the place of melted and minted plate, table services of faïence became the fashion, but it was a fashion followed under stress of compulsion and, directly circumstances permitted, the *noblesse* got new plate again and abandoned the faïence. No matter how beguiling its decoration, it was *earthenware* and they could not forget the quality of its body which, to their minds, seemed rustic and lacking in elegance. They had not the English habit of tea-drinking and Chinese tea equipage made little appeal to them. Fine jars, vases and bowls of Oriental porcelain they could and did appreciate, but it was not until they could obtain dinner services of Western china, or Oriental services made after Western patterns, that they became really enthusiastic "China-maniacs" and willingly supplanted silver plate on their tables with choice porcelain.

Although little or nothing was known in Europe of the technical aspect of making porcelain before the sixteenth century, when various attempts were made with more or less success in Italy, to be followed by further successful essays in the latter part of the seventeenth century in France, and although the vogue of porcelain cannot be said to have become generally popular until the second half of the seventeenth century, when the rapid growth of trade with the Orient and the activities of the various East India Companies, English, Dutch and French, brought the elegancies and charms of chinaware within the reach of ordinarily well to do people, it must not be imagined that porcelain was unknown or unvalued in the West at a much earlier date. As a matter of fact, it was known and highly esteemed for centuries before it became subject of common interest and aspiration, but it was of such rare occurrence and so precious that few besides princes and kings, or the greatest nobles, could hope to possess a piece of it.

Though it is not at all impossible that returning Crusaders may now and then have brought back with them from the East a bit of porcelain, just as they brought back spices, plants and fur-lined night-clothes, there is no definite and indubitable evidence on this score. We must be content to date the authentic history of Europe's concern with Oriental porcelain from the year 1447. Then it was, so we are told by Mathieu de Coussy, the historian of Charles VII, that a letter addressed to the Sultan of "Babylon," bespeaking favour towards French commerce in Levantine seaports, concludes with a request for a present of porcelain to be conveyed to the King of France by his ambassador:—"Si te mande par le dit Ambassadeur un présent à savoir trois escuelles de pourcelaine de Sinant, deux grands plats ouvertz de pourcelaine, deux touques verdes de pourcelaine, deux bouquetz de pourcelaine ouvré," and then the customary polite salutations. The *touque* was a vessel or oval vase; the *bouquet* was a bottle with handles. What value was attached to porcelain may be imagined when it was thus solicited in a diplomatic communication as a present from one monarch to another. Thence onward we find instances, now and again, where the porcelains of the Orient were collected and highly prized by the kings and greatest nobles of Europe. An inventory of the year 1586 shews us that Francis I. of France had amongst his treasures "vases and dishes of porcelain, curiously wrought." We know, too, that the Medici had rare specimens of Eastern porcelain considerably prior to this, while it seems to have found its way to Venice at an even earlier date. In 1567 Queen Elizabeth possessed a much esteemed gift in the shape of a "poringer of white porselyn and a cup of green porselyn." Similar porringers and cups of porcelain were in the possession of some of the great nobles of England not long after, and in the Victoria and Albert Museum there is a splendid octagonal ewer of blue and white Chinese porcelain with exquisite silver mount.

ings bearing the hall-mark of the year 1585. Cairo was the Mediterranean port to which much of the precious porcelain came overland from China, and thence, during the early period, it went through various channels to different parts of Europe where it was eagerly sought.

In the Palace of Versailles there was a Chinese room where were kept the rarest pieces of porcelain presented to Louis XIV, or purchased by him. In 1686 this collection was much enriched by the magnificent porcelains presented to the Grand Monarch by the King of Siam and delivered with great pomp by the Siamese ambassador, but long before this vases, jars, bowls and platters of Oriental porcelain had become familiar objects of decoration not only in the palaces and great houses of France but in England, Italy, Spain, Holland and other countries as well. In fact, ever since the beginning of the seventeenth century the increased development of trade with the Orient had tremendously broadened the acquaintance with porcelain and stimulated appreciation of its value and beauty. As early as the year 1660 there were various merchants in Paris dealing especially in fine porcelain and they were well patronised by a clientéle of amateurs and collectors.

In England, however, it was left for the introduction of tea, coffee and chocolate drinking to popularise and give impetus to the acquisition of china by the general public who had hitherto regarded possession of the precious substance as peculiarly the privilege of the very wealthy. "Gombroon ware" gave place to "China ware" just a little before or about the time of this marked spread of popularity. Up to about 1640 porcelain was called "Gombroon ware" in England from the English trading post at Gombroon, on the Persian Gulf, whence the Chinese porcelains were sent to England; after that, when the East India Company had obtained a concession in Canton, the name for porcelain was gradually changed to "China ware." And not a little of the early "China ware" brought to England consisted of the thin, handleless teacups and the various objects associated with them, as already pointed out. Directly the passion for china was implanted in the popular taste—and a supply was forthcoming to meet the demand—it spread like wildfire. We hear of Mistress Nell Gwynne time and again going down to the docks and poking through the cargoes of newly arrived East Indiamen in order that she might have the first pick of anything that pleased her fancy. Doubtless she gathered in many a choice bit of porcelain on these piratical forestalling jaunts and her practice, we may be sure, not a few others followed as closely as they could. It needed only the example of Queen Mary a few years later to clinch the ardent desire for chinaware on every hand.

To shew how the consuming taste for china continued unabated through the eighteenth century, and how it not only swayed all ranks of society but also aroused genuine enthusiasm amongst men as well as women, we may cite, an amusing incident that occurred about 1765. A ship, in whose cargo was a large quantity of Oriental china, went ashore on the Cornish coast. Presumably it had been intended to smuggle the china and escape the customs duties, for when the customs agents boarded the wreck, as soon as the weather permitted, the ship's company had gone and taken all the papers with them. The chief customs agent, finding some choice teapots and other pieces of china that he greatly admired, in the course of his examination, and regarding them as a professional perquisite, stowed the whole lot in his capacious knee breeches preparatory to going over the side. As he was gingerly descending the ladder to get into the waiting dory, one of his comrades, impatient to be off, bade him make haste and playfully paddled him on the seat of the breeches with the blade of an oar—to the utter ruin of the concealed china and an astounding loud crash!

Horace Walpole was no less enthusiastic a "China-maniac" than the Cornish customs gauger, but it is not recorded that he ever had such a disastrous disappointment in his collecting efforts. He had a good collection of different sorts of china at Strawberry Hill and was always on the alert to add to it, soliciting his friends when they were travelling abroad to bring him back representative pieces from the various Continental china manufactories. In 1785 he writes to Sir Horace Mann, then in Italy:—

"On reading over your 'Florentine Gazette,' I observe that the Great Duke has a manufacture of porcelain. If any of it is sold, I should be glad if your nephew would bring me a single bit, a cup or other trifle, as a sample. I remember that, ages ago, there was a manufacture at Florence belonging to a Marquis Ginori, of which I wished for a piece, but could not procure one. The Grand Ducal may be more obtainable."

What he seems really to have had in mind was a piece of the Ginori china which he had previously failed to procure, for the Ginori china had then attained great fame but there was no Grand Ducal manufacture. But it is not surprising to find Horace Walpole falling into confusion over such tiresome things as facts. The beauty of china, however, strongly appealed to him and he was constantly seeking some new type to gratify his insatiable taste. And

Horace Walpole's attitude was a good index to the popular passion for china, the "china-mania" that affected all ranks of society.

America was not a whit behind England in appreciation of good china and eager desire to possess the best, whether of Oriental or European origin. It was no uncommon thing to send special orders for complete dinner services to the East, and to wait patiently, or impatiently, for the execution of the commission with monograms or armorial bearings on each piece. The vast treasure of fine old china preserved all along the Atlantic seaboard bears eloquent witness not only to the prevalence of widespread "china-mania" in America, but also to the knowledge and discriminating taste of those who first secured this goodly heritage. When a ship laden with china was lured by the wreckers to destruction on the Barnegat sands, the "beach" china, as it was called, found a ready and profitable market amongst purchasers who either knew not whence it came or, at any rate, asked "no questions for conscience sake." But most of the china made its entrance in a regular manner and if anyone cares to examine the old shipping invoices they will gain an amazing but fairly accurate idea of the amount of porcelain it took to satisfy, even partially, the demands of American "china-mania."

With all the enormous demand for Oriental china, it was but natural that attempts should be made in the West to produce the same material, comparable with the Eastern prototypes in substance and decoration. These attempts began in Italy in the sixteenth century. More successful and enduring essays were made in France in the seventeenth century. The eighteenth century saw successful and permanent manufactories of china in England,

France, Italy, Germany and Austria. The earlier attempts resulted in what is known as "soft paste" porcelain, an approximation to the Oriental ware that has much to be said in its favour. During the eighteenth century, beginning with Saxony, European potters mastered the secrets of making "hard paste" or the so-called "true" porcelain of the same quality and characteristics as the Chinese. Thence onward both "soft paste" and "hard paste" china were made in the West, as well as the "bone china" manufactured in England, a substance holding a middle ground between the "soft paste" and "hard paste" porcelains. In America some attempts to produce china were made in the eighteenth century, but though these attempts in one or two instances resulted favourably so far as the quality of the porcelain was concerned, they were not commercially successful and came to an untimely end. It was not until the early years of the nineteenth century that china was successfully and profitably produced on American soil.

Oftentimes, too, when the edge of a bowl or plate is struck it will give forth a clear, bell-like note.

In addition to the whiteness and translucence of porcelain, there is a peculiarly distinctive manner in which its glaze reflects the light, while to the touch the surface is smooth and soft as nacreous shell lining.

THE DIFFERENT SORTS OF PORCELAIN

Porcelain is classified as *hard paste* porcelain and *soft paste* porcelain. There is also a third porcelain composition known as *bone* porcelain, which occupies a more or less middle ground between the *hard paste* and *soft paste* types. It is the fashion in some quarters to refer to hard paste porcelain as *true* porcelain while soft paste porcelain and bone porcelain are termed *artificial* porcelains. However, all three have so much in common, and all three are so widely separated in every respect from other fictile bodies, that it seems much wiser, on the whole, much fairer, and much less provocative of confusion and misunderstandings to adopt the former classification of *hard paste*, *soft paste* and *bone* porcelain.

HARD PASTE PORCELAIN

Hard paste porcelain is distinguished by its *hardness*, its *high resistance to heat*, its *resistance to acids* and its *impermeability to staining fluids*, its *close, compact texture*, its *complete vitrification*, its *translucence*, the nature of its fracture when chipped or broken which is *conchoidal* or *shell-like*, very much like the fracture of a piece of flint, and its *clear, bell-like note* when sharply struck. When we speak of *complete vitrification* it means that the several elements in the composition of the porcelain body are so thoroughly blended and compacted by the intense heat of the firing that the substance appears dense and absolutely homogeneous and is hard and smooth to the touch. This quality is readily apparent in the "biscuit," at the points of fracture where glazed porcelain is chipped or broken, and on the bottom edges of foot-rims that are free from glaze. Complete vitrification also implies that, since the glaze, in the intense heat of the firing, has become virtually part and parcel of the body which it covers, it cannot be chipped off and separated from that body in flakes.

The *materials* of which *hard paste* porcelain is made are, first, *kaolin* or china-clay, a white earthy substance which is a product of decomposition of the felspar contained in granitic rocks; and, second, *petuntse* or china-stone, which contains felspar, the silicate of alumina and potash, or sometimes soda. The felspar is closely allied with granite, or kindred rock, in a somewhat weathered condition and is frequently associated with more or less quartz and mica. The china-clay or kaolin is not fusible, even at the highest temperatures to which the kiln can be brought; the *petuntse*, china-stone or felspar *is* fusible at an high temperature. William Burton, one of the greatest living authorities on porcelain and porcelain technique, notes that "at the high temperature to which the porcelain is exposed during the firing a gradual chemical interchange takes place between the various silicates composing the mixture. The *fusible* silicates, such as the felspar and mica, begin to melt and attack the free silica and the kaolin, and when the changes are complete we get a dense, hard, white porcelain, quite translucent if sufficiently thin. . . . However intensely fired the body may be, it never becomes transparent or clear like a piece of glass, soft paste porcelain is slightly tinged with yellow. Soft paste porcelain has not as great resistance to heat as that possessed by hard paste china.

The *materials* entering into the composition of soft paste china are, first, a white-firing clay, and, second, a fusible silicate such as a frit of glass, sand or broken and pulverised china. When deposits of kaolin were discovered in Europe, the kaolin was made use of.

Most of the early European china was soft paste porcelain and, in nearly all cases it possesses a rarely mellow quality that much of the hard paste china totally lacks. The loveliest and most highly prized old Sèvres china was all of soft paste.

In the process of firing in the kiln the artificial silicates melt, envelope and partly dissolve the clay so that, as Burton points out, "again a material is obtained in which a clear transparent base holds in suspension white and opaque particles, and such substances consequently exhibit something of the soft translucence that distinguishes the porcelains as a class."

BONE PORCELAIN

Bone porcelain, as noted before, may be said to hold a middle ground between hard paste and soft paste porcelain, representing, so to speak, a compromise between them. The *materials* of which the body or paste consists are mainly kaolin, felspar, *petuntse* or china-stone—whichever name you choose to apply to it—and, thirdly, a quantity of bone-ash. This composition was discovered and the process developed in England from about 1750 onward. As Burton aptly points out, "we may regard English bone-porcelain, so far as the body of the ware is

PLATE 6

CELADON VASE, SEA-GREEN GLAZE
Engraved underglaze flowing pattern of peonies above a band of water-leaves at the base

Courtesy of the Victoria and Albert Museum, South Kensington

PLATE 7

A. BLUE AND WHITE CUP AND SAUCER
Rice-grain decoration in the paste; border of *jou-ee* heads in several shades of blue; five blue bats and mark in centre of saucer

B. BLUE AND WHITE CUP
Sides pierced with interlacing coin fretwork

C. "BLANC DE CHINE" CUP
White ware of Fuchien, with prunus blossom decoration in relief

Courtesy of the Victoria and Albert Museum, South Kensington

PLATE 8

BLUE AND WHITE COVERED JAR
Deep blue crackled ground, with large crackles, the blossoms and stems of the prunus decoration reserved in white

Courtesy of the Victoria and Albert Museum, South Kensington

PLATE 9

VASE OF THE SO-CALLED "BATAVIAN" WARE
Glaze of slightly greenish tinge; body a yellowish brown or "dead-leaf" brown with four circular reserved white panels containing peony and leaf decoration in underglaze blue; neck tall with Persian pomegranate or flame pattern in underglaze blue

Courtesy of the Victoria and Albert Museum, South Kensington

concerned, as a true porcelain paste which has been rendered more fusible by the addition of a large proportion of calcium phosphate in the form of bone-ash."

In its distinguishing qualities bone porcelain likewise occupies an intermediate position between the hard paste or natural felspathic porcelains, on the one hand, and the soft paste or artificial glassy porcelains, on the other. It is not generally so white as the hard paste, but more white than the soft paste. Also, it is not quite so hard, nor so impermeable to the action of acid or staining fluids, as the hard paste body, but it is harder and less permeable than the soft paste. Although it holds comparatively a middle ground between the two, yet in its qualities it somewhat more closely resembles the hard paste. In its fracture it is more akin to the hard than to the soft paste. It has the durability of the hard paste and the softer quality of the soft paste glaze.

THE MAKING OF CHINAWARE

IF the reader wishes to follow up in detail all the intimate minutiæ of porcelain manufacture, and to become acquainted with all the technical processes, the books noted in the bibliography at the end of the volume had best be consulted. As we are chiefly concerned here with the aspect of the finished product, it must suffice to point out a few of the salient facts connected with the transformation from the original elements to the ultimate stages of decoration.

After the materials are finely ground, washed and filtered, they are mixed in the desired proportions and the plastic clay is thoroughly worked and kneaded to ensure uniformity of texture. The clay may, perhaps, be "short" and inclined to crumble, or it may be highly plastic and "fat," as is apt to be the case when there is present in the mixture an high percentage of kaolin. The nature of the clay and its degree of plasticity necessarily somewhat determine the methods by which the articles to be made are shaped.

A lump of clay may be "thrown" on the potter's wheel and gradually shaped by the manipulation of the potter's thumbs and fingers as the wheel revolves. This method implies an object of circular form and a proper degree of plasticity on the part of the clay. Again, objects may be moulded, the clay being pressed firmly into moulds of the desired shape. Fluted articles, articles with raised patterns or perforations, and such members as the handles of cups, the handles and spouts of teapots, and the handles and knobs of tureens and vegetable dishes must all be moulded as well as lids, the generality of plates, all plates and platters of form other than circular and, as a rule, most articles with the exception of such jars, bowls and vases of circular form as can be shaped on the potter's wheel. Statuettes and figures, of course, are moulded, unless shaped by the casting process which, however, was unknown in the East. Handles, spouts, knobs and embellishments in high relief, such as figures and flowers, are moulded separately and then attached in their proper places with "slip." "Slip" is a fluid mixture of the clay body, of a thick cream-like consistency. After the separately moulded members are attached in their proper places, the articles are set away to dry until the time comes for them to be fired. Many objects of elaborate and complex shape have to be built up of a number of separately moulded parts.

In casting porcelain a thick "slip" is poured into a plaster-of-Paris mould. The water is absorbed or drained off, and when the clay has dried and hardened to the right extent to hold its shape, the plaster mould is removed.

When the ware has been carefully dried, it is fired. In China it was customary, with a great deal of the porcelain, to apply the fluid glaze, directly to the surface of the air-dried object and then subject it to only one firing at intense heat. Much hard paste porcelain in Europe, however, had a preliminary firing at a dull to full red-heat. This "half baked ware" was afterwards glazed and subjected to a firing at the full temperature necessary, which served to make the glaze become virtually part and parcel of the body. In England the bone pastes were first fired at the most intense heat. Afterwards they were glazed and fired only to a temperature sufficient to melt the glaze and make it adhere inseparably to the body. The same method was followed for firing and glazing soft paste porcelains.

With the exception of underglaze colours, all coloured decoration with enamel colours and all gilding are applied after the article has been through its second or glazing firing and these overglaze enamels and gilding must be fixed by an additional firing at little more than a clear red heat, a temperature much lower than is needed to melt the glaze.

THE GLAZE

The term "glaze" is really only another form of the word "glass," and there is not a great deal of difference in chemical composition between the glaze on the surface of china and the glass which we daily see and handle.

The glaze is a very important factor, not only so far as the aspect of porcelain is concerned, but also as one of the cardinal items of identification. There are many variations of glazing and some of these are peculiar to certain kinds of china; all of them add their quota of individuality and distinction to the ware of which they form the skin. The different glazes vary in their quality which the sense of touch distinguishes as well as in the appearance they reveal to the sight.

The glaze is transparent and ordinarily colourless, or almost altogether so, so that the white body or paste beneath is perfectly visible. In some of the early Chinese porcelains the decoration is effected by the use of one or more coloured glazes, but such glazes are the exception rather than the rule. In still other cases the glaze, although per-

PLATE 10

LARGE CHINESE "IMARI" PLATTER
Glaze of distinct bluish tinge; flowing pattern of peonies, chrysanthemums and Japanese "brocade" *motifs* in blue, red and gold

Courtesy of the British Museum

THE MAKING OF CHINAWARE 25

fectly transparent, is slightly tinged with a greenish, bluish or yellowish tint which, whether intentional or not, often enhances the beauty of the general effect. In some of the old Chinese blue and white porcelain the glaze has a slight bluish tinge which acts as a pleasant bond between the white of the body and the blue of the decoration.

In China the glaze was made of the pure *petuntse* or china-stone, sometimes softened with a little lime, and was applied in a thin fluid state to the air-dried but still unfired objects. They were then fired at an intense heat and finished at one firing, the glaze becoming thoroughly incorporated with the body. In Europe and Japan it was customary to fire the pieces first at a moderate heat of between 600 and 900 degrees Centigrade. Afterwards they were covered with the coating of glaze and subjected to a second firing at the full temperature of from 1350 to 1500 degrees Centigrade, the heat required by hard paste porcelain. Thus the porcelainisation of the body and the fusion of the glaze took place simultaneously.

An accurate mental picture explanatory of this process is most happily conveyed by Burton, in his *Porcelain: Its Nature, Art and Manufacture*. He says:—

"It will be readily conceived that under such circumstances the melting glaze, containing fusible ingredients similar to those used in the body, will also attack and partly dissolve the outer layer of the body substance, and we may picture to ourselves a piece of glazed porcelain of the first class as consisting of many layers of different silicates, some of them of excessive thinness and none of them sharply defined, ranging from the outer skin of the glaze, which in perfect pieces is always the clearest, down to the body itself, which is a felted mass of minute crystalline rods imbedded in a more glassy substance. Only by forming some such mental picture, which is in harmony with the knowledge obtained by a microscopical examination of thin slices of the material, can we understand where the distinctive beauty of porcelain resides. When light falls upon a piece of true porcelain it penetrates these successive layers, which, so to speak, filter, soften and subdue it, so that the lowest depths shimmer and glisten with the light they reflect to the observer's eye through the successive envelopes of more translucent substance."

The process of glazing was different for the soft paste or glassy porcelains and for bone porcelain. The unglazed articles were fired up to a temperature of 1100 to 1150 degrees Centigrade. They were then coated with a glaze that was virtually a glass, rich in lead oxide or borax, and subjected to a second firing, at about 1000 degrees Centigrade, a temperature sufficient to melt and fuse the glaze. Of such glazes Burton observes:—

"Glazes made in this way are always thinner, more transparent and brilliant, more 'glassy,' in a word, than those in the first class for hard paste porcelain, and from their nature and method of formation they lack the subtle depth and unctuous richness of the latter, because they affect the light less as it passes through them."

THE DECORATION

China may be decorated in two ways. *First*, the decoration may be contained in the body of the piece itself and consist of *engraving, embossing, perforations* or fretwork, or of *applied reliefs*. All of these devices are perfected before glazing. This may be called decoration in the white. *Second*, the decoration may be accomplished by means of colours or gilding.

These methods may be employed singly or in combination.

DECORATION IN THE WHITE.—Decoration in the white is effected by engraving or incising patterns in the

THE MAKING OF CHINAWARE

body of an article before it is fired, or the patterns may be impressed by the mould in which the article is first shaped. The engraving or incising process is exemplified in such pieces as the Oriental ware decorated with the rice-grain *motifs*. When patterns are embossed in low relief, they are made by the moulds or, when higher relief is desired, patterns are produced by painting with thick "slip" (a thick fluid form of the clay) upon the surface of the previously air-dried article. When the slip painting, in turn, has dried, the article is ready for glazing and firing. Sometimes the piece of porcelain is first covered with coloured glaze and fired, and then painted with white slip, thus necessitating a second glazing and firing. In certain cases these slip painted reliefs are as delicate as lacework. Examples of the low embossed or raised patterns are to be found in the basket work now and again found on the rims of plates. Perforations or fretwork, in such instances as plate rims, fruit baskets and the old Chinese porcelain lanthorns, often supply a distinctive decoration. Separately moulded reliefs, such as rosettes for the intersections of fretwork, sprigs, flowers and the various sorts of figures employed as knobs and handles are attached with slip to the body of the piece before glazing. In much of the old Chinese Fuchien porcelain these moulded decorations in the white are very beautiful and not infrequently of an elaborate nature.

DECORATION IN COLOUR AND GOLD. The colours used in decorating china are of two sorts, the *underglaze* colours applied before glazing and firing, and the *enamel colours* and gold applied after glazing. Enamel colours and gold thus applied require a second firing to make them fuse with the glaze and become permanent.

The most substantial and reliable underglaze colour is blue, made from cobalt. In the old blue and white ware of China the decorations were painted with this blue on the air-dried bodies of the articles which were subsequently glazed and fired. At a comparatively early date the Chinese developed also an underglaze red. This was difficult to produce, however, and the secret of it was afterwards lost. Another underglaze red followed later but was never nearly so much used as the blue. Underglaze blue was likewise commonly employed by the European makers of porcelain. An underglaze rose was invented in England in the eighteenth century. Foreign potters frequently speak of it as "English pink," and it has been very extensively used. Somewhat later a few other underglaze colours were developed on the Continent and, about the beginning of the nineteenth century, the range of these colours was increased by a good underglaze green and some other colours that were not so pleasing. After all is said and done, blue was the one reliable and serviceable underglaze colour that could always be depended upon and was almost exclusively used, although in many cases overglaze blues likewise occurred.

The overglaze enamels were easy to manipulate and remarkably varied effects were produced with a comparatively limited palette, although by the eighteenth century the Chinese had devised an adequate chromatic range much ampler than the colour resources at their command in earlier times. In Europe, too, especially in France, during the eighteenth century, the colour possibilities were greatly enriched. Enamel colours on the glaze of hard paste porcelain often stand up perceptibly from the surface of the glaze, for the glaze is so hard that the enamel colours, which require a comparatively low temperature for their firing, do not thoroughly fuse with it. On the other hand, enamel colours applied over the glaze of soft paste porcelain very often melt into and become thoroughly incorporated with it so that their presence above the surface of the glaze is neither visible to the eye nor palpable to the touch and you feel nothing but the soft glossy coating of glaze. This absorption of the enamel colours by the glaze both protects them and adds to their lustre.

The third way of applying colour decoration to china is by the use of coloured glazes, previously mentioned. The glaze may be of one colour over the whole of a piece, as in the case of the old Chinese Celadon ware, or glazes of several different colours may be applied to different parts of the same article. This method was used in adorning some of the old Chinese wares. In some cases a piece covered with a single-coloured glaze was further embellished with designs painted upon its surface in enamel colours.

GENERAL ADVICE TO THE STUDENT OF CHINAWARE

IT has been pointed out in the Foreword that there are five factors to keep in mind when judging a piece of china—(1) the body or paste of which it is made; (2) the glaze that covers its surface; (3) the kind of article and its contour; (4) the manner of its decoration; and (5) the mark affixed by its maker. The latter is often lacking as there are a great many pieces of old china that are altogether unmarked.

In the foregoing section, on the making of chinaware, the properties of the paste or body and the nature of the glaze have been explained. It is necessary to state very emphatically, however, that the reader cannot expect to gain a sufficient and accurate knowledge of china merely from books. It is absolutely essential to *see* and to compare the various sorts in order to acquire and cultivate a proper appreciation of the outstanding characteristics that distinguish one kind from another.

Language alone is inadequate to describe and fully define all the subtle variations of quality, colour and texture that enter into consideration and cannot be disregarded. The statement of facts must be complemented by *sight* and *touch*, or at any rate by sight, when it is not possible to handle and feel of the actual objects. The habit of close, critical observation must be encouraged.

The English language is fully as capable as any other —and more capable than most—of expressing the nice differences of quality that appear in the paste, the glaze

GENERAL ADVICE TO THE STUDENT 31

and the colour of the several sorts of china. Nevertheless, there are many variations quite perceptible to the eye that cannot be adequately described in words, for no matter how carefully weighed or meticulously couched the phraseology may be, you can never be sure that the same words or expressions are going to convey identically the same impressions to two different minds.

For example, we may be obliged to describe the pastes of two different kinds of china as *white* and the glazes as *transparent*. There are no other terms by which to designate them. Furthermore, both whites may be of a creamy tone. The term "creamy white" as accurately describes one as the other, so far as words can convey a definitely exact idea, and yet when we see examples of the two pastes side by side we can readily distinguish a difference between one "creamy white" and the other "creamy white." The one "creamy white" is just as much "creamy white" as the other and just as much entitled to the term. The only way in which these differences can be expressed verbally—and it is an insufficient and clumsy way, at best—is to establish some basis of comparison and to say that the paste of A is not so creamy white as the creamy white paste of B. This method must needs be purely arbitrary, and the arbitrarily chosen norm of comparison cannot be a constant, invariable quantity, definitely fixed with mathematical exactitude, but will inevitably vary according to each individual conception.

It is plain, therefore, that acquaintance and familiarity by sight, and acquaintance and familiarity by touch also if it be possible, must accompany and complement the knowledge conveyed verbally. The verbal descriptions constitute an indispensable guide and an equally indispensable check; from the visual and tactual acquaintance comes the real knowledge and likewise the real pleasure.

This intimate acquaintance it is not hard to gain. Outside of one's own personal possessions in the way of china, there is always the opportunity to inspect and study the china treasures of one's friends, who are almost always pleased at the interest and appreciation manifested; there are the antique shops where you are at liberty to scrutinise as closely as you will; and, above all, there are the museums whose collections exist for the purpose of being studied.

Too much stress cannot be laid upon the importance of using the opportunities provided by the museums. You rarely have the chance to touch and handle the museum specimens, it is true, but they are generally well displayed for the purpose of close inspection; they usually have the advantage of indubitable authenticity and therefore serve as representative and trustworthy standards of comparison; and, finally, there are the curators to give such additional information regarding the specimens as you may require. This help they are there to give. It is a part of their duty, and a duty that is almost always cheerfully and graciously discharged.

In the matter of colour and methods of decoration, and likewise in the matter of characteristic contours, a study of the museum specimens will be quite as helpful as it is in the particulars of paste and glaze. With respect to colours, modes of decoration and characteristic contours the experience you gather with keen observation from the wares in antique shops and amongst the possessions of

GENERAL ADVICE TO THE STUDENT

your friends will be even more broadening than the results of museum study, for the museums, no matter how large and complete their collections may be, cannot be expected to display every type of every phase of chinaware ever produced. Such a display would be manifestly impossible. What they aim to do is to shew in each instance the essential characteristics. Having grasped these essential characteristics, it is part of the fascination and stimulus of chinaware study to detect them, trace them and collate them in their manifold combinations which you are certain to meet with from time to time.

The marks of chinaware are often the least reliable sources of identification. While the marks, in many cases, may be accepted as trustworthy, there are many other instances in which they are positively deceptive. Time and time again the marks were deliberately forged, or else made so closely to resemble the marks found on the products of some other factory that there was obviously an intent, on the part of the makers, to deceive the public. Then, again, not a few marks have been applied at some period long subsequent to the date of manufacture. The question of authenticity of marks will be dealt with in each of the ensuing sections.

Both the fashioning and decorating of china are pre-eminently imitative arts. Many of the early Chinese shapes were imitated from earlier bronze vessels. When china began to be made in the West, Chinese shapes were universally imitated. One factory imitated another in its wares. And just so was imitation carried on in endless ways throughout the practice of the whole art. It was precisely the same with decoration. Chinese types were imitated in Japan, and when any decorator initiated a new method in Japan his style was copied in China. The West copied both with avidity, and when the decorators of one European factory originated something different from what had been done before, it was not long before most of the other factories were putting forth products decorated in almost exactly the same manner.

Despite this promiscuous imitation, certain general types of decoration became so to speak crystallised and their pronounced characteristics were unmistakable whether the pieces of porcelain on which they appeared were made in China or Japan, Bow or Worcester, Chantilly or Dresden. Very often there was just enough of the element of individual or local interpretation to add a flavour of varied interest without destroying or obscuring the identity of the mode. The more important of these families of decoration that occur almost universally will be recognised in the key-plate of decorative types at the beginning of the volume. Other types, less conspicuous perhaps but none the less well-defined, are noted here and there with references to examples on which they occur.

The contours of china objects are of great significance, more, indeed, than many people imagine. Quite apart from the skillful technique required for producing shapes of a certain description and the mastery of the art implied in their successful achievement, the contours indicate sundry other things. For instance, plates with rims, although they may have been made in China, were unquestionably made for export to the West. The Chinese prefer plates or dishes of a modified or flat bowl contour devoid of rims. Again, there are certain national tastes and preferences betrayed in the shapes of chinaware, some shapes being peculiarly characteristic of France and

GENERAL ADVICE TO THE STUDENT 35

others just as peculiarly characteristic of England while, of course, there are numerous contours unmistakably Chinese which have persisted through the centuries and inspired numberless derivations in the West (v. Figs. 1 and 2).

But there is still another aspect of contour that ought not to be overlooked. While there are many shapes that have been repeated indefinitely from early times and continue to-day in unabated popularity, nevertheless the prevailing trend of "collective" contour, as exemplified by a number of different pieces of any one date, plainly reflects the design tendencies that made themselves felt everywhere in every branch of art at different well defined periods.

If we care to make a few comparisons, we can easily see these successive design influences manifested in china contours—the swelling rotundity and symmetrical vigour of the Baroque age, when the making of European porcelain was first established upon a permanent basis; the sinuous whimsicalities and polished graces of the Rococo period; the restraint and delicacy of the Neo-Classic dominance; and, finally, the downright severity and bold insistence of the later Neo-Grec era. (Plate 2).

Although shapes of early date may enjoy permanent favour—such, for instance, as various types of teapots (Plate 2)—so that we cannot assume that they were made at this or that period merely on account of their contour, we *do* know, however, that certain shapes first made their appearance at certain epochs and not only enjoyed universal contemporary popularity but were also embodiments of the spirit of design dominant at that time. As striking instances of this sort of thing, the Ginori tureen (Plate 36, B), with oval body and straight, tapering fluted legs clearly betokens the Neo-Classic feeling that pervaded every field of design in the latter part of the eighteenth century; the Derby teapot (Plate 2, D), has a shape eloquent of Neo-Grec supremacy and echoes the contour of silver plate made at the period; the Mennecy vase (Plate 2, J), could not have been designed before the Rococo influence of Louis XV's reign was paramount; and the Saint Cloud vase (Plate 44, A), is plainly indicative of Baroque inspiration in the background of its maker's mind. And so it goes throughout the whole history of chinaware. The key-plate (Plate 2), of representative period contours, at the beginning of the volume, affords a basis for illuminating comparisons on this score.

Finally, a word of advice about acquiring china. If a piece appeals to you by the quality of its shape and the beauty of its decoration, and if you can get it at a fair price, it is worth buying for the joy and satisfaction it will give you to possess it. Study its characteristics and settle its identification, if there is any doubt in your mind about its origin, at your leisure. On the other hand, if you are seeking a specimen of some particular make and date, and if you are not fully satisfied that the piece is what it more or less appears to be, have no hesitation in consulting a museum curator about it and settling the doubt in that manner. A museum curator of ceramics who knows his subject, and is thoroughly conversant with all the niceties of paste and glaze, will be able to give you an unbiassed attribution and, in most cases, will do so quite cheerfully. This is a precaution that is worth taking, especially if the piece in question happens to be of a sort much sought after and likely to command an high price. After all, however,

PLATE 11

A. EIGHT-SIDED BLUE AND WHITE BOWL OF K'ANG HSI REIGN
(1662–1722)
Glaze of slight bluish tinge; decoration in many shades of blue

B. DEEP BLUE AND WHITE PLATE OF LATE MING PERIOD
Glaze of very pale bluish tinge; decoration in several shades of greyish blue outlined in dark blue; "long Eliza" and house scene in centre; waved or shaped rim and border of shaped panels containing flowers and emblems

Courtesy of the British Museum

PLATE 12

TWO EARLY EIGHTEENTH CENTURY BLUE AND WHITE PLATES (CH'ING PERIOD)
Broad rims for export to Europe; glaze of bluish tinge; decoration in two shades of light blue and two shades of dark blue; light brown edge to rim
A. Figures in centre with sparse, suggested landscape; diapered rim with four reserved panels containing figures
B. Peony centre with flower-scroll rim

Courtesy of the British Museum

PLATE 13

EIGHT-SIDED K'ANG HSI BOWL (1662–1722)

Four long sides and four short sides; figures and interiors on long sides, inscriptions on short sides; inside rim chrysanthemum-diapered with four white reserved panels on short sides containing emblems; decoration in several shades of green, pale yellow, smoke, violet and vermilion, line work in black; glaze of slight greenish tinge

Courtesy of the British Museum

PLATE 14

EARLY EIGHTEENTH CENTURY (CH'ING PERIOD) LARGE CIRCULAR PLATTER OR TRAY

Raised rim; central *motif* of peonies, twigs and birds shewing Kakiyemon influence, surrounded by border of *jou-ee* heads; rim diapered with four reserved panels containing lobsters and fishes; decoration in green, vermilion, mauve and pale yellow, line work black, and touches of gold on red flowers; glaze slightly bluish

Courtesy of the British Museum

while there is a certain satisfaction in acquiring a piece of highly-prized ware, prized by the professional connoisseur because of its origin and rarity, there is infinitely more satisfaction to the average person in getting something that appeals because of the intrinsic beauties it embodies. Acquaintance with and appreciation of the varied and beautiful qualities to be found in chinaware, it is one of the prime objects of this volume to stimulate.

ORIENTAL CHINAWARE AND THE WEST

THE CHINAWARE OF CHINA

HISTORY

TO China, the original source and home of chinaware, we naturally turn first in our survey of the porcelain art. Without knowing something of the story of china-making in the Celestial Empire, we cannot understand what took place in the development and fashioning of porcelain in the Western world.

In this section keen collectors of very old and rare Chinese and Japanese porcelains, and the habitual frequenters of museums, will miss not a few varieties of Oriental china with which they are more or less familiar. These varieties are omitted from detailed consideration and likewise from the scheme of illustration not through oversight, intentional slight nor any lacking appreciation of their manifold excellence, but because of their rarity and the great difficulty or unlikelihood of their acquisition by the average person. Furthermore, setting aside the very early wares of rare occurrence, certain choice products of later date were, and still are, eagerly sought after by the Chinese and jealously retained in China so that they almost never find their way out of the country. At the same time, vast quantities of Chinese porcelain, from the seventeenth century onward were made expressly for export. These "export wares" were those that most profoundly influenced the porcelain of the Western world and those, likewise, that have always been most familiar to Occidentals. It seems wiser, therefore, to leave the virtually unattainable sorts to special treatises and to concentrate attention chiefly on those kinds of Oriental china more commonly met with and more possible of acquisition.

Although we are told in some quarters that the manufacture of porcelain began in China before the Christian era, there are no authentic specimens known of earlier date than those produced during the period of the Sung Dynasty (960–1279, A.D.), and these are extremely rare, although imitations and reproductions are by no means uncommon.

In surveying the history of Chinese porcelain, it is necessary to keep in mind the chief periods into which it falls under the various successive imperial dynasties. The following table of dynasties and dates will prove useful as a memory peg and for general reference.

SUNG DYNASTY, 960–1279
YÜAN OR MONGOL DYNASTY, 1280–1367
MING DYNASTY, 1368–1643
CH'ING (TSING) OR MANCHU DYNASTY, 1644—Fall of Empire in Modern Times

Emperors of the Ming Dynasty

Hung Wu	1368–1399
Chien Wên	1399–1403
Yung Lo	1403–1425
Hung Hsi	1425–1426
Hsüan Tê	1426–1436
Chêng T'ung	1436–1450
Ching T'ai	1450–1457
T'ien Shun	1457–1465

Ch'êng Hua............................ 1465–1488
Hung Chih............................ 1488–1506
Chêng Tê............................. 1506–1522
Chia Ching........................... 1522–1567
Lung Ch'ing.......................... 1567–1573
Wan Li 1573–1620
T'ai Chang........................... 1620–1621
T'ien Ch'i............................ 1621–1628
Ch'ung Chêng........................ 1628–1644

Emperors of the Ch'ing or Manchu Dynasty
Shun Chih............................ 1644–1662
*K'ang Hsi........................... 1662–1723
Yung Cheng.......................... 1723–1736
*Ch'ien Lung......................... 1736–1796
Chia Ch'ing.......................... 1796–1821
Tao Kuang........................... 1821–1851

In addition to the list of the dynasties with their dates, the *emperors* of the Ming and Ch'ing dynasties, with their dates also, are given because of the generally accepted custom of speaking of old Chinese porcelain as belonging to the reigns of Wan Li or of K'ang Hsi rather than designating them merely as of the Ming or Ch'ing periods. In fact, the porcelains of the Ch'ing period are seldom or never spoken of as Ch'ing porcelains, but almost invariably are designated in a more specific manner by the name of the reigning Emperor. This usage of terminology doubtless owes its origin to the intense interest in the manufacture of porcelain shewn by the successive Emperors and to the patronage bestowed on the factories whose choicest wares were commissioned for the Imperial household.

It is altogether unnecessary to attempt to commit to

ORIENTAL CHINAWARE AND THE WEST

memory all the foregoing dates. It is quite sufficient for the average person to remember the chief periods—Sung, Ming and Ch'ing—and their dates, and also the dates of K'ang Hsi and of Ch'ien Lung, in the Ch'ing dynasty, before whose names asterisks are set. It was during the reigns of K'ang Hsi and Ch'ien Lung that porcelain making received especial impetus.

THE SUNG DYNASTY

Burton summarises the distinguishing characteristics of the Sung porcelain as simple, and sometimes clumsy, in shape; the body never white, but at best greyish in colour, and occasionally drab or even reddish-brown; the walls of the pieces thick and rarely possessing the quality of translucence; the glazes imperfect and uneven in their distribution, displaying bubbles and drops; and the decoration attained by the use of coloured glazes but never by painting under the glaze.

The significant wares produced during the Sung period were the *Ju yao* (*yao* means "ware"), whose pale green surface was compared to the lightest jade and was said to feel like "congealed lard" to the touch; the *Kuan yao* of the twelfth century, with a crackled green or blue glaze; the *Chün Chou yao* with its blue glaze dappled with purple or plum-coloured splotches; and the *Lung ch'üan yao*.

Unless one is specialising in ancient Chinese porcelains, which are to be found only in the best museums and a few of the most famous private collections, and are quite unobtainable, the last named variety is the only one that needs to be considered. It is the old celadon ware, so highly prized in the Middle Ages, and was exported in considerable quantities to India, Persia, Egypt and other parts of Asia and Africa, a small amount finding its way to Europe from the merchants of Cairo. It is this celadon that has had so many imitations and reproductions and the genuine pieces of which are so valued to-day.

It was called Martabani ware in Persia because it was shipped from the port of Moulmein on the Gulf of Martaban, in Burmah, and by this name it was at one time more or less known in Europe. The name *celadon*, by which it is now generally known, was later applied in allusion to the grey-green dress of the shepherd Céladon who appeared in d'Urfé's *Astrée*.

From the earliest times it was universally esteemed and admired for its beauty and was also looked upon with superstitious veneration because it was commonly believed to possess the magic property of changing colour on being brought into contact with poisoned food or drink. The protection it was thus supposed to afford against poison naturally increased the high regard in which it was held. The "Warham Bowl" bequeathed to New College, Oxford, by Archbishop Warham in 1530 is a piece of this ware.

The body of celadon porcelain is heavy and thick and the pieces are covered with a coloured glaze, sea-green, grey-green, olive-green, blue-green or grass-green. The glaze may be either plain or crackled, but the smooth plain glaze is more usual. Although a certain amount of the celadon ware is undecorated, the pieces generally exhibit more or less embellishment under the glaze, the decorations consisting of vigorously drawn floral *motifs* (Plate 6) and occasionally landscapes and Taoist figures. These decorations are executed in relief, incised, engraved, or stamped into the paste, and were fashioned before the pieces were glazed and fired. The glaze is never so thick that the decoration does not shew through very plainly and the increased thickness of the glaze along the lines of the relief or the incisions often increases the depth of colour at those points.

The other notable ceramic product of the Sung period —the one exception previously mentioned before commenting on the characteristics of celadon—is the *Ting yao* made at Ting Chou in Chihli, a product that came nearer to fulfilling the modern ideals of porcelain quality and excellence than anything previously made.

It is known in the West as *fên Ting* ("rice-flower Ting") or *pai Ting* ("White Ting"), has a thin white or yellowish-white body, and is somewhat translucent and resonant when struck. The decoration consists of delicate ornament, either incised or moulded, and the soft, whitish, tender glaze, more or less dull and opaque, sometimes gathers in "tear-drops" of a straw-coloured tinge. It may be regarded as the immediate ancestor from which sprang the finest subsequent developments in the manufacture of porcelain.

About 1126 the manufacture of *Ting yao* was transferred from Ting Chou to Ching-tê Chên, a place destined under Imperial patronage to become the greatest porcelain-making centre of the world.

YÜAN DYNASTY

During the eighty-odd years of the Mongol or Yüan dynasty's rule in China, the development of porcelain, to a certain degree, was substantially encouraged in one place at least, and the most esteemed product of the period, the *shu fu yao*, made by Imperial command at Ching-tê Chên, it is generally conceded was a direct outcome from the earlier *Ting yao* and an improvement upon it. It was, in fact, a perfect porcelain of pure composition, *hard, white, translucent* and *resonant*. It was a splendid and perfected vehicle ready for the later steps of painted decoration in colour.

MING DYNASTY

With the Ming period, during which all the arts were encouraged and flourished, we mark a notable advance, for painted decoration in colour, both monochrome (Plates 4 and 5), and polychrome, now appears with its manifold fascination, whereas formerly coloured glazes had supplied the sole chromatic resource.

However admirable and praiseworthy may have been the previous achievements in the making of porcelain, it is with the coming of the Ming dynasty that we enter upon the "first really great period of Chinese porcelain." With the exception of the Têhua factory in the province of Fuchien, whose ware will by-and-by receive specific notice, the manufacture of porcelain was now concentrated at Ching-tê Chên, all the other Sung factories having either wholly disappeared or sunk into utter insignificance during the troublous times of the Mongol domination. As a matter of fact, Ching-tê Chên became the Imperial manufactory, directly under the control and constant supervision of State officials, and it enjoyed generous Imperial patronage throughout the ensuing centuries.

This concentration of the resources and the talent of all the most skillful potters, together with the support of keenly interested and appreciative rulers, naturally conduced to developments undreamed of before. Earlier experience was treasured and the best of the preceding wares were reproduced, while new technical methods were devised and new forms of decoration were evolved.

Nearly all the fine Chinese porcelains, from the beginning of the Ming period onward, with which we are familiar in Europe and America have come from the kilns of Ching-tê Chên at one stage or another of its remarkable career, although in some instances the articles made there were decorated at other places, such as Nankin, before being exported to the china-loving West. The only significant exceptions are the "white wares" (Plate 7, C), of Fuchien, for in some way the factory at Têhua managed to retain its identity and independent existence despite the centralisation of all other efforts at Ching-tê Chên.

The first advance in colour decoration was to fashion the design with the different members of the pattern isolated by raised lines in the body. The spaces within these lines were then filled with glazes of different colours. The process seems to have been suggested by the method used for executing designs in cloisonné enamel. Pieces of this sort, attributed to the beginning of the Ming period, are heavy and oftentimes clumsy both in shape and material. The raised lines, defining the different portions of the pattern, are left unglazed and virtually silhouette the figures; the ornament usually consists of diaper patterns, flowers, animals or human figures, boldly drawn and rather crudely, while the glazes used are generally of three colours—ochre yellow, turquoise blue and purple, although an opaque white glaze is sometimes employed also. Contrary to the usual Chinese practice, pieces of this sort appear to have been first fired to a biscuit stage and then decorated with the coloured glazes afterwards, the second firing for the glazes being at a much lower temperature than the first.

The very thin, delicate and translucent white porcelain, developed and refined under the Mongol dynasty from the *Ting yao* of the Sung period, also was further elaborated in its refinement until the so-called "bodiless" porcelain was produced. This fragile triumph of the potter's daring, patience and adroitness is commonly known as "egg-shell" porcelain and has been made, practically without interruption from the reign of Yung Lo, 1403–1424. In the finest specimens of this sort of porcelain the substance of the body or paste is so thin that it seems as though there could be no clay left between the inner and outer layers of glaze.

Notwithstanding the exceeding thinness of this ware, many specimens were enriched with intricate designs incised with a steel tool in the air-dried paste before it was glazed and fired. The best early egg-shell pieces bearing designs executed in this manner were usually of pure white and the ornament was barely visible beneath the glaze unless they were held up against the light or filled with liquid. There is a very early white bowl of this ware in the British Museum with five-clawed dragons traced in white slip under the glaze. When this delicate bit of porcelain is held up to the light the dragons appear like a water-mark in paper.

Another method of decorating this thin white porcelain, requiring the utmost delicacy and deftness of handling, was contrived at about the same time. This is known as the "rice grain" decoration (Plate 7, A) where small pieces the size and shape of a grain of rice are cut out of the thin walls of the piece so that the little piercings form the pattern desired. This is done whilst the body is in its air-dried state; it is then glazed and fired, the glaze filling the piercings and leaving them absolutely transparent.

The perfect production of such articles eloquently testifies to the degree of technical proficiency the Chinese potters had reached by the beginning of the fifteenth century.

The production of blue and white ware (Plates 4 and 5), with the decorations painted in underglaze blue, is the next epoch-making event in the history of Chinese porcelain. Painting with underglaze blue seems not to have been practised to any appreciable extent in China prior to the beginning of the fifteenth century, and it is not at all impossible that the Chinese may have derived this method of decoration from the Persians who had made use of it centuries previously.

The underglaze blue pigment is made from cobalt and the native Chinese supply of this material is of an impure and inferior sort, the presence of manganese and other impurities producing a dull, greyish tone. The cobalt used by the Persians, on the other hand, was very pure and brilliant in colour. Early in the fifteenth century the Chinese seem to have obtained their supply of cobalt from the Persians, or from the people of some other Moslem country, for they always speak of it as Mohammedan blue.

This rich sapphire blue appears in the blue and white porcelain of the reigns of Hsüan-Tê (1426–1435) and of Ch'êng Hua (1465–1487), the early Ming porcelain most highly prized by the Chinese connoisseurs themselves, while the blue and white of the reign of Yung Lo (1403–1424), with its inferior grey-blue, the Chinese collectors consider poor by comparison.

The supply of Mohammedan blue failed in the latter part of the fifteenth century and the Chinese potters were driven back upon their own native materials, with a resultant change in the character of the colour, a change decidedly for the worse. However, during the reign of Chêng-Tê (1506–1521) a further supply of Mohammedan blue was obtained and the blue and white ware of this period is exceptionally fine.

This Mohammedan blue was used in two shades (Plates 4 and 5), and there was absolute harmony and balance between the blues in their distribution and between them and the tone of the glaze. This complete harmony of colouring is one of the factors that renders the old Ming blue and white so delicious in quality and so satisfying. The blue painting of the later Ming period, about the time of the reign of Wan Li, is not graduated nor shaded (Plate 5, A), but applied throughout with the full pigment. Consequently, at its greatest intensity, it produces an almost overwhelming impression; at its best, its decorative effect is amazingly fine.

Early in the Ming period, too, the Chinese potters succeeded in producing a wonderfully beautiful underglaze red from oxidised copper. At first it was used as a ground or solid all-over colour for the outside of such articles as bowls and cups, but later came to be employed for painting designs (Plate 18, A), and was then covered with an especially fine white glaze. An early Chinese connoisseur, in describing a piece of porcelain decorated with this deservedly famous underglaze red, speaks of "three red fishes on a white ground, pure as driven snow, the fish boldly outlined and red as fresh blood, all with colour so brilliant as to dazzle the eyes."

ORIENTAL CHINAWARE AND THE WEST

A few, but only a few, examples of porcelain bearing this underglaze red are to be found in collections on both sides of the Atlantic. Later in the Ming period this excellent red disappeared and its place was taken by another red, an inferior on-glaze colour derived from iron.

In the latter part of the sixteenth century, or the beginning of the seventeenth, as the Ming dynasty was nearing its end, variety in the design and technique of colour decoration comes more and more into evidence. The beginnings of polychrome decoration seem to have been well on their way by the reign of Chia Ching (1522–1566) for the efforts of the preceding reign (Chêng-tê, 1506–1522) in that direction were continued and we find polychrome decoration in reserve on a monochrome ground. There were also some designs wrought altogether in gold on a solid-coloured ground of red or green.*

By the time of Wan Li (1573–1629) we find firmly established the practice of painting with enamel colours on the finished fired glaze, these on-glaze paintings being fused into the surface of the glaze by re-firing at a temperature lower than that of the initial firing.

There were two well-recognised schemes of polychrome decoration with enamel colours painted on the glaze—the three-colour scheme and the five-colour scheme.

---

*As early as the reign of Ch'eng Hua (1465–1488) definite attempts at polychrome decoration seem to have met with a degree of success. Hannover calls attention to the effects produced by the use of different-coloured glazes in combination on the same piece, and also points out incipient efforts at *painted* polychrome decoration, instancing several pieces recorded and commented upon by Chinese connoisseurs and antiquaries, to wit, a wine-cup with a border of green leaves and red grapes and likewise one of the so-called "chicken-cups," a cup on which chickens, insects and flowers are depicted in natural colours. Of these no examples are extant and we must rest content with the recorded statement. Pointing to this as a new colouristic development, Hannover observes: "Here, evidently, is one of the earliest attempts in the direction of the so-called *wu ts'ai*, the complete five-colour brush painting of the later Ming period."

The first, known to the Chinese as *San ts'ai*, was a combination of green, purple and yellow. In the time of the Emperor Wan Li this scheme was amplified and became known as the Wan Li *wu ts'ai* or five-colour scheme, consisting of the green, purple and yellow already mentioned, in addition to underglaze blue and the on-glaze red, derived from iron oxide, that had taken the place of the earlier copper red. From the conspicuous presence and frequent predominance of vigorous green in these three- and five-colour schemes of enamel painted decoration, many of the pieces so decorated are classified as belonging to the *famille verte* (Plate 17, B), which reached its fullest expansion early in the reign of K'ang Hsi.

Although Chinese porcelain, to some degree, had been exported for centuries previously, during the fifteenth and sixteenth centuries this export trade increased steadily and rapidly until, by the end of the sixteenth century, there was not only the Persian, Indian and Egyptian trade to be considered, but whole cargoes of blue and white ware were sent to Europe. As we shall see, a little further on, the trade relations with foreign countries caused a profound reaction upon Chinese porcelain both in form and in the manner of decoration.

CH'ING OR MANCHU DYNASTY

The political disturbances that attended the passing of the Ming dynasty and the establishment of the Ch'ing Manchus were unfavourable to any material progress at the Ching-tê Chên factory, but when order was restored and the Emperor K'ang Hsi was securely set upon the throne in 1662 there began the golden age of Chinese porcelain. During the reigns of K'ang Hsi (1662–1723) and of his two successors, Yung Cheng (1723-1736) and Ch'ien Lung (1736-1796), Chinese porcelain reached the high-water mark of its development in technical perfection, the grace of forms produced, variety of output, and beauty of decoration. Both K'ang Hsi and his grandson Ch'ien Lung took a deep interest in the porcelain factory and their intelligent patronage was an important factor in assuring the triumphs scored during this long period of uninterrupted prosperity and progress.

It would be easier to enumerate the sorts of porcelain that were *not* made during this epoch than to chronicle all the divers kinds that were produced. Nearly all of the earlier types that distinguished preceding centuries were duplicated in addition to the output of the wares that especially characterised the eighteenth century. It is just as well to bear in mind that the great bulk of the Oriental porcelain with which we are acquainted, both in private possession and in museum collections, in Europe and America alike, was made at Ching-tê Chên in the prolific eighteenth century and the latter part of the seventeenth and falls under the general classifications of either K'ang Hsi or Ch'ien Lung china.

Without entering into a full catalogue of the distinctive K'ang Hsi and Ch'ien Lung products of Ching-tê Chên, which will be noted in the ensuing sections, we should remember that within the limits of this period, besides the well known varieties of blue and white ware, the Chinese potters put forth the sorts of porcelain known as the *famille noir*, the *famille verte* (Plate 17, B), in its ultimate development, and the *famille rose* (Plate 17, A), the last named the most beautiful of all the groups designated by their distinctive methods of colouration. To this era also belong the "powder blue" porcelains (Plate 94, A), and that large and highly diversified group generally called "Lowestoft" (Plates 20–27), which was made to the order of foreign merchants and decorated, oftentimes with armorial bearings or monograms (Plates 22, 23, B and 26, B), for individual customers in England and America. This last mentioned type of chinaware has been mistakenly termed "Lowestoft" although by far the greatest part of it was never within miles of the little East Anglian town whose name the general public, aided and abetted by many antique dealers, insist upon attaching to it. This long-standing fallacy dies hard. There *was* porcelain made and decorated at Lowestoft, beyond all shadow of doubt, as we shall see later on, but to apply the name "Lowestoft" to what was purely a Chinese product, influenced by Western preferences expressed to the obliging makers, is altogether absurd.

THE BODY. The body or paste of the oldest Chinese porcelains is heavy, opaque, crude and often full of impurities to such an extent that many authorities are disinclined to consider it truly porcelain. It is not until well on towards the end of the Sung period that a body appears which all agree is undeniably porcelain, a body *hard*, *white*, *translucent* and *resonant*.

It is worth noting that the Chinese themselves apparently attach no particular value to the quality of *translucence*, which we set so much store by. In their estimation, *resonance* is of far greater moment in judging the physical merits of a piece.

The body or paste of Chinese porcelain is by no means of uniform quality, even at any one period. All sorts of variations are to be found from the coarse greyish, reddish

PLATE 15

K'ANG HSI BOWL (circa 1700)

Exterior Nankin yellow ground with fan-shaped reserved panels containing flower, twig and leaf *motifs*; floral decoration, inside and outside, in brilliant green, vermilion, light blue, pale yellow and pale mauve; glaze slightly bluish

Courtesy of the British Museum

PLATE 16

A. K'ANG HSI PLATE WITH FLOWER-SPRAY BORDER
Broad rim for Western export; centre, finely drawn birds and flower sprays; decoration in gold, pale green, greenish blue, pink, black and vermilion, the gold and vermilion predominating, with line work in black; greyish glaze

B. K'ANG HSI PLATE
With broad rim for Western export; border of *jou-ee* heads in vermilion, blue, green and gold; partridge and flower decoration, shewing Kakiyemon influence, in same colours with the addition of light yellow; bluish tinge in glaze

Courtesy of the British Museum

ORIENTAL CHINAWARE AND THE WEST

or yellowish pastes of the very early period to the fine *pure white, hard, translucent* and *resonant* body of the eggshell or "bodiless" porcelain perfected in the early Ming period. Furthermore, we know that at Ching-tê Chên, in the early part of the eighteenth century, various grades of porcelain were being made at the same time. The finest was composed of equal parts of kaolin and *petuntse*, while in the composition of an inferior kind there were four parts of kaolin to six parts of *petuntse*. The least proportion of kaolin that could be used was one part to three parts of *petuntse*.

In many pieces of the purest Chinese porcelain the walls are thick so that the paste is not translucent except at the thinnest parts. The colour of the paste is affected by the purity or impurity of the ingredients entering into the composition, and also by the peculiarities of different local formulas which regulate the proportions of the ingredients employed in mixing the clay. The later paste for the finest wares of the Ching-tê Chên factory, during the reigns of K'ang Hsi and Ch'ien Lung, is pure milky white, while the paste of Fuchien is characterised by a creamy or ivory tinge (Plate 7, C), and the finest pieces betray a slightly pinkish or rosy glow.

The term "soft paste" is often heard in connexion with Chinese porcelain. The term thus applied is absolutely misleading as to the nature of the porcelain in question. There was never any soft paste porcelain made in China. The so-called "soft paste" of the Ch'ing period seems to have been compounded with such a proportion of fusible ingredients that it might be porcelainised at a lower temperature than the ware whose body was compounded in the usual way. The modification appears to have been due to the addition of steatite or soapstone. Unlike the majority of Chinese porcelain, which was fired and glazed at one operation, the so-called "soft paste" porcelain was first fired to the biscuit stage, then painted with its decoration, coated with a lead glaze and fired again at a temperature lower than that of the first firing.

It is highly probable that this was the variety of porcelain mentioned in his letters by the Jesuit, Père d'Entrecolles to whose admirable account we are indebted for much of our information anent the manufacture of Chinese porcelain. He states that this kind of china was remarkably light in weight and that the painted decorations resembled paintings on vellum in their neatness and precision. These are qualities that mark the so-called "soft paste" Chinese porcelain whose surface is somewhat pitted or stippled in appearance and of a pale greyish tint.

The body colour of a good deal of old Chinese porcelain with blue decoration, or with decoration in which blue predominates, as in the imitations of the Japanese Imari ware, appears to be of a slightly bluish tinge like the colour of very poor skimmed-milk from which every atom of cream has been extracted. This tinge is not the body colour but is due, in reality, to the presence of smalt (pulverised cobalt glass) in the glaze, and was purposely introduced for the general harmony of colour. When such a piece is chipped or broken, or where it is not wholly covered by the glaze, the body or paste will be found to be hard, smooth and white.

THE GLAZE. The characteristic composition of the glaze of Chinese porcelain, and the manner of its application, have been noted in the section on The Making of

Chinaware. There are, however, certain amplifications of the statements made there that must be added at this point.

To the manipulation of the glaze is unquestionably due a great measure of the beauty and charm of not a few types of old Chinese porcelain. In certain types, indeed, the body is merely a vehicle to give shape and stability while the glaze plays the rôle of both decoration and finish. The glazes were often wholly responsible for the colour effects and were either applied to the whole piece in one coating or several different glazes were applied at different places in order to produce varied patterns and colour results.

The crackled glaze, which is so highly esteemed and which occurs in varied forms that constitute decorations in themselves, was in all likelihood the result of accident in the first instance. The crackling was caused by the glaze cooling and contracting more rapidly than the body underneath it, thus breaking into sections separated by fine surface lines or cracks.

Having discovered the cause of this phenomenon, the potters turned it to good account and were soon able to produce crackled ware at will and, what was more, even to regulate the size of the crackle which came to be designated as large, medium and small, the last being graduated from the size of trout scales down to a semblance of fish roe. The effect of the large and medium-sized crackling was sometimes accentuated by rubbing either red pigment or India ink into the minute cracks.

Vari-colored or "transmutation" glazes were at first the result of accident but were soon brought wholly under the potter's control. As these glazes, along with the other coloured glazes, some of which have already been mentioned, were really decorations quite as much as they were the bodily finish and protection of the ware, they will be more fully noticed under Types of Decoration.

The glaze is transparent and, when perfectly applied, is evenly distributed over the whole surface of an article. It is only on pieces where the mechanical technique is not perfect that the glaze runs and collects in "tear-drops."

When quite pure and perfect, the glaze is colourless and absolutely smooth of surface. When it shews a slight tinge of colour, this tinge is either the result of intent or else due to some impurity in the composition of the glaze.

The slightly dappled, vellum or matt-like appearance of the glaze on the so-called "soft paste" Chinese porcelain has already been noted. This dappled or matt-like surface of the glaze is often to be seen also on the so-called "Lowestoft" china.

There is a monochrome coloured glaze seemingly peculiar to the Ming period. It is a smooth glaze uncrackled, coated over a grey or white crackled porcelain, and is much esteemed in tones of green.

ARTICLES MADE AND CONTOUR. The articles commonly made of porcelain included vessels for temple or sacrificial use, the vessels for domestic shrines, all manner of writing paraphernalia, every description of vase, jar and bowl for flowers—for the Chinese are an essentially flower-loving people and require a large supply and variety of such things—wine-cups, trays, teapots, tea-caddies, teacups, plates, platters, bowls, bottles, drum or barrel-shaped garden seats, flower-pots, lanthorns, fish-bowls, covered jars for sweetmeats or ginger, plaques for the embellishment of furniture, figures or statuettes, and an whole host of minor odds and ends.

PLATE 17

A. EIGHTEENTH CENTURY FAMILLE ROSE OCTAGONAL PLATE
Rim of characteristic rose pink; polychrome centre on white ground, with "Mandarin" figures, vases, jars and table

B. EARLY EIGHTEENTH CENTURY PLATE
Decoration in characteristic *famille verte* colouring; diaper border enclosing inner border composed of emblems and flowers; centre, in shaped panel, shewing steps, house and flower vase

Courtesy of the British Museum

FIG. 1. Characteristic Chinese porcelain shapes

58 THE PRACTICAL BOOK OF CHINAWARE

FIG. 2. Characteristic Chinese porcelain shapes

Besides these, there were the table services and other miscellaneous articles made for general export to Europe and America, and oftentimes made to the special order of individual patrons.

The native Chinese shapes of the earliest porcelain pieces were in many cases derived from still earlier bronze or brass articles, such as various bronze temple vessels, and they perpetuated the forms of their prototypes. These pieces usually possessed grace and directness of contour; they were always interesting. A number of the characteristic Chinese shapes are given in the accompanying line cuts.

Increasing trade relations between China, on the one hand, and Persia and India, on the other, especially from the beginning of the fifteenth century onward, resulted in a multiplied variety of contours. Persian and Indian shapes were gradually adopted—although the Chinese have ever been notoriously conservative—and became in time a part of the Chinese contour repertoire, while certain other shapes were employed almost exclusively for articles manufactured for export to the countries just mentioned and apparently made little appeal to native Chinese taste. Some of the representative Persian shapes adopted and naturalised by the Chinese potters are shewn on the accompanying pages, especially in Figure 2.

In addition to the shapes obviously derived from bronze vessels and continued in pottery and porcelain, there were other naturalistic shapes, suited to plastic rendering, that the potters devised and perfected at an early date. Early in the Ming period, along with the severe contours of ancient bronzes translated into porcelain, we find lively imitations of animals, fruit and flowers. The potters displayed great aptitude in adapting these forms to expression in their own medium.

When Oriental china began to be shipped in large quantities to Europe, a certain reflex influence set in from the Western purchasers. It was not long before the customers of the different East India companies gave orders to be fulfilled in China, and accompanied these orders with patterns and designs of what they desired to have executed for them at the factory of Ching-tê Chên. These commissions the Chinese cheerfully and obligingly fulfilled oftentimes giving the new articles they were fashioning a peculiarly Oriental (Plate 20, B) interpretation, but for their own use and pleasure they held to the time-honoured forms to which they had been accustomed and never really adopted the Western shapes as they had some of those derived from Persia several centuries previously.

TYPES OF DECORATION. The types of decoration for Chinese porcelain during the period with which we are chiefly concerned—that is, from about the middle of the seventeenth century to a little before the middle of the nineteenth—were exceedingly varied, and it will conduce to a comprehensive grasp of the subject if we follow for the most part the classification made many years ago by Sir Wollaston Franks when he arranged the collection in the British Museum. This classification is so logical and all-inclusive that it has very generally been followed as a standard ever since. The classification makes five main divisions and is as follows:

A. *Decoration depending on the Glaze alone.*
   1. Glazes plain white or creamy.
   2. Coloured Glazes uniform in tint.
   3. Flambé and other Glazes, varying locally in Colour, but the whole applied at the same time.

PLATE 18

A. EARLY EIGHTEENTH CENTURY PLATE WITH FIVE BATS
White ground surrounding mark in centre; decoration in shaded red with dark line work

B. EARLY EIGHTEENTH CENTURY OCTAGONAL PLATE
Alternate sectors of dark blue and white; decoration in green, gold, vermilion and pale yellow; gold diaper and chrysanthemums on dark blue grounds, flowers and vases in centre and white sectors

Courtesy of the British Museum

PLATE 19

A. EIGHTEENTH CENTURY CUP AND SAUCER, DECORATED AT CANTON
Decoration in deep cobalt blue with superimposed gilding; white glaze

B. SEVENTEENTH CENTURY CUP AND SAUCER
Border of emblems and emblems on outside of cup; decoration in brilliant green, light blue, vermilion and pale yellow; glaze nearly white

Courtesy of the British Muesum

PLATE 20

A. K'ANG HSI PLATE (1662–1722)
Herring-bone diaper rim edge and border of empanelled flower groups, enclosing centre with "Mandarin" figures; decoration in light and dark vermilion with touches of gold; bluish glaze

B. EIGHTEENTH CENTURY "JESUIT" PLATE
Border of flower scrolls and winged cherubs, and centre depicting the baptism of Christ; decoration in dull vermilion and gold; greenish glaze

Courtesy of the British Museum

PLATE 21

A. EIGHTEENTH CENTURY PLATE WITH MOULDED AND WAVED RIM

Decoration akin to manner of so-called "Lowestoft" china; six panel border of small figures and flowers, elephant and rider in centre, enclosed by Rococo scrolls, Western influence in design; decoration green, deep pink, light blue, gold and vermilion; glaze slightly greenish

B. "LOWESTOFT" MUG, MADE TO WESTERN ORDER

Small scattered "Dresden" flowers and English inscription enclosed in Rococo scrolls; decoration pink, brown, dull blue, gold, vermilion and light green; glaze slightly greenish

Courtesy of the British Museum

ORIENTAL CHINAWARE AND THE WEST

B. *Decoration in Slip, generally white, over the Glaze.*
C. *Decoration with Underglaze Colours.*
   1. Copper-red.
   2. Cobalt-blue.   (This includes all the "blue and white" ware.)
D. *Glazes of more than one Colour, painted on the previously fired biscuit.*
E. *Decoration with Enamel Colours over the Glaze.*
   1. Coral.
   2. *Famille noire.*
   3. *Famille verte.*
   4. *Famille rose.*
   5. Chrysanthemum and Peony.
   6. "Mandarin."
   7. "India."
   8. Chinese Imari and Kakiyemon.
   9. Reserved Panels in Ground Colour.
   10. Jesuit.
   11. Lowestoft.

The foregoing classification does not make a separate division of modelled decoration found on white ware especially the white ware of Fuchien (Plate 7, C), already referred to, with ornaments modelled in high relief and applied; neither does it make a separate division for patterns engraved in the paste before firing and glazing and subsequently enriched with enamel painting over the relief.

A. *Decoration depending on the Glaze alone.*
   1. *Glazes plain white.* This does not mean the ordinary ware made for subsequent decoration in colour, but the finer-textured pieces with an ivory-like appearance, whose beauty of form and mellow, ivory-like colour constitute their charm (Plate 7 C). China of this sort, which usually occurs in rather small objects, is ordinarily known as *blanc de Chine*.

   In this section may also be classed crackled ware, with a transparent colourless glaze over a white body or over a coarser greyish paste.

2. *Coloured Glazes uniform in tint.* Reference has already been made to the skill with which the Chinese potters contrived glazes of various colours, the colour being inherent in the glaze itself and produced by the materials in its composition. Besides the Celadon glaze (Plate 6) and its greyish and greenish variations already noted, often with underglaze engraving, there were glazes of various turquoise shades, royal blue, deep blue, blue verging almost to black, *sang de boeuf,* mule's blood, pigeon's blood (a glaze approaching ruby red), liver colour, tomato red, ruby, coral, lilac, pink, lavender, *clair de lune,* crushed strawberry, purple, peach bloom, "dead-leaf" brown and sundry other gradations of brown, *café au lait,* tea-colour, Imperial pale yellow, lemon yellow, straw colour, orange and grey.

The glazes known as "soufflé" and "jasper" belong in this monochrome glaze class. The "soufflé" glaze may be of any colour. The name refers to the mechanical *manner* in which the effect is produced. Jacquemart, quoting and translating Père d'Entrecolles, says: "This is how it is obtained. The colour, made of the proper consistency, is placed in a tube, one end of which is covered with a close gauze; by blowing through the other end, little drops filled with air are precipitated upon the enamel. These burst when coming in contact with the sides of the piece, and reduce themselves into little contiguous circles, forming a network like the finest lace. Sometimes the soufflé colour is blue, more often of a carmine red, which, at first sight, gives to the piece the appearance of a violet-like enamel. This decoration often fails; the little drops do not burst, but form, on the contrary, into little veins, which run half-melted into the starch-blue glaze. Hence results a peculiar decoration very agreeable to the eye—jasper, not less sought after than the soufflé itself."

3. *Flambé and other Glazes, varying locally in Colour, but the whole applied at the same time.* In these splashed, mottled or *flambé* glazes—"transmutation" glazes, the Chinese call them—the varied effect is largely dependent upon chemical changes that

ORIENTAL CHINAWARE AND THE WEST

take place in the substance of the glaze itself during the firing process and often produce striking contrasts and modulations of colour. One type of transmutation glaze of the "Chün-yao," so say the Chinese connoisseurs, ought to be "red as cinnabar, green as the plumage of the king fisher, and purple, brown and black as the skin of the egg-plant."

B. *Decoration in Slip, generally white, over the Glaze.*

Porcelain decorated with devices in slip over the glaze was usually of a strong-coloured ground so as to throw the pattern in white slip into stronger relief. This sort of decoration was applied mostly to vases, jars and bowls.

C. *Decoration with Underglaze Colours.*

This sort of decoration was painted on the air-dried body *before* the application of the glaze and *before* firing.

1. *Copper-red.* Reference has already been made to the old copper-red decoration, and also to the later iron-oxide red under glaze.
2. *Cobalt-blue.* This class includes all the enormous family of "blue and white" ware. The white porcelain supplies the ground; the decorations are in blue alone. The most usual types of decoration found in "blue and white" ware are:
   a. *Miscellaneous* (Plate 11, A), including dragons, flowers, birds, animals, landscapes, pagodas, shaped panels or medallions, bridges, mountains, trees, fishes, fishermen in punts, insects, baskets and pots of flowers, houses, hunting scenes, pheasants on rockeries, peonies, bamboos, peony and lotus scrolls, asters, magnolias, and sundry other subjects.
   b. The prunus or so-called "hawthorn" (Plate 8) blossom pattern, executed either in blue on a white ground or in white on a blue ground.
   c. The "Mandarin" (Plate 5, B) type, so-called because the chief subjects are figures, usually of persons belonging

to the Mandarin class. Under this division should also be placed the tall, willowy ladies standing beside vases of flowers, irreverently known as "long Elizas." The seventeenth century Dutch traders called them "lange Liszen" and the term, translated as "long Elizas," has clung ever since (Plate 11, B).

  d. "India" china. This large class includes all the porcelain made for export to Europe and America and is characterised, to a great extent by shapes that are essentially European (Plates 11, B and 12), such as tureens, vegetable dishes, sauce boats, gravy boats and cream jugs. The decorative *motifs* are virtually the same as in the preceding classes.

  It might be well, however, to add to this class the china made for export to Persia (Plate 5, A), and India on which scrolls, flowers, tree and other devices were used that were not at all Chinese but essentially Persian in character and derivation.

3. *Powder-blue.* Powder-blue porcelain (Plate 94, A), was decorated with a solid coating of cobalt blue that was *blown*, not brushed, upon the air-dried body before glazing and firing. This method of application in minute drops of fluid pigment imparted the powdered appearance.

4. *Mazarine blue.* This is a blue in which the ground is solid and has not the mottled aspect of powder blue, hence the different name to distinguish the two types.

It should be added that with both powder blue and mazarine blue there are often reserved spaces or panels in white (Plate 94, A), so that the blue does not wholly cover the surface of the piece. Various devices occur in these reserved spaces, and are rendered either wholly in blue or else in polychrome.

On much blue and white china the decoration is rendered in several shades of blue (Plates 4, 5 and 11), usually two, but sometimes more. Attention must also be

ORIENTAL CHINAWARE AND THE WEST 65

directed to the great variations that occur in the quality of the blue—it may be a pure cobalt colour, or blackish, greyish, or even almost purple at times. The pale silvery blue might be especially characteristic of one period, while the full-bodied blue would be equally characteristic of another.

D. *Glazes of more than one Colour, painted on the previously fired biscuit.*

Allusion has already been made to this method of decoration in the section on *History*.

E. *Decoration with Enamel Colours over the Glaze.*

This division includes a broad range of distinct and well recognised types of decoration. They are:

1. *Coral-red*, the *motifs* being rendered in red alone (Plate 18, A), on the white porcelain, or the ground colour being coral-red with devices in gold.
2. *Famille noire*, so-called because the ground is either a lustrous green-black glaze or enamel, while the decorative *motifs* appear in white, green, yellow and brown. The usual subject is the prunus blossom, and the colouring is always restrained.
3. *Famille verte* (Plate 17, B), so-called because the prevailing or dominating colour is a vivid enamel leaf green. The other colours are underglaze blue or on-glaze blue, an iron red, purple and yellow. While the green dominates, it does not necessarily monopolise the colour scheme. The subjects depicted are largely historical—emperors, eminent scholars, famous warriors, statesmen, and scenes from celebrated plays and romances. Floral *motifs* and *genre* scenes are also of frequent occurrence.
4. *Famille rose* (Plate 17, A), so-called because a beautiful rose-colour, a later addition to the porcelain painter's palette, is a conspicuous colour and often imparts the prevailing tone. Along with this distinctive rose-colour all other colours, many of them hitherto new to Chinese porcelain, were freely used so

5

that the *famille rose* is *par excellence* the polychrome class. The *famille rose* began to dominate about the second quarter of the eighteenth century and continued in high favour till the early years of the nineteenth. All manner of subjects are represented in the *famille rose* decoration and the drawing is usually of the greatest delicacy and refinement.

5. *Chrysanthemum and Peony* (Plate 14). This class is sometimes so designated because of the well defined type of decoration in which chrysanthemums or peonies, or both together, are the dominating *motifs*. This type occurs in both the *famille rose* and the *famille verte*.

6. "*Mandarin*" *china* (Plate 13). This class has the same *motifs* as already noted for the "blue and white" "Mandarin" group, the difference being that they are in polychrome.

7. *Chinese Imari and Chinese Kakiyemon.* This group consists of imitations of the Japanese Imari and Kakiyemon types. There was such a demand from Europe for these Japanese wares that the Chinese saw their market being injured by Japanese competition and therefore promptly produced types of the same sort. The red, blue and gold Chinese Imari (Plate 10), is often much finer and more beautiful ware than the Japanese originals. The Chinese Kakiyemon (Plate 14), also, is exceedingly beautiful.

8. "*India*" *china* (Plates 16, A, 19, 23, 24, 26). The same distinction applies here as in No. 6.

9. *Reserved Panels in Ground Colour* (Plate 15). This class occurs also in the Powder-blue division, the *famille verte*, and the *famille rose*. The polychrome devices in the shaped reserved panels are usually flowers, birds, figures or landscapes. A great deal of china with divers shades of brown glaze and reserved panels with blue decoration (Plate 9) was exported to Europe by the Dutch merchants and is generally known as "Batavian" ware.

10. *Jesuit china,* so-called because it was decorated with scriptural or ecclesiastical designs supplied by the Jesuit missionaries. The "Baptism" plate (Plate 20, B), shews a good example of such decoration. The renderings were purely

ORIENTAL CHINAWARE AND THE WEST 67

Oriental, as may be seen by looking at the writhing cherubs in the border which more resemble malignant animals than celestial creatures.

11. *"Lowestoft"* (Plates 21, 27). Under this head comes all that great body of china exported to Europe and America throughout the greater part of the eighteenth century, decorated with armorial bearings, monograms and cyphers, bearing numerous small polychrome flowers, thoroughly European and not at all Oriental in character.

In casting up an enumeration of the foregoing, we must not overlook the importance to general decorative effect of the scroll borders (Plates 12, B, 16 and 20), and, even more, of the many varied diaper patterns (Figs. 3, 4 and 5, and Plates 17, B, 12, A and 14), that were employed for the enrichment of rims and borders and, often enough, composed whole grounds, imparting a rich texture full of interest in both colour and line. These diapers occur constantly in almost all classes.

In point of decorative interest, we cannot attach too much importance to the diaper patterns in the embellishment of Chinese porcelain. Some idea of the rich variety to be achieved by their use may be gathered from a careful scrutiny of the examples given in figures 3, 4 and 5. And these are only a portion of the repertoire. When employed in monochrome, as on the blue and white chinaware, they afford a fascinating enrichment; expressed in a variety of colours, they cause the porcelain to glow with vibrant life. To the apt use of diapers is due no small part of the charm of Oriental china.

Amongst the many subjects that appear in the decoration of Chinese porcelain, besides the *motifs* already mentioned may be numbered symbols (Plates 11, B, 13

FIG. 3. Characteristic Diaper Patterns used in the decoration of Chinese porcelain

PLATE 22

A. BEAKER VASE *B.* COVERED JAR

Part of eighteenth century "Lowestoft" mantel garniture with armorial bearings and small scattered "Dresden" flowers, made to Western order; decoration cobalt blue, light pink, bluish green, gold, black and dull vermilion; glaze of greyish tone

Courtesy of the British Museum

PLATE 23

A. SMALL EIGHTEENTH CENTURY "LOWESTOFT" BOWL
Made to Western order with armorial bearings, small scattered flowers, and diapered border inside rim; decoration green, pink, gold, vermilion, cobalt blue, and deep violet; glaze slightly bluish

B. EIGHTEENTH CENTURY GREEN "LOWESTOFT" SAUCEBOAT
Western shape and Western manner of design; decoration deep rich green, deep pink, gold, and touches of deep cobalt blue; glaze slightly bluish

Courtesy of the British Museum

FIG. 4. Characteristic Diaper Patterns used in the decoration of Chinese porcelain

FIG. 5. Characteristic Diaper Patterns used in the decoration of Chinese porcelain

and 5, B), emblems, charms, characters, lozenges, coins, rhinoceros horns, fillets, sugar cane, bamboo, storks, tortoises, fir-trees, cocks, mirrors, fish nets, bats (Plate 18, A), mythical animals, such as kylins, swastikas, sceptres, chess boards, rats and vines, squirrels, arrows, three-legged toads, musical instruments, drums, horses, oxen, hares, monkeys, sheep, dogs, boars, lions, tigers, elephants, deer, foxes, camels, cats, ducks, pheasants, quails, peacocks, parrots, butterflies, bees, silkworms, and endless fruits, plants, flowers and trees, every one of which has some symbolical significance. The peculiar figures termed symbols, Sir Wollaston Franks notes, "are generally eight in number, although the individual forms are apt to vary." The number eight is favourably regarded by the Chinese, doubtless because of the *Pa-kwa* or eight mystical trigrams and also because it is a number

ORIENTAL CHINAWARE AND THE WEST

whose units can be arranged symmetrically. These sequences of eight may be classed in three chief divisions: (1) the emblems of the eight immortals, which are of Taoist origin and not of very common occurrence; (2) the eight lucky emblems of the Buddhists, which are to be found in every possible place and manner of expression; (3) the *pa-pao* or signs of the eight precious things. These last vary widely in their expression and seem not to be connected with any particular religion.

Symbols or emblems can usually be distinguished from other ornaments by the fillets or streaming ribbons entwined about or attached to them. In ordinary life fillets are narrow strips of red cloth which the Chinese tie round or attach to any object they think has the efficacy of a charm. These fillets typify the rays or aura emanating from the charm and are to a charm what the nimbus is to a saint or deity. A number of characteristic symbols or emblems, with fillets attached, are shown in figures 6 and 7.

The symbolism of Chinese decoration is inexhaustible. There is a story wrapped up in every piece of Chinese ornament and there is not a cup, saucer, plate or vase that will not repay investigation on that score alone. You can eat your dinner from a Chinese plate and along with each morsel of beef or mutton you can also trace a romance or get a lesson in Confucian morals, if you care to read the language of the symbols before your eyes.

THE MARKS. The marks on Chinese porcelain may occur in three classes—date marks, hall and other allied marks, and symbol marks. The date marks may be in both plain and seal characters. Marks usually are found on the base of a piece and most commonly are painted in blue.

FIG. 6. Typical emblems or symbols used in the decoration of Chinese porcelain

FIG. 7. Typical emblems or symbols used in the decoration of Chinese porcelain

On some of the later pieces they are in red. They may also be engraved in the paste or stand out in relief.

Little reliance can be placed upon them, for they have been habitually forged and misapplied, and it is more than likely that falsified marks have been made, over and over again, to the order of exporters. This practice has gone on for centuries. By the average person the mark on a piece of Chinese porcelain may as well be considered merely an interesting item of decoration and naught else. The mark may tell the truth, but more probably it tells a lie. Under ordinary circumstances, it is much safer and more satisfactory to disregard the mark and judge a piece by its more visible and tangible qualities. If you are really concerned about the mark, go to an acknowledged expert in Chinese porcelain and he can tell you what the mark *says* and also what he *thinks* the piece really *is*. His opinion will be worth considering.

JAPANESE CHINAWARE

History. Japanese porcelain is thought to have had its beginning with the handiwork of a certain Gorodayu Go-Shonzui. It is related that he visited China at the beginning of the sixteenth century and worked for five years in the factories of Ching-tê Chên. When he learned all he could in that time, he returned to Japan, taking with him a supply of porcelain materials from China, and made a number of pieces of blue and white porcelain. Not knowing where there were deposits of kaolin and *petuntse* in his native country, he had to stop making porcelain when his materials gave out.

In the opening years of the seventeenth century Risampei, a Corean potter settled in the province of

ORIENTAL CHINAWARE AND THE WEST 75

Hizen, so the story goes, discovered the necessary kaolin and *petuntse* in the neighbourhood of Arita. Kilns were established at Hyakken and it is probable that blue and white ware was made there. The kilns were afterwards moved to Arita to be near the source of supplies.

The use of brilliant enamel colour on Japanese porcelain is inseparably associated with the name of Kakiyemon. Kakiyemon was connected with the works at Arita and, according to the story told, he and a companion, Tokuemon, set out to China in 1646, bent on discovering the secret of Chinese enamel colours. At Nagasaki they chanced upon the captain of a Chinese junk who gave them the information they sought and thus saved them the trouble of a long journey. They went back to Arita and it was not long after this that Kakiyemon originated the beautiful manner of decoration known by his name. After Arita, other porcelain factories were established in the same province, such as Nabeshima and Mikawachi, under the control of the great feudal lords and not a little fine porcelain was produced at these places.

In the provinces of Kioto, Owari and Kaga other porcelain factories sprang up and various sorts of wares were made, restrained in character with delicately drawn designs in underglaze blue or else decorated with a few enamel colours in a reticent manner and with excellent good taste. The Japanese always greatly admired the old Chinese celadon wares, and these also they used as models for their work.

One of the dominant characteristics of Japanese porcelain is its reticence of colouring and design. The decoration was always kept well within bounds and exuberance of composition was virtually unknown. It is not fair to judge Japanese taste in porcelain design by the Imari ware made for export. If anyone is to be blamed for the crudities and vulgarity that often appear in such ware, it is the Dutch traders who suggested that what the Japanese porcelain makers had done extremely well should be "improved" by mussing up the design and adding heavy blobs of colour. A great portion of the Imari ware that found its way to the West was of a description that the Japanese would not countenance for their own use, and it was made only for export at the behest of the Dutch East India merchants.

Some of the most distinguished porcelains of Japan were produced at the different factories in the latter part of the eighteenth century and first half of the nineteenth. As there was no one important centre of porcelain production, like Ching-tê Chên in China, there was not only great diversity of individual style in the wares made at the several factories, but there was also much difference in the quality of the paste and glaze. The output during this period was not large, except in the few instances where the porcelain was made almost solely for export, and for that reason the quality in more than one of the factories was maintained at a rather high standard.

THE BODY. In general, the quality of the body in Japanese porcelain was not so good as that which distinguished the ware made at the great factory of Ching-tê Chên in China. The Japanese paste was more glassy looking and seemed of thinner consistency. Compared with the Chinese pastes, it appeared to lack the finer qualities that go to make a really excellent body. For one thing, it seems as though the materials for the Japanese paste had not been prepared in the same careful, scrupulous and

PLATE 24

CHINESE "LOWESTOFT" HELMET CREAM PITCHER AND SUGAR BASON c.1790
Paste white, glaze faintly bluish; orange ground colour, Classic figures in black; gilding

Courtesy of the Pennsylvania Museum

PLATE 25

A. EIGHTEENTH CENTURY CHINESE
"LOWESTOFT" CUP
All decoration finely drawn in black

B. EIGHTEENTH CENTURY CHINESE
"LOWESTOFT" SAUCER
Decoration finely drawn in black in imitation of the Worcester
transfer prints engraved by Hancock and others

Courtesy of the Pennsylvania Museum

PLATE 26

A EIGHTEENTH CENTURY CHINESE "LOWESTOFT" TEAPOT
Made to Western order, with shield, monogram and heraldic mantlings; decoration deep blue, red and brown, with gold bands and small gold stars powdered on deep blue ground

B. LATE EIGHTEENTH OR EARLY NINETEENTH CENTURY CHINESE "LOWESTOFT" TEAPOT
Monochrome landscape in Western manner; decoration brown and gold

Courtesy of the Pennsylvania Museum

PLATE 27

A. CHINESE "LOWESTOFT" PLATTER WITH DECORATIONS IN APPLE GREEN
Courtesy of the Pennsylvania Museum

B. CHINESE "LOWESTOFT" COVERED DISH WITH
UNUSUAL DECORATION OF STRAWBERRIES
Courtesy of the Pennsylvania Museum

patient manner as the Chinese. Furthermore, the clay mixture apparently was not so plastic as the Chinese and perhaps because of this failing it was customary to fire the ware to a biscuit stage before glazing and then fire it a second time after glazing. There was also oftentimes a tendency for the pieces to warp and crack in the firing. The result of all these conditions was that much of the Japanese porcelain seems thick and clumsy when compared with Chinese porcelain of the same period.

The paste of the Imari commercial ware was thick, heavy and coarse and the body of the early Kutani porcelain was greyish and seemingly composed of impure materials. On the other hand, the paste of the Hirado porcelain, with which great pains were taken, was of rich, fine solid quality and clean white, closely resembling Chinese paste. The Nabeshima body, too, which was carefully prepared, was of good, clean, dense texture and wholesome colour. Likewise, the later Kutani paste was milky white, though somewhat soft in substance. The early Arita paste with the Kakiyemon decorations was of a beautiful creamy white which made an admirable foil for the coloured enamel embellishments. The paste of the Owari porcelain, though milky white was of a rather soft, chalky nature. At several of the factories very fine eggshell porcelain was made and for this purpose the paste had to be most carefully prepared, so that it exhibited the qualities we naturally look for in porcelain of an high order.

THE GLAZE. The glaze commonly used, especially the glaze on the Imari commercial wares, which contained an appreciable quantity of lime, was almost always minutely pitted so that it presented a semblance to fine muslin. It was less solid than the Chinese glaze and this musliny aspect from tiny bubbles seems to have been due to incomplete fusion. In colour it had often a cold greyish tinge. Its whole appearance is very different from the close texture and oily sheen of the Chinese glaze. By way of contrast, the glaze of the Hirado porcelain, made from more carefully prepared materials, has a velvety, lustrous aspect. The Nabeshima glaze and the later Kutani are both of good quality, though the latter shews a somewhat dull surface.

ARTICLES MADE AND CONTOUR. There has never been as great diversity in the articles made by the Japanese as there was in porcelain of Chinese manufacture. While the Japanese made plates, platters, bowls, cups, saucers, teapots, jars and vases and, for their own use, such articles as incense boxes, incense burners, rice bowls, wine cups, and the various things required for the elaborate tea ritual, they were not in the habit of making dinner, tea, coffee and chocolate sets, with all the etceteras for the Western market, as the Chinese did. There were also the human figures, grotesques, birds, and animals which were made in large numbers.

The contours, almost without exception, are simple and straightforward and, to a certain extent, shew the influence of Chinese shapes.

TYPES OF DECORATION. The types of decoration commonly practised included painting in underglaze blue, painting with enamel colours, gilding, ground colours, coloured glazes, ribbing, piercing and fretwork. The Japanese palette was limited to a comparatively few enamel colours, and nearly all of their *motifs* shewed reticence and restraint in treatment. Many of the sub-

PLATE 28

LARGE JAPANESE IMARI PLATTER
Flowered and foliated border, enclosing garden scene and "long Eliza" figures; decoration red, dark blue and gold; glaze of greyish tone
Courtesy of the Victoria and Albert Museum, South Kensington

jects were treated in a purely conventionalised or symbolic form, a circumstance that rather enhanced their decorative value than otherwise.

Religious subjects supplied not a few themes for decoration. There were also landscapes and river scenes, the beloved mountain Fujiyama, animals, birds—in the depiction of which they were peculiarly successful—fishes, mythical creatures, flowers, trees and sundry symbols.

The local specialities in decoration are noted in the section devoted to the individual factories.

THE MARKS. The marks on Japanese porcelain usually indicate the names of the factory and the potter. The name-mark of the Japanese Emperor is sometimes added. These marks may be incised in the paste, impressed in the paste with a seal or stamp, or painted either in underglaze blue or with enamel colours. Much of the best Japanese porcelain is altogether unmarked. The Japanese marks are far more to be relied upon for accurate information than are the Chinese, except the marks on Japanese ware made solely for export. These last are purely fantastic inventions.

ARITA CHINA—1605 TO PRESENT DAY

HISTORY. This factory was established when Risampei, the Corean, found porcelain materials near Arita. Its most beautiful and famous product was the Kakiyemon ware (cf. Plate 51, A), named for the painter who devised this means of decoration in a few colours—iron-red sometimes verging to orange, lilac, a fine enamel blue, grass green, and dull gold—and with a limited range of *motifs* comprised in a sparse composition of dragons, phœnixes, tigers, fluttering birds, quails or partridges, bamboos, pines or plum trees.

The red, blue and gold Imari ware (Plate 28), so-called from its place of export—was also made here, the patterns being largely derived from old brocades; hence the term "brocaded."

Blue and white ware, decorated chiefly with diapers and scrolls, was made at Arita, the underglaze blue being of a rather poor, muddy quality. Celadon porcelain, too, was produced; likewise very exquisite egg-shell porcelain, decorated with underglaze blue or with enamel colours.

NABESHIMA (OKAWACHI) CHINA—c.1660 – c.1868

HISTORY. This factory, also in the province of Hizen as well as Arita, was established under the patronage of the feudal lord about 1660. The paste and glaze of this china are, in many instances, better than the paste and glaze of Arita.

A type of china was made here whose decoration closely resembled the Kakiyemon ware of Arita. Another sort had decorations in underglaze blue, less brilliant than the Chinese blue. Celadon porcelain was likewise made. The favourite decorative *motifs* for the blue and white china were cherry-blossoms, hydrangeas, peonies, chrysanthemums and other floral subjects, along with conventionalised birds and butterflies, in conjunction with conventional scrolls and diaper patterns. The ware was not marked but had a comb pattern encircling the foot-rim. This same comb pattern is sometimes seen on Kaga porcelain.

HIRADO (MIKAWACHI) CHINA—1712-1868

HISTORY. This factory was established at Mikawachi in the province of Hizen, under the patronage of the feudal lord. In 1750, Matsura, the lord of Hirado converted it into a private factory and from then until 1830 the finest porcelain in Japan is reputed to have been made there. The paste and glaze were of a quality far superior to anything produced in the other factories.

The painted ware was decorated altogether in underglaze blue and the drawing exhibited exquisite delicacy. Some of the ware shewed engraving and modelling in the paste, delicate piercings and frettings were employed, and egg-shell pieces were also made. Modelled figures, too, were fashioned and glazed with coloured glazes.

KUTANI (KAGA) CHINA—1664-1750; 1779-1822; 1832 TO PRESENT DAY

HISTORY. The Kutani factory in the province of Kaga was established by the feudal lord of Daishoji in 1664. Several different sorts of ware were made. One was distinguished by a beautiful green glaze, along with soft greenish blue, purple and yellow glazes, disposed in scrolls, diapers and floral patterns over outlines traced in black on the biscuit. Another sort was painted with red, green, blue, yellow and purple enamel colours, along with silver and gold. Landscapes, flowers, a single bird on a twig, and similar naturalistic subjects (Plate 29) supplied the themes together with symbolical ornaments and diaper patterns. In still another sort, red was predominant. The decoration of red scrolls and diapers was disposed in panels containing landscapes, mythical animals and flower *motifs* in green, yellow, purple and red. A subdivision of this variety had a red ground colour, with patterns wrought in gold, silver, bright green, yellow and purple. The making of these wares came to an end about 1750. After that date several revivals took place, one of which had a red ground colour whereon the patterns appeared in gold.

KIOTO CHINA

There were not a few porcelain-makers of great ability and good taste who flourished in Kioto at one time or another from the middle of the eighteenth century down to the end of the period with which this book deals. Eisen, who worked about 1760, was the first of these. The wares they made were of excellent quality and beautiful in decoration, but as none of their products exercised a material influence on chinaware in the Western World, the reader desirous of pursuing the subject further is referred to books treating especially of Japanese porcelains.

ITALIAN CHINAWARE

MEDICI CHINA
FLORENCE—1580-1613 (?)

HISTORY. Francesco I de' Medici, Grand Duke of Tuscany, in 1580 established at Florence a manufacture of soft paste porcelain. The factory was in the Boboli Gardens. Bernardo Buontalenti played an active part in this undertaking, and it is said that soon after its inception porcelain vases and other articles, of the finest quality, were produced and decorated in blue. This was the first European porcelain of which we have any certain knowledge and of which undoubtedly authentic examples exist.

Fewer than fifty authentic pieces are now known to be in existence. These comprise vases, dishes, bowls, (Plate 30), plates, cruets, bottles, flasks, basons and ewers. They are all in museums or else in well-known private collections.

The mark, painted in blue, consists of the dome of the Cathedral in Florence, above a capital F, occasionally with slight additions or variations.

The manufacture was discontinued in the early years of the seventeenth century.

GINORI OR DOCCIA CHINA
DOCCIA, BY SESTO, NEAR FLORENCE—1735 TO PRESENT DAY

HISTORY. The Marchese Carlo Ginori, in 1735, founded the porcelain factory at Doccia, an estate belonging to his family at Sesto, about six miles from Florence. As a Tuscan, he had all the initiative, readiness, for enquiry and hard-headed common-sense characteristic of his race. Endowed with both energy and tenacity of purpose, he chose to follow the old Tuscan tradition that strongly sanctioned mercantile, industrial and agricultural activities on the part of the nobility. Through application and diligence he occupied a prominent position in Florentine affairs and became a senator. As part of the services he rendered the State there were sundry special commissions, entrusted to him in view of his sterling capacity, public spirit, and the confidence reposed in him by the Grand Duke.

At one time he was engaged in reclaiming a part of the Maremma, a formidable task that meant draining a section of the waste, malarial marsh lands and converting them to purposes of productive farming. This involved much canal cutting, road making, bridge building, the planting of settlers from various quarters, and the establishment and care of divers industries. Along the coast, he exerted himself to develope coral fisheries, attracting thither Neapolitans skilled in their conduct. By well directed efforts he also materially furthered the interests of Tuscan shipping.

In one place, where the conditions seemed suitable, he introduced Angora goats, hoping to promote the manufacture of cashmere shawls. What measure of success

PLATE 29

A. JAPANESE EIGHT-SIDED BOWL; EIGHTEENTH CENTURY

With polychrome flower decorations inside and out; decorations in cobalt blue, light bluish green, vermilion, gold and creamy yellow; glaze of slightly bluish tinge

B. JAPANESE KUTANI PEAR-SHAPED BOTTLE OR VASE; EIGHTEENTH CENTURY

With polychrome flowers; decoration in dark blue, green, vermilion, pale rose and yellow; glaze of slightly greyish tinge

Courtesy of the British Museum

PLATE 30

BOWL OF MEDICI CHINA; LATE SIXTEENTH CENTURY
Decorations in blue, paste creamy white, glaze soft and waxy with slight bluish tinge
Courtesy of the Victoria and Albert Museum, South Kensington

PLATE 31

GINORI PLATTER, 1737; THE FIRST PIECE WITH POLYCHROME DECORATION MADE AT DOCCIA

Cream-coloured waxy paste: slightly raised moulding at edge of rim, with guilloche of mulberry and green, thin orange band, polychrome flower sprays on rim, figure with purple over-robe, green sleeves and coral red under-robe

Courtesy of Factory Museum at Doccia

PLATE 32

A. GINORI ICE PAIL, c.1760
Waxy paste, clear glaze; polychrome flower sprays scattered in Dresden manner, rose mulberry band at rim

B. GINORI SOUP PLATE, c.1760
Shaped rim with pineapple or basketwork moulded ornament and moulded ribbings, polychrome flowers in Mennecy manner, with scattered flowers and fruits in centre

Courtesy of Factory Museum at Doccia

rewarded this venture we know not, but the attempt was indicative of Ginori's alertness and determination to make the most of every opportunity for improvement that offered. While Governour of Livorno—he had then embarked on his porcelain-making experiments—at his own expense he sent a ship to the East Indies expressly to fetch some of the clay and other materials used by the Chinese in making porcelain.

The Marchese Ginori was a man of cultivated tastes and was readily susceptible to the "China-mania" that had taken Europe by storm. He was also blessed with prevision or prophetic imagination. Whether his ambition was fired by the memory and knowledge of the Medici porcelain, previously made in Florence, and by a laudable desire to renew and develope in his native country an enterprise so gratifying to his sense of beauty, or whether, as a result of his enquiries and observations, convinced that Italy possessed the materials requisite for an industry he foresaw would have a fruitful issue, it is impossible to say. In all likelihood both motives played a part in forming his ultimate determination. At all events, he set up his kilns and started the making of porcelain at Doccia. Quite apart from the character of the chinaware produced, the success of this establishment, which has continued in active operation to the present day, is remarkable because it was never assisted by Government subsidies or patronage as were so many other ventures of a like sort in other countries, with the exception of England and America.

Going to Vienna on a diplomatic mission, in 1737, the Marchese Ginori there met Karl Wandhelein, a chemist who had previously had some considerable experience in the manufacture of porcelain. Him Ginori engaged to come to Doccia and direct the nascent industry on which he had embarked two years before. Along with Wandhelein it is said—apparently with sufficient foundation—there came to Doccia one or more artists from Vienna or Saxony. Even the very early products shew the presence of someone experienced in design. Both the founder and his successors made it a point not only to have the ordinary workmen trained in modelling and decoration, but also to have their children taught these arts as well so that the traditions of the factory might pass on from generation to generation. In a way Doccia was really a little school of industrial art. Whoever the first modellers and decorators may have been, they were followed by a series of experts as competent as we should expect Florence to produce. The factory museum at Doccia, in which there is a complete chronologically arranged record of production, testifies to the prowess of these assistants.

Wandhelein appears to have been a capable director and in due time, though not until many costly experiments had been tried, the factory was enabled to place its products on a commercial basis. It has been said that eighteen years elapsed before the venture began to bring in any appreciable returns of profit. This statement, however, altogether lacks authentic substantiation. Whatever difficulties may or may not have had to be surmounted, this we know—the industry, from the very outset, was supported by the enterprise, energy and enthusiasm of Ginori alone.

The china made at Doccia exhibited many phases of style and decoration and in nearly all of them it is possible to recognise easily the sources of inspiration in different sorts of china made elsewhere. Some of the influence is distinctly Chinese, as was the case in nearly all china factories during much of the eighteenth century. This was natural for the art of chinaware was essentially a Chinese art and it was to be expected that Chinese precedents should be held in high esteem. Besides, the china art is an imitative art. Even the Chinese copied or adapted many of their early porcelain forms from bronze, brass and other metal shapes and, despite their proverbial conservatism, in much of their later ware they did not scruple to make use of elements derived from outside sources. Again, many of the influences to be discerned in the Ginori china are plainly of European origin. The Doccia factory was founded about ten years before Bow and Chelsea, five or six years before Vincennes, and only a few years later than St. Cloud and Chantilly, yet the impulses received from the greater French porcelain factories and some of those in England can be detected without difficulty, to say nothing of the strains derived from Dresden and Vienna. In regarding this reflex action exerted upon the output of Doccia by the work of other factories we must, however, remember this. Through former centuries Italy had lavishly supplied other countries with inspiration in all the arts; the eighteenth century was pre-eminently a period of borrowing back the commodity she had so freely given forth aforetime. Nevertheless, Italian hands always managed to give an individual twist of interpretation to borrowed *motifs*, imparting a distinctly national flavour. So it was in the making of Ginori china, and in this characteristic lies much of its charm. Again and again we find a strongly individual adaptation of several distinctive methods of borrowed decoration combined on one piece. Early in the nineteenth century the Ginori family bought many of the moulds from the Capo di Monte factory, at Naples, along with the right to use the Capo di Monte mark on reproductions made from these moulds.

The Doccia factory until a recent period remained wholly under the control of the Ginori family. Since a corporation was formed and an amalgamation effected with the Richard company, of Milano, the Ginori family have retained a controlling interest.

THE BODY. During the early years, the body or paste used was what they called *masso bastardo*, a composition which Brongniart places amongst the "hybrid" or *soft pastes*, apparently taking exception to the quantity of magnesia and the clay of Monte Carlo. In speaking of the kaolins of Campo and Chiusi, near Porto Ferraio on the Island of Elba, he notes that they are talc clays rather than true kaolins. He therefore designates the early Ginori china "hybrid" or *soft paste* porcelain, reserving the term "true" or *hard paste* porcelain for the later products. Although Brongniart is loath to count the *masso bastardo* as hard paste, nevertheless it was certainly not soft paste in the French sense nor the "bone" porcelain made in England. From the very start, Doccia followed the hard paste ideals of Dresden and Vienna, and there was never a distinct period of soft paste development as there was in France. Whatever may have been the imperfections of materials and composition, judged by Dresden standards, the *masso bastardo* seems to have been as "true" porcelain as some of the old Chinese bodies that have always been accounted hard paste.

The cost of importing clays and minerals from Germany would have been prohibitive; the Ginori factory, therefore, used native materials as closely as possible approximating the qualities of the kaolin and felspar used at Dresden. The paste made from these materials had a slightly greyish tone and a smooth texture.

When the deposits of kaolin and felspar were found at St. Yrieix in the south of France, these materials were used and the paste became a pure white. Since that date the characteristic Doccia paste has been white, hard, translucent and resonant.

THE GLAZE. The early glaze was soft, unctuous and exceedingly mellow, but not always evenly distributed, sometimes shewing a tendency to run. The later glaze was clear, brilliant and absolutely even in distribution, both glaze and body being technically perfect.

ARTICLES MADE AND CONTOUR. Almost from the outset Doccia has made all manner of tableware, vases of all sorts, candlesticks, sconces, all the various accessories for writing and dressing tables and figures and groups in biscuit. About the middle of the eighteenth century flowers were extensively modelled and naturalistically coloured. As the century advanced the pieces in biscuit were not confined to busts, figures and groups, but clock cases, table garnitures, vases and many other items were fashioned in the same substance.

The contours during the early days were to a great extent of Rococo type (Plate 33, B), with occasional interpretations of Oriental shapes. From about 1765 onward the contours were predominantly of Neo-Classic inspiration (Plate 35), while at the end of the century and in the fore part of the nineteenth the shapes shewed the impress of Neo-Grec and Empire styles.

TYPES OF DECORATION. At an early date in its history Doccia was using a varied array of decorative logical *motifs;* a prevalence of Pompeian and Etruscan features; and a more lavish use of gilding are the characteristics that especially mark this period.

THE MARKS. The marks used at the Doccia factory varied more or less at different periods. That of most common occurrence was the six-pointed star in one form or another. The six-pointed star and the star with many points are usually in red; the double triangle, which is really a variant of the six-pointed star, is often in gold on the finest pieces; the mullet with the double triangle may be found in blue or gold on pieces of exceptional quality. Capo di Monte reproductions, made from the purchased Capo di Monte moulds, bear the crowned N of Capo di Monte.

VENICE CHINA
VEZZI, 1720-1740; COZZI, 1764-1812

HISTORY. The first successful attempt to make porcelain in Europe is believed to have been in Venice about 1470. It is recorded that a certain Maestro Antonio, an alchemist, made bowls, vases and other small articles which were said to be of a very light and translucent porcelain, quite as good as, or even superior to, the porcelain of "Barbary." In 1508 a payment is recorded for seven bowls of *porcellana contrafacta*, which evidently means imitation porcelain. It is more than likely that this ware made by Maestro Antonio was soft paste porcelain. None of it is known to exist; nothing further is known of its making. The earliest European porcelain of which visible evidences remain was the Medici porcelain made in Florence.

PLATE 33

A. GINORI OVAL PLATTER, c.1775
Shaped moulded rim; Chinese peony decoration with prevailing red, blue and gold

B. GINORI COVERED DISH, 1770
Without coloured decoration, cream-coloured waxy paste, clear glaze; Louis XV. contour shewing Rococo influence, moulded pineapple or basketwork ornament about rim, and moulded gadrooning; delicately modelled flowers, leaves and stems applied

Courtesy of Factory Museum at Doccia

PLATE 34

A. GINORI PLATE, c.1815
Very hard, white body, clear glaze; ground of rim a deep red, charged
with elaborate gilt decoration in French Empire *motifs*
Courtesy of Factory Museum at Doccia

B. GINORI PLATE c.1780
Shaped moulded rim; paste hard and white; decoration of Oriental
origin, chiefly in red, blue and gold
Courtesy of Factory Museum at Doccia

PLATE 35

A. GINORI URN-SHAPED VASE OR JAR, c.1790   B. GINORI CHOCOLATE POT, c.1790
Paste hard and white; vertically striped decoration shewing con-   Classic impulse seen in oval medallion and guilloche bandings;
temporary French influence   French vertical stripings and other items interpreted in character-
istic Italian manner

Courtesy of Factory Museum at Doccia

PLATE 36

A. GINORI SWEETMEAT DISH, c.1780
Wedgwood influence in central medallion, scattered polychrome flowers and fruits in Dresden manner; hard, white paste, clear glaze

B. GINORI TUREEN ON LEGS, c.1780
Paste hard, slightly creamy in colour; Neo-Classic influence seen in oval shape, straight, fluted legs and collared feet

Courtesy of Factory Museum at Doccia

The next venture at porcelain making in Venice was in the eighteenth century. The brothers Vezzi, wealthy goldsmiths, had acquired patents of nobility. Having determined to establish an hard paste porcelain factory, in association with two other Venetians of rank, they employed Christoph Conrad Hunger as director and began operations in 1720. Hunger had previously worked at Dresden and at Vienna, and had the reputation of being the ablest porcelain expert of the day. Some workmen from Dresden are also believed to have been employed. The kaolin for the Vezzi china is said to have been brought from Saxony, but this seems highly improbable. The chinaware made was of very superior quality and closely resembled the wares of Dresden. Francesco Vezzi died in 1740 and the factory was discontinued.

From 1758 to 1763 there appears to have been a small porcelain factory conducted by a man named Hewelche and his wife, supposed to have come from Dresden. Little is known about this undertaking, and virtually nothing can be stated with certainty.

In 1764 Geminiano Cozzi established a soft paste porcelain factory near San Giobbe in Venice and made a great variety of beautiful wares. The enterprise proved a great commercial success and the factory did a flourishing business until 1812, when it was discontinued.

THE BODY. The hard paste of the Vezzi china was never a cold staring white, but of a somewhat warmer, creamier tone than Dresden china. It was, too, a little more glassy in appearance. Soft paste was also made by the Vezzi. The soft paste of the Cozzi had a slightly greyish tinge.

THE GLAZE. The Vezzi glaze was good, clear and very like that of Dresden. The Cozzi glaze was of excellent quality, but more satin-like and mellow.

ARTICLES MADE AND CONTOUR. The articles made at the Vezzi factory included not only the usual varieties of tableware, vases, flower pots and other ornamental objects, but also a number of figures and statuettes. During the term of Hunger's directorship, 1720 to 1725, the contours closely followed Dresden precedents. After Hunger's departure, the Dresden lead was less closely followed and the contours became more florid and more characteristic of the mid-eighteenth century Venetian phase of the Rococo manner.

The Cozzi factory also produced an highly diversified range of wares, over and above the usual table services and kindred articles of universal demand. Figures and groups, both glazed and painted, and also in the biscuit, were regularly made. By the time the Cozzi factory started, 1764, the excesses of Rococo design had passed so that the contours chiefly reflected the Neo-Classic trend, but with that mellowness and occasional whimsicality often imparted by Italian hands.

TYPES OF DECORATION. At the Vezzi factory, moulded or impressed ornament, modelled and applied ornament, pierced ornament, painting in underglaze blue and with on-glaze enamel colours, and gilding were all constantly used. The *motifs* were commonly figures, flowers (Plate 42), landscapes, harbour scenes, country scenes, birds, monkeys, and scrolls. Oriental *motifs* were often employed and were sometimes curiously blended with Venetian *motifs*. During the late period an iron-red was a favourite colour, although underglaze blue and a full palette of enamel colours, along with gilding, were in use throughout the entire period of the factory's existence.

At the Cozzi factory, all the same decorative processes were in use. The *motifs* were in large measure the Neo-Classic versions of those mentioned in connexion with the Vezzi factory, and other purely Classic devices pertaining especially to the later period, although some pronounced *chinoiseries* were still used, the taste for which seems to have lingered. In colour, there was a predilection for iron-red by itself, although all colours were in general use. Some of the decorations were in gold alone. The gilding done at the Cozzi factory was especially fine.

The Marks. During the period of Hunger's directorship at the Vezzi factory, 1720–1725 the pieces were unmarked. From 1725 to 1740 the mark in red or blue varied from "V" to "Venezia" with all manner of intermediate abbreviations. The mark of the Cozzi factory was an anchor drawn in red, blue, or gold, sometimes with the painter's initials above it. It is possible that the letter "C" may also have been used.

CAPO DI MONTE CHINA—1743–1821
CAPO DI MONTE—1743–1759
PORTICI—1771–1773
NAPLES—1773–1821

History. The Capo di Monte porcelain factory was established by Charles III, King of Naples, and installed in the palace of Capo di Monte in 1743, where it continued in operation till 1759, when Charles III succeeded to the throne of Spain and left Naples. This porcelain factory was a matter of the deepest interest to the King, and tradition says that he often worked in it with his own hands. At the annual fair, in the piazza before the palace, the products of the factory had a special stall and the King was furnished daily with a list of the sales made and the names of the purchasers. When Charles left Naples in 1759 he took with him to Madrid the best models and moulds, and about forty of the most skillful workmen.

From 1759 to 1771 operations were suspended. Then King Ferdinand IV re-established the works in the Villa Reale at Portici. In 1773 the factory was again moved and set up in Naples, where it continued to work under State direction and support until 1807, when it was sold to a company. It was closed in 1821.

THE BODY. During the first period, only soft paste porcelain was made, and the body was yellowish, greenish, bluish or dead grey in tone, the colour shewing considerable variation. The tinge was not always pronounced, and the ware was translucent.

From 1771 to about 1806 both soft and hard paste bodies were used. After 1806, or thereabouts, only hard paste was produced. The hard paste was pure white, hard, translucent and generally of excellent quality.

THE GLAZE. The glaze of the soft paste was soft, rich and satin-like to sight and touch. The hard paste glaze was clear and brilliant without being glittering.

ARTICLES MADE AND CONTOUR. The common impression of Capo di Monte china is onesided and quite erroneous. People ordinarily think of it as a sort of ware much over-decorated with small figures modelled in high relief (Plate 40, A), and further accentuated by lavish gilding and vigorous colouring in which pink, rose and purple are dominant. This manner of ware was peculiar to Capo di Monte, it is true, but it was by no means the only thing made there. A few of the pieces responsible for this impression may be genuine, but most of those ordinarily met with are counterfeits, manufactured by the gross to sell to gullible tourists. And by no means all of these counterfeits are made in Italy. As a matter of fact, a great many other and very different things were made at the royal factory, but unfortunately they are almost altogether unknown.

During the first period, besides tableware, vases, jars, flower pots, sconces and the like, there were made numbers of small snuff-boxes, patch-boxes, inkstands and similar articles on which it was possible to lavish the modelled and highly coloured decoration just mentioned—the kind of decoration that ninety-nine people out of an hundred associate with the name of Capo di Monte. Then, too, special pieces such as consoles, mirror-frames, clock-cases and chandeliers were made. All of these creations were agreeable to the Rococo taste of the age and were generally of more or less pronounced Rococo contours.

During the second period a number of biscuit pieces were put forth in addition to the wares previously enumerated. The contours, especially in the case of tableware and vases, became far more restrained and shewed the increasing influence of Neo-Classic conception. Painted decoration on the flat surface began visibly to triumph over applied modelling.

During the last period, when the factory was in Naples, all the preceding wares were made in considerable quantity, but there was a tendency to increase and emphasise the production of biscuit pieces. With Pompeii and Herculaneum as immediate sources of inspiration at the very doors, it is not surprising to find the Classic trend in contour becoming more and more pronounced.

TYPES OF DECORATION. Both for painted decoration and for decoration modelled and applied, we find great plenty of marine *motifs*—shells, dolphins, periwinkles, coral, fishes and the like. It has been suggested that some of these popular shell forms more than likely inspired the shell salt-cellars not long afterwards made at Bow. There is certainly a striking similarity between the Bow shell salt-cellars in plain white and the plain white shell forms made at Naples. Not a little of the early Capo di Monte china was wholly without colour; the modelled forms were not suggested by the white ware of Fuchien, but the general type probably was. Some of the white undecorated pieces, without modelled and applied ornament, are very simple and exhibit much dignity and charm of contour.

A number of pieces were painted with Oriental *motifs* interpreted in a very European manner. These were soon succeeded by unmistakably European themes in the way of natural flowers, fruits, birds, figures, pastorals, love scenes, landscapes and harbour scenes. Oftentimes the decorations were painted *en camaïeu*, crimson, bluish-violet and black being especially favoured for this purpose. Small landscapes and harbour scenes were often thus rendered in monochrome, either enclosed within panels and medallions or unenclosed.

Towards the latter part of the century and in the early years of the nineteenth two strong tendencies became apparent—first, a disposition to substitute painting and colour on a flat surface, whether in the form of ground

PLATE 39

A. SCEAUX ICE-PAIL, POLYCHROME FLOWER DECORATION
Courtesy of the Victoria and Albert Museum, South Kensington

B. GINORI OVAL PLATTER, c.1760
Shaped moulded rim, polychrome flower decoration in manner of **Mennecy**

Courtesy of Factory Museum at Doccia

colours, carefully executed Classic *motifs* or landscapes and harbour scenes of a general character, for modelled, applied and coloured ornament; second, a pronounced bias in favour of the *motifs* directly derived from Pompeii and Herculaneum (Plate 40, B). To the latter tendency we are indebted for the so-called "Pompeian" china which supplied an impulse felt throughout Europe. The cameos and medallions were rendered with exquisite taste, and these as well as the arabesques exercised a profound influence on the china decoration of the age. From the time the factory was transferred to Naples, the revived Classic style in both contour and decoration was followed almost exclusively. There were also many local incidents of sea and mountain, including the various moods of Vesuvius, introduced into the decoration. Grey, green, blue, yellow and Pompeian red were some of the ground colours much used and these, sometimes along with touches of black, afforded admirable foils for Classic subjects in panels and medallions, or for the reserved panels enclosing flowers, birds, country scenes or harbour views. The gilding was always notably good.

THE MARKS. During the first period the mark was the Bourbon fleur-de-lys, impressed in the paste or painted in blue. It was also occasionally applied in red or gold. In the later periods the mark was "N", usually surmounted by a crown, but sometimes without. It was commonly in blue, but now and again it occurred in red or else impressed in the paste. While the factory was at Portici the marks "R. F." and "F. R. F." occur. The genuine Capo di Monte ware with modelled and applied figures is generally unmarked, and the flesh tints are exquisitely

THE PRACTICAL BOOK OF CHINAWARE

soft; the Ginori reproductions of the same ware are usually marked with the crowned "N" or otherwise and the flesh tints have a stippled appearance.

LE NOVE CHINA—1762–1835

HISTORY. In 1761 or 1762 Pasquale Antonibon began to make soft paste porcelain at Nove, near Bassano, in his faïence factory. Antonibon had the fortunate faculty of being able to attract men of talent to work with him, and the results of this are manifest in the china. The Antonibons, father and son, made soft-paste porcelain until 1802, when the factory passed out of their hands till 1825. The factory then reverted to the former owners and they continued to produce porcelain till 1835. After that time only faïence and divers other sorts of earthenware were made.

The chinaware issuing from the Nove factory possesses great artistic distinction (Plate 41). The paste was a beautiful creamy white and the glaze was mellow and clear. There was great diversity in the matter of decoration. The jardinière illustrated (Plate 41), is clearly in the manner of Sèvres. Flower decorations are numerous, oftentimes in polychrome, occasionally in green and gold, now and again in purple. Ground colours were used very frequently and were always good. Birds, landscapes, Classical and mythological subjects likewise appear as *motifs*. The factory is said to have made figures in biscuit.

The mark was "Nove," either with or without a six-

PLATE 37

A. AND *B.* GINORI FIGURES, c.1775
Creamy white paste, clear glaze; exquisite modelling, partial polychrome decoration
Courtesy of Factory Museum at Doccia

PLATE 38

A. AND *B*. GINORI CUPS AND SAUCERS, c.1765
Decorations *en camaïeu*
Courtesy of Factory Museum at Doccia

C. GINORI REPRODUCTION OF
CAPO DI MONTE FIGURE
From Capo di Monte mould; flesh tints
and partial coloured decoration
Courtesy of Factory Museum at Doccia

pointed star in blue or red or, sometimes, in gold. Occasionally the star occurs without the name. Some of the Nove China, between 1802 and 1825 when the factory was in the hands of Giovanni Baroni, has the initials "G. B." above the name "Nove."

$$* \quad * \quad * \quad \overset{\frown}{\underset{\text{NOVE}}{GB}}$$

VINOVO CHINA—1776-1820

HISTORY. With the assistance of Pierre Antoine Hannong of Strasburg, Giovanni Brodel established an hard paste porcelain factory at Vinovo, near Torino, in 1776. Brodel found Hannong a most difficult person to work with and retired from the business in 1778. In 1780 it was sold to Dr. Gioanetti, an eminent chemist. Under him the factory produced a considerable quantity of china up to 1815, when Dr. Gioanetti died. Under his successor the business declined so rapidly that the factory was closed in 1820.

The paste at first was of a yellowish tone and the glaze was often defective; the later ware was of fine grain and had an excellent white glaze. The decorations, though not distinguished, were pleasing and the colours were good. Flowers, polychrome and monochrome, garlands and ribbons, medallions, landscapes, flowers and arabesques in gold, and numerous *motifs* of Classic provenance make up the repertoire. In general style the Vinovo china resembled the wares of the independent Parisian factories of the late eighteenth century.

The mark was "V" with a cross above it, in either underglaze blue or on-glaze blue; occasionally the mark was incised, or else applied in black, brown, red, or gold. In exceptional cases the "V" may be omitted or the cross may be omitted.

† ⩲V̇. ⩲V̇.⁄DG L.V̇.

ROME PORCELAIN—1790–1831

History. The hard paste porcelain made by Giovanni Volpato at Rome from 1790 to 1831 was restricted to groups and figures in biscuit. They were copies from antiques and the sculptures of Canova.

TREVISO AND ESTE CHINA

History. At Este, between Padova and Ferrara, a soft paste porcelain factory was established in 1780 which made both tableware and figures in biscuit. Little is known about it, but the few pieces that can be traced to Este display merit. The Este mark may be the word "Este" accompanied by a date or may be of the form shewn in the cut.

In the latter part of the eighteenth century a small quantity of soft paste porcelain was made at Treviso, consisting mostly of tableware. The pieces are marked "Treviso" with G.A.F.F., or F.F., in addition.

D·B

FRENCH CHINAWARE

ROUEN CHINA—1673-1696

HISTORY. The earliest manufacture of porcelain in France, of which we have any reasonably sure knowledge, was that established under letters-patent by Louis Poterat in 1673 at Rouen.

In 1664, it is true, Louis XIV had granted to Charles Reverend a patent for the making of porcelain in Paris, and there are several allusions in works of the time apparently indicating that in or near Paris attempts to produce porcelain were made before 1670. There are several specimens of early work, too, which it seems impossible to identify as the products of either Rouen or St. Cloud. These seem to indicate the existence of a short-lived enterprise whose records have been lost. It is, therefore, the manufacture inaugurated by Poterat at Rouen that we must regard as the first authenticated production of porcelain in France.

The letters-patent issued to Poterat in 1673 granted him an "exclusive monopoly for the fabrication of plates and dishes, pots, and vases of porcelain like that of China . . . . for the period of thirty years." This privilege was conferred in consideration of his foreign travels and diligent application whereby he had mastered the technical secrets enabling him to establish a new industry in France. An official report, made at the instance of M. de Pontchartrain in 1694, discloses the facts that porcelain was made at the factories of both Louis Poterat and his father; that the works were well kept; and that although they possessed the secret of making porcelain, very little of it was made, most of the output consisting of faïence. Louis Poterat died in 1696 and the conduct of the works then fell to his brother. The latter, however, seems to have been incapable of continuing the business successfully and the making of Rouen porcelain was discontinued.

The Rouen china was soft paste porcelain and the body, of a rich, creamy quality, has a slightly greenish hue. The glaze is less "glassy" in appearance than the glaze of much other soft paste porcelain and exhibits a very pale sea-green tinge.

There are only about fifty pieces of Rouen china known to be in existence, and almost all of these are decorated altogether in blue, although a few specimens exhibit other colours in combination. One piece in the museum at Rouen shows a decoration in blue, green and red. The blue is darker, denser and often greyer than the blue usually seen on other early soft paste porcelains, and the colour seems to have been applied not *under* the glaze but *on* the raw glaze before it was fired.

It is noteworthy that the decorations were invariably in the contemporary French manner of ornament that characterised the reign of Louis XIV. It is all the more remarkable that no *motifs* of direct Chinese provenance occur when we remember that the making of porcelain was an openly avowed imitation of Chinese methods, was stimulated by Chinese examples, and that in nearly every other case Chinese types of decoration were borrowed and applied without hesitation.

SAINT CLOUD CHINAWARE — c.1696 – c.1773 (?)

HISTORY. "I saw the potterie of St. Clou, with which I was marvellously well pleased, for I confess I could not distinguish betwixt the pots made there and the finest China ware I ever saw. It will, I know, be easily granted me that the painting may be better designed and finished (as indeed it was) because our men are far better masters of that art than the Chineses; but the glazing came not in the least behind theirs, not for whiteness, nor the smoothness of running without bubbles. Again, the inward substance and matter of the pots was, to me, the very same, hard and firm as marble, and the self-same grain on this side vitrification. Farther the transparency of the pots the very same. . . . . I did not expect to have found it in this perfection, but imagined this might have arrived at the Gomron ware; which is, indeed, little else but a total vitrification, but I found it far otherwise and very surprising, and which I account part of the felicity of the age to equal if not surpass the Chineses in their finest art.

They sold these pots at St. Clou at excessive rates, and for their ordinary chocolate cups askt crowns a-piece. They had arrived at the burning on gold in neat chequere works. He had sold some tea equipages at 100 livres a sett. There was no moulding or model of China ware which they had not imitated, and had added many fancies of their own, which had their good effects and appeared very beautiful."

Account of a Journey to Paris in the Year 1698, by Doctor Martin Lister, published in London, 1699.

Besides this testimony to the merits and charms of Saint Cloud chinaware by the eminent Doctor Lister, who had accompanied the Duke of Portland to Paris on a diplomatic mission and was afterwards physician to Queen Anne, there is the witness of royal interest in the works and appreciation of its products. *Le Mercure Galant*, in October 1700, contains this notice:

"I have forgotten to write to you that the Duchesse de Bourgogne, when she had passed through St. Cloud and turned along the riverside to visit Madame la Duchesse de Guiche, made her carriage stop at the door of the house where the MM. Chicanneau have had established for some years now a manufactory of fine porcelain, which without doubt has not its like in all Europe. The princess found pleasure in seeing several pieces of very good shape made on the wheel. She saw some others painted in patterns that were more regular and better done than those of the Indian porcelain. Then she went to see the faïences being made in the manufactory, and afterwards MM. Chicanneau conducted her into their office, where she saw quantities of fine and beautiful porcelains in their perfection, with which she was so pleased that she promised to come again. She did not leave without shewing her satisfaction by the gratuities she gave to the workmen."

Established as it was under the shadow of the Château de Saint Cloud, the factory seems not only to have enjoyed a measure of interest and patronage from the Duc d'Orléans, but also to have attracted not a little favourable notice from the King and the great personages of the Court on their comings and goings between Versailles and Paris, and its success in a commercial sense was probably due in large measure to these advantageous circumstances.

The establishment at Saint Cloud began, it appears, as a faïence factory. By 1670 it was important enough to be given a large commission for orange pots and flower vases for the gardens of Versailles, as well as being called upon to supply numerous other decorative requisites from time to time. Its wares justly deserved their high reputation.

Antiquarian research has discovered that there was a painter named Chicanneau in Poterat's factory at Rouen and it is thought that he there first found out the secrets of porcelain-making and then carried them to Saint Cloud. At all events, the letters-patent of 1696—from which year we may date the official manufacture of porcelain at the Saint Cloud factory—granted by Louis XIV to "Barbe Coudray, the widow of Pierre Chicanneau, and to Jean-Baptiste, Pierre and Geneviève Chicanneau, brothers and sisters, children of the aforesaid Coudray and the aforesaid Pierre Chicanneau, and the undertakers of the faïence and porcelain works established at Saint Cloud," mention the porcelain-making experiments of Pierre Chicanneau the father, note his success in producing pieces approximating Chinese porcelain in excellence, and state that the children have carried on the work and, prior to the year 1696, "have arrived at the point of making porcelain of perfect quality."

Historical data regarding the porcelain works of Saint Cloud are not plentiful in contemporary French memoirs, but it appears that off-shoots of the establishment at Saint Cloud were started in the faubourg St. Honoré and in the faubourg St. Antoine in Paris, where similar wares were produced, by members of the Chicanneau family. These splits were seemingly caused by family dissensions with ensuing legal processes and great expense. It is said that the factory at Saint Cloud was destroyed by fire in 1773 and that the owners, thanks to long wrangling and law costs, had not money enough to rebuild it. This misfortune presumably put an end to the manufacture of Saint Cloud china. The Saint Cloud works, however, can boast the distinction of having been the first French enterprise of the sort that succeeded in maintaining a long continued existence.

THE BODY. The china of Saint Cloud is one of the soft paste porcelains. It has a creamlike yellowish tinge, and where chipped or broken the fracture shews a close, regular granular texture.

THE GLAZE. The glaze is clear and shews very few bubbles to break its evenness. It is more brilliant than the Rouen glaze and has a very slight creamy tinge. Blisters rarely occur. There seems also to have been some use of coloured glazes for there is in the Victoria and Albert Museum a little water jug, with attached cover, moulded top and bottom, with an overlapping scale or pineapple skin *motif*, and covered with a pale green glaze, evidently made in emulation of the old Chinese Celadon ware.

ARTICLES MADE AND CONTOUR. The articles most commonly made at the Saint Cloud factory included cups, saucers, jugs, teapots, coffee pots, chocolate pots, tea, coffee and chocolate services, trays, dishes, plates, platters, tureens, sugar-bowls or basons and tableware generally, knife handles, statuettes, grotesques, vases, bowls and flowerpots.

Porcelain figures are said to have been first fashioned at Saint Cloud and, between 1710 and 1724 under the direction of Dominique Chicanneau, "all other kinds of imaginable things." Grotesque figures and branched candlesticks in the form of tree trunks appeared, it is stated, as early as 1731, but these branched candlesticks mentioned by contemporary writers seem not to have survived.

The contours of the various pieces were at first mainly of Chinese derivation for European china-makers at the outset, almost without exception, tried to reproduce both Oriental shapes and Oriental decoration as nearly as they could in order to compete with the china imported from the East.

PLATE 40

A. CAPO DI MONTE CUP
Modelled decoration in relief, strong polychrome treatment; creamy soft paste
Courtesy of the British Museum

B. NAPLES PLATTER AND TUREEN IN POMPEIAN MANNER
Hard white paste, clear glaze; gold decorations, pale green figures on black ground in medallion
Courtesy of the Victoria and Albert Museum, South Kensington

PLATE 41

LE NOVE JARDINIÈRE
Bands in yellow-green with gold diaper, flowers in dull madder, blue, yellow, violet and vermilion; glaze slightly uneven and of yellowish tinge

Courtesy of the Victoria and Albert Museum, South Kensington

PLATE 42

A. VENETIAN CUP AND SAUCER
Heraldic devices in dull Indian red; decorations in gold, violet and a little green; glaze cold white

B. VENETIAN TRAY WITH SHAPED RIM
Floral decoration in light violet, yellow, deep green and Indian red; cold white glaze

Courtesy of the Victoria and Albert Museum, South Kensington

PLATE 43

A. SAINT CLOUD FLOWER POT, IN THE WHITE
Gadrooned rim and base, moulded flower and foliage decoration in low relief, modelled handles; creamy white soft paste, slightly greenish glaze
Courtesy of the Victoria and Albert Museum, South Kensington

B. SAINT CLOUD TEAPOT, IN THE WHITE
Moulded prunus-blossom *motif* in relief, modelled handle and spout; creamy white soft paste, slightly greenish glaze
Courtesy of the Victoria and Albert Museum, South Kensington

FRENCH CHINAWARE

Later there was a gradual modification and an addition of shapes less distinctively Chinese and more European in character. It is worth noting that at Saint Cloud the same contours and the same decorations were continued in use over a long period of time.

METHODS AND TYPES OF DECORATION. White pieces with modelled ornament (Plate 43, A), were produced in fairly numerous quantity, evidently inspired by the white ware of Fuchien (Plate 43, B), which was greatly admired in Europe. These pieces depended for their charm on the moulded and applied ornaments and included such objects as small figures or statuettes, knife handles, cups, saucers, covered jars, jugs, bowls and sugar dishes, and flower-pots. Prunus blossoms and sprigs in relief (Plate 43, B), flowers, sprays and rosettes appeared on the porcelain surface.

While the plain white ware decorated with applied reliefs (1) met with favour, a great many of the pieces bearing moulded reliefs were also enriched with patterns in underglaze blue (2), the colour decoration being so disposed as to accentuate the value of the modelling (Plate 44, B). (3) A few of the pieces with modelled reliefs were decorated with red, yellow, purple, green and dark brown along with the blue. (4) Pieces of Chinese shape, but without moulded reliefs, bore polychrome decorations, for the most part in designs closely copied from Chinese models. (5) A later development employed European designs, blue and polychrome, in the lighter and more graceful *motifs* of the Baroque manner (Plate 44, A), that characterised the reign of Louis XIV; these appeared first on pieces of Chinese shape. Together with these patterns and modified shapes (6), a more flowing manner of modelled reliefs came into use, the combination resulting in what was, perhaps, the most typical phase of Saint Cloud chinaware.

THE MARKS. The marks were carelessly used and are not certain guides. A sun pressed into the paste was the first mark. A later mark consisted of the letters S C, in blue, with a small cross above and the letter T underneath. In company with this mark are often found numbers or detached letters, which may be the numbers of certain patterns or the initials of the decorators. Sometimes these blue initials are surrounded by little crosses. A fleur-de-lys is said to have been used sometimes but some doubt exists on this score.

LILLE CHINAWARE—c.1711 - ?

HISTORY. In 1711 Barthélemy Dorez exhibited to the Mayor and Council of Lille specimens of porcelain that he and his nephew, Pierre Pélissier, had fashioned; at the same time he sought permission to set up a porcelain factory in connexion with his faïence establishment and likewise asked certain concessions. The Council granted his petitions and subsidised his works, the subsidy being regularly continued till 1720 by which time the undertaking seems to have been firmly on its feet. The brothers Dorez offered to sell their enterprise to the King who, however, declined to buy it but gave them certain privileges and exemptions that could not infringe the rights of the French East India Company nor offend the Duc d'Orléans who was patron of the Saint Cloud factory. These privileges did not include permission to open a warehouse in Paris for the sale of their wares, and without this outlet they had not a sufficient market to maintain their enterprise. The manufacture of Lille porcelain was discontinued not long afterwards, but it is not known in exactly what year this occurred.

The products of the Lille factory were chiefly confined to imitations of the wares of Saint Cloud, and it is often difficult to distinguish with any degree of certainty between the pieces issuing from the two establishments, especially when sufficient marks of identification are lacking. The chief difference between the porcelain of Lille and that of Saint Cloud seems to have been that the former lacked the finish and interest of decoration shewn by the Saint Cloud china, and that the glaze shewed a greater tendency to blister. The paste was the same at both Lille and Saint Cloud.

The mark D occasionally appears on pieces decorated in blue, as well as the mark Æ. The mark L, accompanied by a cross, may indicate Lille or it may be one of the varied marks employed at Saint Cloud.

L   D⟊.   L⟊

CHANTILLY CHINA—1725-1789

HISTORY. The Prince de Condé, lord of the château and domain of Chantilly, was the patron of the porcelain factory and provided the funds to enable Ciquaire Cirou to carry out experiments. Letters-patent were issued to Cirou in 1735, and therein it is set forth that, for the ten years preceding, he had endeavoured at Chantilly to make porcelain of the same quality as the Japanese; that he had excelled the Dresden porcelain; and that he purposed selling his wares not only in France but abroad as well. In view of these declarations, the King accords Ciquaire Cirou licence, for twenty years, to make at Chantilly all manner of china in imitation of Japanese porcelain.

The Prince de Condé was an eager connoisseur and had collected a number of fine examples of Imari ware. In this collection were some excellent specimens of Kakiyemon decoration, and these seem particularly to have inspired much of the early Chantilly decoration—very appropriately, indeed, as imitation of the Japanese porcelain was avowedly one of the chief objects proposed by Cirou. (Plate 45.)

Chantilly never took the lead in originating new styles. The factory was started with the ideal of good imitations, and its successive directors contented themselves with producing admirable adaptations of the successive styles put forth elsewhere. Nevertheless, despite any evidence of originality, the work of Chantilly possessed great distinction and charm, and its appealing beauty ensured constant popularity so long as the factory lasted. It continued until 1789, on the eve of the Revolution, and, after the time of Cirou, was under the directorship of Antheaume, Potter, de Baynal and Lallement in order.

THE BODY. The body of Chantilly china was a soft paste, very like the paste of Saint Cloud, of an even granular texture, with a mellow, creamy or slightly yellowish tinge. It seems, however, to have been more solid and stable in the firing, inasmuch as large flat pieces, such as platters, could be made successfully. These appear not to have been put forth at Saint Cloud.

THE GLAZE. There were two distinct types of glaze used at Chantilly, one during the early years of the factory's existence, the other adopted at a later date. The early Chantilly glaze contained oxide of tin which gave it a milky-white, opaque quality that not only enhanced the brilliancy of the decorations but also imparted a strongly individual aspect to the ware and increased its resemblance to the Japanese prototypes.

Subsequently, in order to meet the demand of competition with Sèvres and Mennecy-Villeroy, this glaze was abandoned and a transparent glaze adopted in its stead.

ARTICLES MADE AND CONTOUR. The chief products of the Chantilly factory included dinner services, tea and coffee sets, cabarets or solitaires, trays, jugs, statuettes, grotesque figures, flowers, birds, sconces and candlesticks, modelled bouquets, knife handles, ink-pots and writing paraphernalia in general, boxes, caskets, powder boxes, vases, pomatum pots, snuff boxes, patch boxes, covered jars, and various other objects of common use.

At first Japanese forms were largely used as models, and many of the platters, dishes, trays and sugar bowls were of lobate form which seems to have been especially favoured. Chinese types of contour, too, were considerably followed, not only for tea-services and articles of tableware but also for the modelled figures and grotesques.

At the same time a great many distinctively French forms were adopted and executed with consummate delicacy, refinement and charm. Subsequently, the work done at Sèvres supplied not a little material for imitation and the Chantilly renderings were in no wise inferior to their models.

TYPES OF DECORATION. The types of decoration characteristic of Chantilly china include the polychrome Kakiyemon *motifs* (Plate 45), of flowers, sprigs and birds; the more stayed and conventionally disposed Imari *motifs* with dominant blue, red and gold; Chinese polychrome *motifs*; underglaze blue decorations of flower sprays (Plate 46, A and B), modelled and applied ornaments for white ware, and modelled flowers and figures for knobs and handles on tableware, which were decorated with colour; little scattered flowers and sprays in imitation of the Dresden manner; compositions of fruits, flowers and birds in a clear green etched with black; polychrome flowers, fruits and birds like those used at Sèvres; embossed patterns of basketwork and other *motifs* for plate rims and necks of jugs; perforations (Plate 46, C), and the yellow, blue, green, and rose grounds in the style of Sèvres, with the accompaniment of gilding, reserves, and multi-coloured flowers. These last, it may be added, were so successfully carried out that it is virtually impossible to tell many of them from Sèvres pieces of the same description unless the marks be examined.

THE MARKS. The usual mark employed at Chantilly was a carefully drawn hunting horn applied in on-glaze red. Late in the eighteenth century the same mark appears in blue, oftentimes accompanied by letters and figures meant to specify different individual pieces. The fact that instances occur where the Chantilly mark has been removed and the Sèvres mark substituted by falsifiers shews how close was often the resemblance between the two wares.

MENNECY-VILLEROY CHINA—1735-1773 OR 1774

HISTORY. The factory of Mennecy-Villeroy was started in 1735 by François Barbin under the patronage of the Duke, Louis-François de Neufville de Villeroy, one of the great nobles of the Court of Louis XV. Apparently the venture was undertaken, and porcelain was manufactured, without the authorisation of royal letters-patent. Royal sanction, it seems, was not granted until 1748, and then it was restricted with stipulations that Barbin must not employ any workmen who had ever worked at Vincennes and that he must not imitate the wares made there.

The earliest pieces made at Mennecy were imitations of Saint Cloud china. Somewhat later, the opaque tin glaze of Chantilly was used and Chantilly wares were copied. At length the factory found itself, so to speak, and developed a manner of its own. Although the creations of Vincennes and Sèvres were closely imitated, nevertheless a certain individual character was imparted to the Mennecy china.

Jean-Baptiste Barbin, who had succeeded his father as director of Mennecy, was himself succeeded about 1766 by the MM. Jacques and Jullien, who not only managed the works but became its owners as well. One was a painter and the other a sculptor. In 1773 or 1774 the factory of Mennecy-Villeroy came to an end after venturing to make pieces in biscuit besides producing some of the most fascinating china of the eighteenth century, of much artistic excellence.

THE BODY. The Mennecy-Villeroy porcelain had a soft paste body of a yellowish or dark ivory tinge, and was made in emulation of the Saint Cloud body. The faint yellowish or amber tone gave it a peculiarly mellow quality and rendered it a warm and sympathetic ground for the coloured decoration applied to its surface.

THE GLAZE. The glaze of the earliest efforts is faulty and uneven, and although the technical shortcomings were soon remedied, there was rarely or never quite the same perfection of finish in this respect that characterised the work of several of the other contemporary factories. At one time an opaque glaze was used, much like the early Chantilly glaze which, however, it did not equal.

ARTICLES MADE AND CONTOUR. Amongst the articles made at the Mennecy-Villeroy factory the modelled pieces in biscuit deserve special mention because of their artistic excellence and because of the initiative implied in undertaking them. An advertisement of March, 1766, announcing the coming sale of the factory and its stock of wares—this was just before Jacques and Jullien became the proprietors—enumerates "cups, saucers, antique vases, groups, pedestals, mustard-pots, gravy-boats, dishes, covered dishes, cruet-stands, powder-boxes, sugar-boxes, sugar bowls for the table, and fruit baskets of various forms."

Besides these, the factory customarily made a varied assortment of pieces including flower pots, pot-pourri jars, milk jugs, coffee and chocolate pots, teapots, water jugs, ewers and basons, wall brackets and sconces, small clock cases, mirror frames, candlesticks, statuettes, snuff-boxes, pomatum pots, patch boxes, knife handles, and sundries for household embellishment or use upon writing tables or dressing stands. There seems to have been a

PLATE 44

A. SAINT CLOUD COVERED JAR
Decoration in underglaze blue, *motifs* in Louis XIV manner; creamy soft paste, glaze slightly bluish

B. SAINT CLOUD COVERED JAR
Moulded decoration in relief coloured, pink, yellow, blue and violet, stems and leaves green and blue green; creamy paste and glaze

Courtesy of the Victoria and Albert Museum, South Kensington

PLATE 45

CHANTILLY GRAVY BOAT

Characteristic lobate form, with modelled flower knob; Kakiyemon decoration in light blue, light green, pale yellow and vermilion; creamy soft paste, glaze slightly bluish

Courtesy of the Victoria and Albert Museum, South Kensington

PLATE 46

A. AND *B*. CHANTILLY FLOWER POT AND LOBATE COVERED DISH
Creamy soft paste, slightly greenish glaze; decorations light and dark greyish underglaze blue

C. CHANTILLY OVAL FRUIT DISH

Edges of perforations in mulberry, light blue ribbons on handles, flower sprays in mulberry yellow and green; creamy soft paste, glaze nearly white

Courtesy of the Victoria and Albert Museum, South Kensington

PLATE 47

MENNECY-VILLEROY VASE
Characteristic flower decoration in rose, mulberry, yellow, green and dull blue; rim line of burnt Siena; soft paste of creamy ivory tone, clear glaze

Courtesy of the Victoria and Albert Museum, South Kensington

FRENCH CHINAWARE

marked preference for vertical rather than flat pieces, and consequently plates and platters were comparatively rare products.

During the sway of the Chinese taste the Mennecy factory made use of a number of Oriental shapes, but most of its products exhibit purely European contours. Those in the Rococo manner shew much grace and charm, particularly the pieces of simpler character, although some of the more elaborate efforts (Plate 2, J) were rather overdone in their tortured intricacy.

The knobs on the lids of tea, coffee and chocolate pots, sugar bowls (Plate 48), and covered dishes, and the handles of tureens and dishes, were well modelled and daintily picked out with colours.

TYPES OF DECORATION. The Mennecy types of decoration, at the outset, were patterned after the early methods of Saint Cloud and Rouen, use being made of the characteristic *lambrequins* of the latter factory wrought in blue. Then followed decorative painting in bright, glowing reds, greens, yellows and blues in the subsequent manner of Saint Cloud and Chantilly, both in the Kakiyemon vein and in the more realistic French and Saxon styles (Plate 48). The most characteristic Mennecy decorations were those patterned after the modes of Vincennes and Sèvres, although the Mennecy decorators always managed to impart a certain individuality to the pieces they put forth. Chinese as well as Japanese *motifs*, of course, were employed to some extent, but the greater part of the decorations were wholly European in character.

Occasionally Sèvres ground colour processes were followed, such as using a *bleu du roi* ground enriched with "partridge eye" diapering, gilding and polychrome flowers in reserve. A number of cups, saucers, snuff-boxes and other small articles were produced which displayed pastoral scenes and figures after the fashion of Watteau and Lancret, executed with exquisite finish.

A purplish rose colour was characteristic of Mennecy decoration (Plate 47), and occurs very frequently, while yellow, rose, lilac and blue are rather predominant in the flower painting. As gilding was a jealously maintained prerogative of the royal factories, and was forbidden Mennecy, so that there were times when it could not be practised extensively or openly, it was necessary to find some substitute to use as a finish for certain schemes where gold would ordinarily have been employed. This substitute is discovered in the yellow, blue and, more especially, the rose-coloured lines with which the mouldings, edges (Plate 47), and other suitable points were habitually embellished. These colour lines add greatly to the charm of the decoration and we may now be glad that gilding was banned.

Polychrome painting of flowers and other *motifs* was also prescribed by royal letters-patent as the sole privilege of Vincennes and Sèvres. Although there were long periods when this regulation was not enforced, and when the other porcelain factories employed colour as freely as they pleased without molestation or interference, there were also occasions when the privilege was insistently maintained. At such times there was no choice but compliance and Mennecy, Chantilly and Saint Cloud had to be content for a season with monochrome decoration until the lines were relaxed again. About 1766 there was such a period of stringency. When the anti-polychrome regulation was enforced, the factories other than Vincennes and

Sèvres were at liberty to use any one colour desired in decorating a piece of china, and flowers, birds, and other *motifs* were all presented in blue, yellow, rose or mauve, as the case might be, *en camaïeu* as the method was called. Not a few of these decorations *en camaïeu* are very beautiful and possess great distinction.

THE MARKS. The unmistakable Mennecy mark consisted of the letters D. V. (presumably signifying Duc de Villeroy). On the earlier work, this mark was painted in enamel colour; later it became customary to scratch or engrave it on the paste before firing. On some of the Sèvres imitations the two crossed "L's" of Sèvres are *painted* beside the D. V. incised in the body.

D.V.

VINCENNES CHINA—1740–1745–1756

HISTORY. The porcelain factory at Vincennes owed its inception to three fugitives from Chantilly—the brothers Dubois, painter and sculptor, who had been dismissed for flagrant ill conduct, and one Gérin. Having secretly got possession of the Chantilly processes, they set about the manufacture of porcelain on their own account. About 1740 they disposed of some of their products in Paris and, as a result, obtained the interest of M. de Fulvy through whose good offices the King granted them permission to occupy some buildings adjacent to the château of Vincennes. M. de Fulvy also got them a grant of money. They took into partnership a man named Gravant, who likewise had knowledge of porcelain-making processes and was ready to invest a considerable sum in the enterprise.

The porcelain they made appears to have been unreliable in quality at first and a large proportion of their pieces got spoiled in the firing. Much of the trouble was directly attributable to the general ill-behaviour and drunkenness of the brothers Dubois—there seems to have been no fault with their formulas or processes—who eventually made off, leaving a disorganised and bankrupt concern on Gravant's hands. Gravant, however, had mastered all their porcelain secrets and succeeded in winning the substantial support of M. de Fulvy and a number of courtiers and financiers so that he was able to put the factory on its feet for the time being.

In 1745 a company was formed, with privileges granted by the King who himself took a direct and lively interest in the undertaking and aided it financially. Under these favourable auspices the staff was strengthened by the addition of the most competent people it was possible to secure. Hellot, a distinguished chemist, took charge of the chemical management; Duplessis, a goldsmith and sculptor, supervised the modelling; and the artist Bachelier, along with Mathieu, the King's enameller, took charge of the decorating.

Although the financial condition was always precarious until the factory ultimately became a royal establishment, artistic success crowned the efforts put forth and so distinguished were the achievements that early in 1748, when the Queen received an handsome presentation vase from the factory, the Dauphine Marie-Josèphe, "a finished diplomatist, ordered a similar vase as a present for her father, Frederick Augustus, Elector of Saxony, to shew him that the Vincennes porcelain was quite equal to that of Dresden." All the great nobles of the court became ardent patrons of the works, and plans were laid for increasing the volume of the output in view of the demand both in France and abroad. The memoirs of the Duc de Luynes mention naïvely that "the English want only white porcelain, but as they might use this to paint upon, they [the pieces of porcelain] are sold just as dear as the painted ones."

Triumphs of marvellous production continued without cease. One of the notable achievements was the fashioning of porcelain flowers that possessed the utmost verisimilitude to the living blooms and were immensely popular. From the memoirs of the Marquis d'Argenson we learn that:

"The King has ordered from the Vincennes works porcelain flowers, naturally painted, with their vases——more than 800,000 livres worth——for all his country houses, and especially for the château of Bellevue of the Marquise de Pompadour. Nothing else is spoken of in Paris, and truly this unheard of luxury causes great scandal."

Also, Soulavie, in his memoirs of the Duc de Richelieu, writes:

"Madame de Pompadour, doing the honours of her residence to the King, displayed before his eyes a whole flower garden. She expected him one day in this charming château of Bellevue, which had cost him so much, and when he entered it, she received him in an apartment at the far end of which was a hot-house with an immense flower bed, although it was a hard winter. As fresh roses, lilies and pinks predominated, the enraptured King could not sufficiently admire the beauty and the sweet scent of these flowers. But nature had been made game of. These vases, flowers, roses, lilies, pinks and their stems—everything was porcelain—and the sweet perfume of these heavenly flowers was the effect of their essences, volatilised by art."

The fashionable world went quite mad over these porcelain flowers, and for a time the major part of the factory's business lay in filling orders for them.

Notwithstanding all these outward successes, the factory was just beginning to work at a small profit when the deaths of both M. de Fulvy and his brother threw the financial affairs of the company again into complete chaos so that it was necessary, in order to avert catastrophe, to appeal for the more direct aid of the King. The outcome of the negotiations was that in 1752–3 the factory of Vincennes was declared the "*Manufacture Royale de Porcelaine*" and became an institution directly under the King's protection and support. As such, it continued until it was merged in the royal manufactory of Sèvres in 1756.

THE BODY. The Vincennes body was a soft paste, regarding the composition of which there are extensive historical data, as well as detailed descriptions of the processes employed. The earliest paste produced by the brothers Dubois was prepared presumably according to the Chantilly formula, but its appearance was slightly greyish and its behaviour in the kiln was not invariably satisfactory. As already explained, much of the trouble was due to negligence. Evidently some change in the composition of the paste was made or else greater care was exercised in its preparation about the time of the reorganisation after the flight of the Dubois brothers. The quality was noticeably improved and brought to a pure, mellow white. Hellot said of it, "M. Gravant's paste [the old paste of Vincennes more carefully prepared after the departure of the Dubois element] produced a biscuit of the same grain as that of the Chantilly porcelain, but much whiter . . ."

This beautiful white soft paste body, possibly with a few slight modifications subsequently introduced by Hellot, continued in use during the whole life of the Vincennes factory.

THE GLAZE. The glaze of the Vincennes porcelain was throughout of a beautifully clear, transparent quality. In some of the very first pieces made it is possible to find flaws, usually concealed, however, by the adroitly painted decoration, but at an early period in the factory's career these imperfections were successfully eliminated.

ARTICLES MADE AND CONTOUR. The articles made at Vincennes fill a rather varied and comprehensive list. Furthermore, they may be divided into two grades, the ordinary tableware and usual articles of household enrichment and utility, on the one hand, and the elaborate pieces upon which special efforts were bestowed, on the other.

The first named class included bowls, jugs, sugar-bowls or boxes of several different sorts, cups and saucers, plates, platters, dishes, butter-dishes, soup tureens, mustard pots, cheese dishes, jardinières, watering-pots, flower-pots, tea, coffee and chocolate pots, vases, candlesticks, covered jars, cabarets, flower-holders, sconces, clock cases, mirror frames, patch boxes, snuff boxes, powder boxes, cream jugs, fruit baskets, sweetmeat dishes and many like articles of common requirement. A few statuettes, decorated in colour, may also be placed in this category.

To the second belonged the modelled flowers (Plate 49), made and coloured to approximate life, the groups and busts in biscuit produced during the royal period, with vases and other objects of special importance.

Elegance and purity of contour were distinguishing

characteristics of the Vincennes china throughout the greater part of the factory's existence. Even from the very outset, there was apparently little recourse to definitely characteristic Oriental shapings in the way of direct imitations. A certain amount of Oriental influence there was bound to be, but there seems to have been a prevailing tendency to develope contours in a national vein. As soon as Duplessis became a member of the staff, he bestowed great attention on the modelling and many of the products were marked by those subtle and delicate refinements of line (Plate 49), that we are accustomed to associate with the best instances of eighteenth century French design in all branches of art. Many of the pieces had straight sides and flaring tops or displayed a pleasant blending of oval and lobate forms. Subtlety and simplicity were happily combined, and it was not until the passion for producing pretentious "shew pieces" became an overmastering motive and ran away with discretion that many of the contours became unduly elaborate and intricate in their Rococo complexities.

TYPES OF DECORATION. In the letters-patent issued when the factory was in its infancy it was explicitly set forth in unmistakable terms that the purpose of the enterprise was the manufacture of porcelain *after the style of Saxon porcelain*. Of course the main hope back of this expressed aim was that the porcelain of Vincennes should equal or excel the porcelain of Dresden in point of paste and glaze, but the desire for superlative excellence of decoration was by no means of trifling import.

Amongst the very early pieces are examples with scattered flowers and insects, in the Dresden manner, adroitly painted in polychrome to conceal imperfections

PLATE 48

A. MENNECY-VILLEROY COVERED JAR
Characteristic flower decorations in deep green, rose, yellow and light purple; soft paste of creamy ivory or amber tinge, white glaze

B. MENNECY-VILLEROY COVERED DISH
Flower decorations in blue, purple, rose and olive green; characteristic mauve or mulberry lines at edges and rims; soft paste, of creamy ivory tinge, white glaze

Courtesy of the Victoria and Albert Museum, South Kensington

PLATE 49

THREE VINCENNES VASES
Painted and modelled decoration, gold, yellow, pink and mulberry, leaves cold green; creamy white soft paste, glaze creamy and slightly uneven
Courtesy of the Victoria and Albert Museum, South Kensington

PLATE 50

A. TOURNAY FLOWER POT B. ARRAS FLOWER POT

White paste, clear glaze; bands dark blue with gold arabesques, medallions in smoky violet, birds naturalistic colouring   Moulded ornament, decorations in dark underglaze blue; creamy paste, glaze slightly greenish

Courtesy of the Victoria and Albert Museum, South Kensington

in the body or glaze, in the fashion previously noted. The products of Vincennes, and of its successor Sèvres, are noteworthy for the almost complete absence of Oriental *motifs* in their decoration as well as in their contour. The tendencies were always peculiarly European and French. One of the few instances of the employment of Oriental decorative *motifs* occurs in the prunus sprigs and blossoms in relief on early products that displayed no colour save reticent bandings and a few touches upon such moulded features as handles.

Enormous pains were taken to ensure the perfect naturalistic colouring of the modelled flowers and bouquets that were so popular, whether the flowers appeared as separate creations in the form of detached bouquets and sprays or were applied as attached embellishments (Plate 49), to the body of a vase or dish or the branches of a sconce.

Flowers, likewise, were painted with equal care on the surface of the porcelain and were as meticulously executed as were the modelled blossoms. Sprays of flowers thus painted formed one of the favourite types of decoration. At the outset gold was not used, but as the secret of gilding porcelain was bought from a Benedictine friar when Gravant, supported by M. de Fulvy, reorganised the establishment after the Dubois *dèbacle,* gilding soon made its appearance on Vincennes china and played an increasingly conspicuous rôle in the decoration as time went on. When the factory became a royal undertaking, the right to use gold was considered its special prerogative and other factories, as already noted, were forbidden to use it or put it on their china.

Under the chemists Hellot and Macquer, many new

colours were added to the porcelain decorator's palette so that with everything from bright red and carmine, soft rose and lilac, to all gradations of greens, yellows and blues at their disposal the china painters suffered no limitations. One result of this unrestricted colour range was that subtle shadings and greater naturalism in floral renderings supplanted the earlier conventionalised treatment.

Much use, too, was made of ground colours with spaces in reserve in which were polychrome knots of flowers, birds, figures and landscapes. The most important and famous ground colour, *bleu du roi*, appeared just before the middle of the century. This splendid underglaze colour was so intense that it usually had to be modified by a network of gilded lines, or some similar device to break it up. Several years afterwards, Hellot devised the turquoise blue, an enamel or on-glaze colour that was peculiarly characteristic of the later decoration of Vincennes and the subsequent decorations of Sèvres.

Besides the types of decoration hitherto mentioned, there were delicate interlaced ribbon patterns in conjunction with minute diaperings, tiny flowers, birds and gilding. There were also piercings, fretwork, and embossings, as well as the more prominent moulded work of rims, handles and knobs, all of which afforded opportunities for manifold enrichment with colour and gold.

Birds of brilliant and varied plumage often appeared as the chief items of polychrome decoration and were, indeed, characteristic of one well recognised Vincennes type. Small landscapes, woodland and pastoral scenes, in the finished and somewhat minute manner of the day, were employed with great frequency either on shaped panels in reserve or without the accompaniment of any

PLATE 51

A. DRESDEN CHINA PLATE WITH KAKIYEMON DECORATION
Decoration and colouring characteristic of Kakiyemon mode

B. SÈVRES SMALL COVERED JAR
Characteristic apple green ground colour, with reserves and flowers

Courtesy of the British Museum

surrounding ground colour. Again, both woodland scenes and flower subjects were painted *en camaïeu*, the edges or rims of pieces so decorated being enriched with a line of gold. Yet another type of decoration consisted of leaves, flowers, sprays and garlands, or of arabesques, painted in gold on the white body of the china.

THE MARKS. Up until the time when Vincennes became a royal factory there seems to have been no definitely recognised mark, although a few pieces of early style bear either the two interlaced L's or two L's standing by themselves with a point between.

When the works came under the direct control of the King, it was ordered that the mark should thenceforward be the royal cypher, the familiar interlacing L's, of which that on the right is reversed. Pieces for the King's personal use, or intended as royal presents, sometimes displayed a fleur-de-lys above the cypher. From 1753 onwards it was customary to date the pieces by a letter between the L's, the date letter for 1753 being A, and so onward.

SCEAUX CHINA—1749- ?

HISTORY. At the instance of one Jacques Chapelle—a versatile person who, amongst other accomplishments, possessed a knowledge of china-making—a company for the manufacture of porcelain was formed at Sceaux in 1749. The nucleus for this enterprise was a faïence factory already well established. Through the good offices of the

Duchesse du Maine, Chapelle engaged to secure royal consent for the manufacture of porcelain.

All arrangements had been made down to the least detail, and the work-people engaged were ready to start work, but the expected royal consent failed to materialise. The privileges already granted Vincennes presented one obstacle, and another still more serious was the opposition of Madame de Pompadour. Consequently, for the time being, the new organisation had to be satisfied with making a species of faïence called *Faïence Japonée*.

In 1763 the MM. Jacques and Jullien—the same who acquired Mennecy in 1766—took over the establishment and, in 1772, Richard Glot became director, Jacques and Jullien then concentrating all their interests at Mennecy. Although royal consent was lacking, porcelain was undoubtedly made at Sceaux, surreptitiously, perhaps, but none the less certainly, from the time Jacques and Jullien began to manage the works.

The Duc de Penthièvre, High Admiral of France, became patron of the factory in 1775 and, shielded by his puissant influence, they dared to make porcelain quite openly, although not until 1784, when the Vincennes-Sèvres monopoly was somewhat modified, did they obtain the full right to employ polychrome decoration and gilding. Such decoration, however, they had probably made use of long before.

The Body. The soft paste body was the same as that of Mennecy, which is quite natural considering the intimate connexion in personnel that existed between the two factories, Jacques and Jullien directing both Sceaux and Mennecy simultaneously for several years.

THE GLAZE. The glaze of Sceaux, likewise, was identical with that of Mennecy.

ARTICLES MADE AND CONTOUR. The articles made at Sceaux were, in general, the same as those made at Mennecy and included all those things incidental to the furnishing of tables, dressing stands and writing tables, as well as divers other accessories for house embellishment. The contours, too, bore a close resemblance to those of the factory with which there were such intimate relations.

TYPES OF DECORATION. As might be expected, under the circumstances, there was an obvious similarity between the methods of decoration employed at Sceaux and those in vogue at Mennecy. There is this to be said, however. The flower and bird designs, which were particularly favourite *motifs* in both places, were often better conceived and more deftly executed at Sceaux, a fact that gives the Sceaux china a special touch of distinction. During the period when the use of gilding was denied, rims, borders and edges usually displayed a finish of rose-colour (Plate 39, B), in lieu of gold, the effect of which is very engaging.

THE MARKS. The usual mark shews the letters S X incised in the paste, although many pieces which it is reasonable to attribute to Sceaux shew no mark at all.

S X

TOURNAY CHINA—1750-

HISTORY. Although Tournay is now in Belgium, the products of the Tournay factory are included under the head of French china because Tournay was under French rule when the porcelain made there won its reputation.

Peterinck began making porcelain at Tournay in 1750, and the work prospered so much that a few years later the factory employed a large force of work-people and put forth a very considerable volume of wares.

There were two grades of china produced at Tournay, one including pieces of the finest character that could compare favourably with the output of any of the other French porcelain factories, the second being inexpensive and well calculated for all ordinary domestic use. Both kinds were produced simultaneously over a considerable period, but after a number of years the finer grade was discontinued. The ordinary grade is still made there.

THE BODY. The soft paste body of Tournay china was of somewhat different composition from that used at the French factories already considered, and it required a much shorter time for firing. In colour it has not the noticeable yellowish or amber tinge characteristic of the Chantilly or Mennecy body, but it is not so white as the soft paste body of Vincennes or Sèvres. It is also somewhat more porous in texture than the others.

While the usual processes of moulding and throwing were followed in shaping the pieces at Tournay, the process of casting (v. section on The Making of Chinaware) was also used. This process, it is believed, was first employed in the Tournay factory.

THE GLAZE. The Tournay glaze is clear, transparent beautifully smooth and evenly distributed, without runnings or "tear-drops."

ARTICLES MADE AND CONTOUR. Amongst the articles of the finer ware were vases, flower-pots, tableware and table garnitures, tea, coffee and chocolate services, candlesticks, sconces, and the sundry elegancies of equipment for writing and dressing tables. The second grade included table services also, and all the articles of everyday domestic utility for which porcelain was suitable. In the matter of contour, both Oriental and European models afforded a basis for adaptation.

TYPES OF DECORATION. One of the most favourite types of decoration consisted of flowers, either scattered in the Dresden manner or else grouped in sprays and more organised compositions. These were very carefully executed, and the factory was particularly fortunate in the use of an excellent iron oxide red.

When the fashions set by Sèvres had become all-prevalent, the Tournay decorators followed suit with admirable ground colours and polychrome *motifs* in reserve (Plate 50, A). The Tournay factory was successful not only in producing a good underglaze *bleu du roi* but also in imitating other items of Sèvres embellishment, such as the "partridge eye" device, diapers and reticulations of gold, and birds of brilliant plumage along with the floral *motifs* and ribbon patterns.

Little landscapes and woodland scenes in the pastoral manner of the day were largely made use of as well as figures, the latter in the form of cherubs or *amorini* or else as compositions based on Classic precedents. Both landscapes and figure subjects often appeared *en camaïeu*, as a rule, however, in conjunction with a certain amount of gilding.

The commoner wares were chiefly decorated with flowers, either scattered or arranged in sprays or connected garlands. These decorations were executed, for the most part, in blue, although polychrome painting was employed to some extent.

THE MARKS. The mark of the finer grade of Tournay china consisted of two crossed swords accompanied by four crosses, and was applied either with gold or in on-glaze colour. The inferior grade bore only workmen's individual marks or some factory symbol indicating the pattern of the piece.

ORLÉANS CHINA—1753-1811 (?)

HISTORY. The Orléans porcelain factory, under Sieur Gerréault, began its career in 1753 with the Duc de Penthièvre as its patron, the same nobleman whom we have already met extending his protective interest to the factory at Sceaux, although his patronage at Sceaux was not exercised till many years later.

This venture was authorised by the Council of State and was distant far enough from Paris not to be perpetually harassed by the opposition of neighbouring competitors and claimants of exclusive privileges. Up until 1770 the factory produced soft paste porcelain; after that date all its products were of hard paste. The factory continued in operation until 1811, it is known certainly, and may have gone on for some years longer. A good deal of china must have been produced, but it was very fragile. Consequently, it is comparatively rare.

THE BODY. The Orléans soft paste body was highly vitreous, very translucent, white in colour, and of beautiful quality. The hard paste body used after 1770 was extremely vitreous or glassy at first and exceptionally brittle, but the composition later became more satisfactory.

PLATE 52

A. SÈVRES CUP AND SAUCER   *B.* SÈVRES CUP AND SAUCER

Typical Directoire shape; creamy paste, clear glaze; decorations in gold and polychrome, flower knots in brilliant pinks, blues, violets, greens and yellows

Typical diapered *motif*, bands in yellow-pink and gold, flowers in yellow, mulberry and blue, medallions naturalistic, paste creamy, clear glaze

Courtesy of the Victoria and Albert Museum, South Kensington

PLATE 53

SÈVRES TEAPOT

Typical vine and trellis design; white paste, clear glaze; top and base uneven deep blue, columns shaded madder, leaves grey green, red berries, gold banding

Courtesy of the Victoria and Albert Museum, South Kensington

PLATE 54

A. SÈVRES OCTAGONAL PLATE   *B.* SÈVRES CUP AND SAUCER

Hard white paste, clear glaze; Classic figure in medallion and arabesque border with *putti*; decorations deep green, rose, yellow, light purple and gold

Hard white paste, clear glaze; decorations blue, purple, rose, olive green and gold

Courtesy of the Victoria and Albert Museum, South Kensington

PLATE 55

SÈVRES JUG
Characteristic Empire shape; ground burnt Siena, Classic arabesques in deep brown, panels highly naturalistic in colour, bands, spout and handle gilt

Courtesy of the Victoria and Albert Museum, South Kensington

THE GLAZE. The glaze on both the soft paste and the hard paste bodies was very brilliant and glassy and lacked the sympathetic mellowness displayed by the glazes of such factories as Chantilly, Mennecy, or Sceaux.

ARTICLES MADE AND CONTOUR. Table services, tea, coffee and chocolate sets, and pieces of kindred use composed the principal output, although a certain number of statuettes and vases were also produced. The contours were chiefly of European character, well shaped, and with all the moulded details impeccably designed and executed. During the hard paste period the prevalent Neo-Classic forms made their appearance.

TYPES OF DECORATION. In the soft paste period the decorations were often in the form of scattered flowers done in underglaze blue. The other type chiefly employed consisted of bouquets, knots and garlands painted in polychrome and enriched with gilding.

During the hard paste period scattered flowers and garlands composed the usual decorative *motifs* and gilding was also used.

THE MARKS. The marks of the early period consist of a label above the letter C. At some time early in the nineteenth century the mark became a round vignette with the word "Orléans." It was applied in gold or in onglaze colour.

SÈVRES CHINA—1756 TO DATE

HISTORY. The first chapter of the history of Sèvres is the history of Vincennes, which we have already traversed in detail. One of the shareholders of the factory of

Vincennes, realising full well the more or less precarious financial condition of the establishment, endeavoured to interest Madame de Pompadour in its affairs, hoping that her intervention might be instrumental in placing everything on a firm footing.

Madame de Pompadour, who was a person of great good taste and felt a deep concern in everything connected with the welfare of art in France, promptly took the matter up and straightway proceeded to fasten the King's interest more securely and directly on the development of the royal porcelain manufactory. A piece of ground was selected at Sèvres, and, to make a long story short, in due time the necessary buildings were erected and the Vincennes establishment with its whole personnel transferred there.

The trying experimental stages attending the early years of any enterprise had all been passed through. Sèvres began with an already complete background of ripe experience and established tradition and, so far as processes were concerned, there was an absolutely clear path ahead to spring full-grown into fame and the glories of superlative achievement. There were defects in the organisation and management of the factory, it is true, and these were serious enough to have landed an establishment without royal support in total bankruptcy, but the King's interest and pocket, both manipulated by Madame de Pompadour, bridged over the difficulties and made it possible to produce china of unparallelled excellence and beauty.

Madame de Pompadour manifested no less solicitude about the design and quality of the factory's products than she did over the ways and means of maintenance.

Her tastes in the matter of the designs followed and executed can readily be traced; her care for material prosperity can be judged from the following extract, taken from the memoirs of the Marquis d'Argenson where it is recorded that:

"Madame de Pompadour talks about nothing but the great advantage that the State will derive from the manufacture of porcelain in the Saxon fashion, and even in having excelled the Saxons in it. A royal shop for the sale of this porcelain is opened in the rue de la Monnaie, and there is exhibited a service which the King is going to send to the King of Saxony as if he wanted to bid him defiance, and provoke him by shewing him that he had even excelled his porcelain manufacture. At one of the King's suppers the Marquise de Pompadour said that those who did not buy as much of this porcelain as they could afford were not good citizens, to which someone answered that, 'Since the King had bestowed so many donations in the encouragement of this manufactory, those at Charleville and at St. Etienne for the manufacture of weapons, useful to us in another way, are neglected, and three-quarters of the work-people go over to foreign countries.'"

Financial difficulties, however, continued. Most people found the ware too expensive, especially as they could buy Dresden porcelain and Oriental china at a much lower figure. At last, in November 1759, in order to save the situation, the King undertook the whole monetary responsibility of the works, an edict was issued ordering the factory to be administered for His Majesty, and the shareholders were paid off with interest-bearing notes, properly secured. Thus did the factory of Sèvres become crown property.

At the instance of M. Boileau, who had grown up with the business management of Vincennes and had contrived to make himself absolutely indispensable, the Lieutenant-

General of Police put forth an edict forbidding all persons to make, model, paint or gild porcelain, or to sell the same, under the severest penalties. This edict likewise forbade manufacturers of so-called common porcelains, who had hitherto enjoyed certain privileges, to use gilding, to make figures, flowers, or other modelled pieces except as embellishments for their own wares, or to employ any colour other than blue, applied after the customary Chinese patterns, for decorating their products.

This, of course, called forth a stormy outburst of indignation and protest. Factories like Mennecy and Chantilly enjoyed the patronage of powerful nobles whom the King did not wish to offend and, furthermore, he saw the unwisdom of ruining a number of factories and causing needless unemployment. Accordingly, by another decree, set forth in February 1766, the making of porcelain in imitation of the Chinese was permitted, but the managers of the factories were straitly charged in the decoration of their china to use no colour other than blue, except they chose to paint a piece wholly with some other single colour *en camaïeu*. They were likewise forbidden to use gold, or to make statuettes or ornaments in high relief out of porcelain, either glazed or unglazed. These monopolistic restrictions explain why Chantilly and Mennecy china of a certain period was decorated either in blue, or in some other colour *en camaïeu*, and without the grace of gilding.

In spite of these drastic measures that crippled the liberty of other factories, Sèvres still laboured under money troubles and the King was ultimately obliged to meet deficits from his privy-purse. If some of the energies and talent had been turned to making more china for the average market, instead of concentrating almost all efforts on magnificent regal productions, there would have been more substantial profit and less anxiety. Nor need artistic excellence have suffered in the least. Chantilly and Mennecy, to mention no others, produced beautiful chinaware of a quality and price not prohibitive to the purse of those who could afford reasonable luxury. And they found profit in doing so.

As it was, the management of Sèvres, inspired by extravagant notions of splendid ostentation, pinned their faith mostly on effulgent *chefs d'œuvres*, cabinet pieces marvellous to behold, but quite beyond ordinary reach. "Most of the pieces appear to have been intended for the King's service, for the furnishing of the royal palaces of Versailles, the Trianon, Marly, Bellevue, Meudon, St. Germain, and Fontainebleau. He used them as presents for his relatives, his friends, his courtiers and his ambassadors. They were also made use of as diplomatic presents, sometimes, perhaps, as diplomatic bribes." Naturally, when the commercial considerations were either wholly eliminated or else so minimised that they counted for naught in the grand total, it required a kingly purse to meet the costs of production, and even the kingly purse was not always adequate to the demands without a good deal of pinching and paring. When the royal purse was utterly depleted and Louis XV, like his predecessor, had to send all his silver to the mint, then Sèvres made wares for popular consumption and prospered.

The early sumptuous period of Sèvres soft paste porcelain lasted from 1756 to 1769. In the latter year began the manufacture of hard paste porcelain conjointly with the soft paste. A great quantity of the factory's productions were still of the magnifical type and, so it seems, of equally magnifical price. To encourage the artists responsible for the designs and decoration, and also to help the sales, the King had exhibitions of porcelain every year in the Palace at Versailles. These he not only attended in person, but he actually played the part of shewman and salesman. A contemporary source gives us a lively picture of these occasions:

"Every New Year's Day they bring into the galleries at Versailles the newest and choicest pieces of Sèvres porcelain, which the King himself distributes among his great lords for their money; he fixes the prices himself and they are not cheap. We presume that the price must be pretty high on account of the financial situation, but we shall speak about that later on. It is certain that some of the noble lords are not ashamed of taking a cup, or some little ornament, when they think they are not observed. Seeing a count take a cup in this way, Louis XV sent to him next morning the cashier from Sèvres with the saucer that he had been unable to take, and a bill for the pieces. One day the King saw that an *abbé* refused to purchase a piece on account of its price, but in order to persuade him the King immediately promised him a benefice."

In time the wealthier public gradually became educated up to the price of the wares of Sèvres and collectors bought the choice vases, flower-pots and figures, both glazed and in the biscuit, on the production of which the ablest sculptors, painters and modellers of the day had spent their best efforts, but popular requirements were still too little considered, and the factory was usually run at a loss or now and then barely managed to pay expenses. These latter occasions were of rare occurrence.

When Louis XVI succeeded to the throne, royal interest in the factory was continued unabated, both on the part of the King himself, who took deep pride in the Sèvres achievements, and also on the part of the Queen, for Marie Antoinette dearly loved the graces which the painters, the sculptors and the modellers so beguilingly expressed, and often visited the works. The story is told that one day the Queen, on looking at a quantity of recently decorated porcelain, deplored the fact that she saw abundance of roses, tulips, daffodils and other flowers of all colours save blue, a colour to which she was very partial. Hettlinger, one of the directors, at once thought of using the cornflower as a decoration to please the Queen, and thenceforth it became vastly popular as a *motif*, not only at Sèvres but at all the other porcelain factories as well.

The King's enthusiasm was very obviously attested both by his continuance of the annual exhibitions in the Palace at Versailles and by the active part he took in the preparations for them, on which occasions he was sometimes more of an hindrance than an help, as we may gather from a letter written by Hettlinger:

"I have already said that an exhibition of porcelains takes place at the end of every year up to the day of the 'Three Magi.' It is held at the Royal Palace, but the public are allowed to come and examine and buy the pieces. The King occupies in Versailles, besides the State rooms, the *Petits Appartements*, where he passes his private life. Three of these rooms are cleared of their furniture, and the porcelain pieces are exhibited on tables. This year he did not wait until the arrival of the work people, but must himself be unpacking the pieces, breaking not a few, and mixing everything up so that it took us hours to put it straight. The King delights in his manufactory at Sèvres, and he said to one of his confidants, 'Our brave Sèvres men will soon be here. I must make haste to shoot some game.'"

But royal interest in the prettinesses of the work did not help matters much, and certainly did not assist the financial management. Fifteen years before Louis XVI succeeded to the throne, the materials requisite for making hard paste porcelain had been found in France, endless experiments had been carried out, and a number of hard paste porcelain factories had sprung up in various parts of the kingdom, although hard paste was not made at Sèvres until some years after the native materials had become available.

These recently established hard paste porcelain works were forging steadily ahead and were seriously affecting the market of Sèvres. Although there were still in effect the restrictive edicts that gave Sèvres a virtual monopoly of fine porcelain making in France, and clipped the wings of private enterprise, those edicts were not rigorously enforced. There was laxity on the part of government officials, there were evasions on the part of the newly arisen factories and, what was most significant of all, some of the greatest nobles of the realm and, indeed, members of the royal family had lent their names and active patronage to divers of these independent ventures even when they were not financially interested in their success, as they were in more than one instance.

Things gradually went from bad to worse in the business affairs of Sèvres, until at last the King was obliged to retrench and greatly curtail the staff which, of course, only made the position of the independent factories stronger. Even under these disadvantageous conditions, marvellous work was performed in the royal factory and triumphs of porcelain design and decoration were produced right up to the very eve of the Revolution.

During the Revolution the factory was in sorry plight and so were the workers, but under the Napoleonic

PLATE 56

A. SÈVRES CUP AND SAUCER

B. SÈVRES CUP AND SAUCER

Typical Empire shape; hard white paste, clear glaze; decorations gold, black, pale green, shades of brown and dull blue, ground biscuit coloured or buff

Hard white paste, clear glaze; gold arabesques on rim of saucer and cup, flower decorations light green, light yellow and deep shades of rose, blue and violet

Courtesy of the Victoria and Albert Museum, South Kensington

PLATE 57

LATE EIGHTEENTH CENTURY BOWL AND EWER
Made at one of the porcelain factories near Paris; decorations in very deep blue and gold; pure white, hard paste, clear, transparent glaze

Courtesy of the Victoria and Albert Museum, South Kensington

PLATE 58

A. CAEN JUG, EMPIRE SHAPE
Paste white, glaze of slightly greenish tinge; oblong medallions in sepia with black border, other decorations in gold with light greenish grey leaves

B. EMPIRE JUG WITH GOLD DECORATION
Made at one of the porcelain factories near Paris; white paste, clear white glaze; silhouette hunting scene in gold

Courtesy of the Victoria and Albert Museum, South Kensington

PLATE 59

A. NIDERVILLER FLOWER POT   *B.* VALENCIENNES COVERED SUGAR BASON

White paste, glaze of slightly bluish tinge; decoration *en camaieu* in   White paste, cold white glaze; decorations in gold, blue, pale bright
smoky violet, gold handles and bandings   violet and light green

Courtesy of the Victoria and Albert Museum, South Kensington

FRENCH CHINAWARE

régime order was restored and the establishment was again put on its feet, for Napoleon saw in it a means of contributing to the splendour and outward display of pomp about which he was so solicitous and which he knew how to use to such good purpose. In this era much magnificent but over-elaborate porcelain was produced. The great physicist Brongniart became director and bent his energies to perfecting the hard paste body. It was at this time, in the early years of the nineteenth century, that the making of the beautiful soft paste porcelain at Sèvres was definitely abandoned.

The factory of Sèvres has grown into a great national institution and has rendered invaluable services to the porcelain art, but as this volume is not concerned with the essentially modern developments of chinaware, we shall leave it at this point, merely adding that in the museum at Sèvres are admirable and comprehensive collections of china which it is well worth while for any china-lover to inspect.

THE BODY. In the section on Vincennes china the early story of the soft paste body was told. After the factory of Vincennes was removed to become the foundation of the Sèvres factory, the chemical staff of Sèvres were constantly conducting experiments, and whenever there was a chance to effect an improvement, the improvement was straightway made, until the paste was brought to absolute perfection—*pure milky white, hard,* and *translucent.*

This perfect body, with its tender translucence, continued to be used without a competitor for favour until 1769, when hard paste was added to the list of products. Oftentimes the walls of the soft paste pieces were thinner at Sèvres than they had been made at Vincennes; this increased their translucence and also their fragility. The soft paste in the biscuit pieces sometimes shews a very pale amber tinge, which adds a warm glow and mellowness to the general aspect.

The hard paste produced underwent the same constant and rigid scrutiny as the soft paste had undergone at an earlier date, and the same revision of formulas for its composition. It was the tendency of the chemists in charge to aim at technical perfection rather than sympathetic quality, beauty, or adaptability for decoration. The soft paste was the most perfect vehicle ever achieved for decorating, far more so than the hard paste. But much was sacrificed in the endeavour to reach technical perfection in the hard paste, and there was a tendency to make it too "severe"—cold, hard, metallic and glittering in quality.

Brongniart, who abandoned the manufacture of soft paste porcelain, bent his efforts toward making the hard paste conform absolutely with the hardest type of Chinese porcelain. Under Brongniart the hard paste was made harder than previously, and the type he introduced is still employed for table services. It was not until late in the nineteenth century that this attitude was at all modified. The Sèvres hard paste body is absolutely *white, hard, translucent* and *resonant* and needless to say, flawless.

THE GLAZE. The glaze used at Vincennes had been brought to perfection before the removal to Sèvres. It had a lustrous, luscious richness, and at Sèvres it was maintained at its highest state of clarity, colourless transparency, glassy smoothness, and evenness of distribution.

The glaze used on the first hard paste porcelain made at Sèvres, and continued down to 1800, was calcareous, that is, it had chalk or lime in its composition, and was much less glossy than the glaze of the soft paste porcelain. As a matter of fact, it was relatively opaque, and hence the early hard paste exhibits a pearly whiteness. This early glaze was an especially kindly medium for colours and for enamels in relief. Brongniart changed this glaze for one made from the natural pegmatite of St. Yrieix, near Limoges, and it is this later glaze that so often seems glittering and unsympathetic.

ARTICLES MADE AND CONTOUR. Apart from the objects *de luxe*, the "shew pieces," to which reference has already been made, the modelled flowers, the splendid vases and other ornaments intended for the King's service or to be given as presents to foreign monarchs and ambassadors, the wares made at Sèvres number dinner-services of both simple pattern and the more elaborate designs of Duplessis, trays, sugar-bowls, inkstands, jardinières, tea, coffee and chocolate services, milk jugs, table garnitures, sconces, candlesticks, basons and ewers, tobacco and snuff-boxes, patch boxes, covered jars, watch cases, buttons, cane-heads, thimbles, perfume and pomatum pots, needle-cases, *bonbonnières*, bowls, pot-pourri jars, gravy-boats and sauce-boats, vases of a dozen different styles, fruit baskets, dessert services, clock cases, cups and saucers, plaques or panels for furniture—these in the reign of Louis XVI—small flower jars, and jewel caskets. Besides these there were the portrait medallions, busts, groups, and figures of biscuit porcelain modelled by the most eminent sculptors.

As previously pointed out, the contours followed at Sèvres were distinctly French. It is the nature of the French genius, even when a model is admittedly drawn from some foreign source, so to assimilate and adapt it and endow it with new individuality that it wholly ceases to be what it was and becomes a new thing instinct with Gallic character. Whatever inspiration in contour was derived from Oriental sources was so reshaped in the hands of the Sèvres designers that it became French in the transmutation.

During the reign of Louis XV the contours of Sèvres porcelain were a faithful index to the prevalent trend and spirit of contemporary design as we see it reflected in architecture, furniture and painting. Subtle shapings and curves were the order of the day, and we find these elements accommodated to chinaware, as well as everywhere else. Long before Louis XVI came to the throne, however, a change of taste had set in and superseded the well recognised Rococo manner that we particularly associate with the reign of Louis XV.

A strong tendency toward greater purity and simplicity of line was unmistakable. The chinaware of Sèvres promptly registered all the changes of style from the exuberant fancies of the Rococo mode to the more austere forms of Neo-Classic provenance. Without loss of grace, the many playful curves and subtle shapings gave place to straight lines or restrained flaring contours (Plate 54, B). When the Directoire and First Empire came, the urbanity and suave but cheerful dignity of Neo-Classic contours yielded, in turn, to the aggressive and insistent severity of robust Neo-Grec forms (Plates 55 and 52, A), inspired by newly-quickened archæological enthusiasms. In short, whatever was the dominant attitude in the minds of Frenchmen toward matters of style and design, that attitude was straightway mirrored in the products of Sèvres whose design was a peculiarly sensitive index to every slightest variation of national taste.

TYPES OF DECORATION. The types of decoration that characterised the porcelain of Sèvres, notwithstanding their manifold variety, reflected the procession of style influences just as surely and accurately as did the contours. We find the Rococo manner, at its best, exemplified from about 1756 to 1769. Before this, however, there were indications of the coming change, and during the reign of Louis XVI the spirit of the decorations manifested an altogether new aspect. Delicacy, elegance and restraint succeeded to exuberant and playful fancy, to be in turn ousted by the incisive severity of the Directoire mode which was soon to be followed by the ostentatious pomp and circumstance of the Empire fashion. All of these epochs had their own well defined preferences in both colouring and the character of decorative *motifs*, and these preferences were interpreted in the china of Sèvres no less than in every other visible manifestation of decorative art.

It must be remembered that Sèvres had fallen heir to all the decorative developments of Vincennes and had only to go on amplifying and adding to the stock of thoroughly organised tradition acquired by inheritance at the outset. There were, to begin with, the various types of flower and bird painting followed by the Vincennes decorators and there were the wonderful ground colours that the Vincennes chemists had already devised. To these colours, in 1757, was added the beautiful *rose Pompadour*, popularly and *wrongly* called rose *du Barry*.

The development of the Sèvres style of decoration was the natural outgrowth of the methods in vogue at the Vincennes factory. There was no break in the tradition.

It was a continuous progression, to a large measure in the hands of the same men. The chief difference to be noted, so far as the early work of Sèvres is concerned, is that the decorations in many instances gradually became richer and more sumptuous than those customarily employed at Vincennes and new colours and gradations of colour were added.

The *bleu du roi*, as previously mentioned, was too intense and vibrant to use in large masses alone and was ordinarily modified by fine gilded reticulations in a regular pattern, by vermiform gold lines, by the "partridge eye" *motif*, or by a circular diaper in gold. Besides the *bleu du roi*, the Sèvres blue and turquoise blue as ground colours, there were *rose Pompadour* (just mentioned), apple-green (Plate 51, B), grass-green, lilac, daffodil yellow, claret colour, a pale canary yellow which was developed at a rather late date, brown tortoise shell and green tortoise shell grounds, and the underglaze chrome green, which last was developed during the Empire and, although striking, cannot be considered beautiful or in any way worthy to be compared with the earlier grounds.

The panels reserved on the white ground of the porcelain, in conjunction with these ground colours, were surrounded and defined with gilded or coloured scrolls or bands of ribbon. In the case of one jardinière, now preserved in the Wallace Collection, with a ground colour of *rose Pompadour*, the oval reserved panel is surrounded with a broad green ribbon touched with gold. On these reserved panels were customarily painted with the utmost delicacy woodland scenes, pastorals, groups of figures, harbour scenes, military subjects, scenes of society, gallantry or love, and a diversity of mythological subjects, or else they were decorated with flowers in polychrome or birds of gorgeous plumage. Although subjects of this sort had been marvellously well executed at Vincennes, at Sèvres there was a marked increase in the delicacy and refinement of presentation. This is not to be wondered at when a number of the ablest artists of the time were constantly employed—such men as Le Guay, Lecot, Dodin, Armand, Aubert, Bouillat, Mérault, Sioux, Chabry, Pithou, Bouchet and Rosset, to name only a few of them.

The modellers and sculptors were no less distinguished in their profession. There were Duplessis, Falconet, Bachelier, Le Riche, Perrotin and Levaux, while in modelling the originals for the biscuit portrait busts and groups there were such men as Pigalle, Clodion, Caffieri, Boizot, Julien and, above all, Pajou. Many more names of painters, sculptors and modellers might be added to the list, did space permit, but if anyone wishes to pursue the details further on this score a complete roll may be found in the bulletins of the Sèvres museum.

When ground colours were not used, with reserved panels for the elaborate painted decorations, rims, bands or other parts of grounds were sometimes filled with diapers of lattice (Plates 52, B and 53), or trellis work or with "partridge-eye" forms composed of sea-green or bright blue dots in conjunction with minute gold dots on the white ground of the porcelain to give additional texture and enrichment. There were also landscapes and country scenes executed on a white ground *en camaïeu* in crimson, rose, blue or rose mulberry, with gilding on the rims and at other appropriate places.

Not a little of the tableware was decorated with flowers in polychrome, scattered or in bouquets (Plate 52, A and B), and often the scattered flowers were very minute. There were also garlands, festoons and wreaths (Plate 54, B), of both flowers and foliage (Plate 56, B), while fruit was often used on dessert services. Armorial bearings likewise played an important part in the decorations, along with monograms and cyphers.

Besides tiny forget-me-nots, little cornflowers and rosettes set at the intersections of latticework (Plate 52, B), there were graceful arabesques (Plate 54, A), patterned after those of Pompeii or adapted from the frescoes of Raphael; there were medallions with cameo heads and figures; there were rectangles, ovals, octagons, hexagons, and panels of other shapes filled with Classic figures; there were country scenes and peasant figures (Plate 56, A); there were innumerable border patterns with scrolls, cartouches, cornucopias and various symbols and attributes, and there were elegant Etruscan *motifs*.

The Directoire brought Phrygian caps and an host of Roman republican and Imperial *motifs*, while the Empire brought a brief dominance of Egyptian themes and a larger and more permanent following of Greek and Roman devices supplied by Percier and Fontaine.

The gilding was always excellent (Plate 56, B), whether the whole design was painted in gold or whether the gold was employed as an enrichment, either flat or burnished. The "jewelled Sèvres" with transparent raised enamels laid on gold that appeared like inlaid jewels on the surface of the porcelain, was one of the triumphs of combined gilding and enamelling.

PLATE 60

A. DRESDEN "ONION PATTERN" SOUP PLATE
Hard white paste, cold white glaze; decoration in deep blue

B. DRESDEN CUP AND SAUCER
Hard white paste, cold white glaze; typical Dresden flower decoration in two shades of green, mulberry, vermilion, greenish yellow and dull blue

Courtesy of the Victoria and Albert Museum, South Kensington

PLATE 61

A. EARLY DRESDEN CHOCOLATE POT

White paste, cold white glaze; decoration *en camaïeu* in rose mulberry, red and gold banding, Louis XIV. arabesque *motif* around neck

B. EARLY DRESDEN JUG

White paste, cold white glaze; gilding and polychrome flower and insect decoration in light yellow, mulberry, dull bluish green and vermilion

Courtesy of the Victoria and Albert Museum, South Kensington

PLATE 62

A. DRESDEN FIGURE OF LACE MAKER*

White paste, glaze slightly bluish; decoration in pale yellow, deep violet, light blue, green and viridian

*This figure represents Barbara Ottman who introduced pillow lace-making into Germany in 1561

B. DRESDEN JARDINIÈRE

White paste, glaze slightly bluish; modelled ornament and moulded ornament in paste; decoration in gold, mauve, yellowish green, vermilion and mulberry

Courtesy of the Victoria and Albert Museum, South Kensington

PLATE 63

A. NYMPHENBURG FLOWER POT
Paste cold white, clear white glaze; gold and blue arabesque border, flowers in mauve, pale yellow, dull blue, vermilion and two greens

B. HÖCHST SAUCE BOAT WITH MOULDED ORNAMENT
Paste white, cold white glaze; decoration in mulberry, pale blue, green, yellow and vermilion

Courtesy of the Victoria and Albert Museum, South Kensington

FRENCH CHINAWARE

THE MARKS. The Sèvres mark was the royal cypher, the two "L's" interlaced and facing each other. The date letter or letters stood between the two L's and afford an accurate means of dating the pieces.

BOURG-LA-REINE CHINA—1774-1788

HISTORY. The factory at Bourg-la-Reine, not far from Sceaux, was founded in 1774 by the MM. Jacques and Jullien who have appeared twice before, once in connexion with Sceaux and once as the managers of the factory at Mennecy-Villeroy. The Bourg-la-Reine factory was started under the protecting patronage of the Comte d'Eu, and it is believed that Jacques and Jullien embarked on this new enterprise upon relinquishing the works of Mennecy-Villeroy, either through sale or upon the expiration of a lease.

Considering who were the heads of the factory, it is to be expected that the wares produced at Bourg-la-Reine should be substantially the same as those of Sceaux and Mennecy. The china produced at those two places commanded a ready market and the work of Bourg-la-Reine was merely a continuation of the earlier work of Jacques and Jullien. When the pieces are unmarked it is well-nigh impossible to distinguish between the products of the three factories.

Nearly all the edges of the Bourg-la-Reine pieces have a line of rose-colour. Very few were gilded, and those so decorated were probably amongst the latest products after the inhibitions respecting gilding had been removed. The pieces of Bourg-la-Reine china that are marked have the letters B. R. incised in the paste.

B. R.

ARRAS CHINA—1782-1788 (?)

History. In 1782 the Arras factory was undertaken by two ladies named Deleneur. They were previously faïence dealers in Arras and engaged in the manufacture of porcelain at the instance of the Governour of Flanders and Artois, who supplied the necessary funds. This he did partly because of his jealousy of Tournay, partly because of the extensive importation of English china, which he wished to stop.

The body was a soft paste, yellowish white in colour, somewhat resembling the paste of Mennecy or Sceaux. It was chiefly decorated in blue (Plate 50, B). The mark consists of the letters A R painted in underglaze blue and occasionally a painter's initial appears alongside.

Competition was too keen and other wares were cheaper so that the factory was not profitable and was abandoned after five or six years.

AR

SAINT-AMAND-LES-EAUX CHINA—1815 TO DATE

HISTORY. Dorchies Herbo, a Fleming, started the porcelain factory of Saint-Amand-les-Eaux in 1815 and produced a fine white soft paste body. Counterfeiters of porcelain have often availed themselves of this ware to dress up with decorations and sell as specimens of the old soft paste Sèvres. Along with Tournay, the factory of Saint-Amand-les-Eaux is the only establishment that has continued the making of soft paste porcelain to the present day. The common porcelain of this factory is painted with simple designs in underglaze blue.

PARIS CHINA

HISTORY. From about 1760 onward, but chiefly in the later years of the eighteenth century, a number of porcelain factories sprang up in Paris and in its immediate suburbs. They were engaged chiefly in the manufacture of hard paste porcelain, consequent upon the discovery of the necessary materials in the south of France, and were able to pursue their course comparatively unmolested, partly through diplomatic evasion, partly through the laxity of enforcing the regulative edicts that prevailed during the reign of Louis XVI. They unquestionably infringed the prerogatives claimed by Sèvres, but this infringement was generally connived at by those in authority and was actively encouraged by many of exalted station, in one case even by the Queen, Marie Antoinette, herself.

Of these minor factories, many of which produced admirable china both in point of structure and tasteful decoration, those most worthy of attention were Vincennes (not to be confounded with the old Vincennes factory which was merged in Sèvres), the "*Manufacture du Comte d' Artois,*" the factory of Vaux, the Fabrique de la Courtille, the Fabrique de la rue de Reuilly, the Fabrique de Monsieur at Clignancourt, the Fabrique de la Reine, rue Thiroux, the Fabrique du Duc d'Angoulême, rue de Bondy, the Fabrique de la rue Popincourt, and the Fabrique du Duc d'Orléans.

The products of these factories are always turning up and most of them are so excellent (Plates 57 and 58, B), that anyone might well rejoice at getting them. Nor is this excellence to be wondered at when we remember that not a few of those men who started these factories, or directed them, had gained their knowledge and ability, both technical and artistic, in no less a training school than the factory of Sèvres.

When the deficits of Sèvres were appallingly large in the reign of Louis XVI, and it was well-nigh impossible for the King to find the wherewithal to maintain the works at their full capacity, he was obliged to reduce the staff. Every reduction sent adrift men who were capable of making and decorating porcelain in the manner of Sèvres and, when the enforced retrenchment deprived them of their wonted employment in the royal factory, it was only to be expected that they should seek an outlet for their experience elsewhere and carry on the kind of work for which they were best fitted.

Started as these factories were, late in the century when the passion for hard paste porcelain was strong and when France now had the materials within her own territory whereby she could equal the long-envied products of the German factories and secure the same commercial advantages, it was the most natural thing in the world that they should all pursue the making of hard paste porcelain.

As all these factories were in operation late in the century, the china they made exhibited the contours and decoration characteristic of that epoch when restraint and reticence began to take the place of the more florid exuberance that had previously prevailed. In contour, purity of line, and in decoration, the disciplined elegance of Neo-Classic *motifs* contribute a charm that distinguishes much of the chinaware put forth by these establishments. Their wares may be less famous than the products of other better known factories, but they are none the less beautiful and deserving of sincere appreciation.

VINCENNES (HANNONG) CHINA—1767–1786 (?)

HISTORY. Before Sèvres engaged in the making of hard paste porcelain, and while experiments with that end in view were being eagerly pursued, negotiations were carried on with the Hannongs, a family of Strasburg potters who unquestionably possessed the secrets of making hard paste porcelain and produced it first at Strasburg and afterwards at Frankenthal. These negotiations do not shew M. Boileau, the guiding spirit of the management at Sèvres, in a very creditable light. Boileau, having obtained Hannong's secrets and pumped him dry of every item of useful information, not only refused to live up to his stipulated agreements but acted with the greatest harshness, persecuted the Hannongs, and made it impossible for them to manufacture porcelain within the kingdom of France. The whole affair was a piece of inexcusable trickery and sharp practice.

In 1767 permission was granted a certain Maurin des Aubiez to set up a faïence factory at Vincennes, and this permission to make faïence was a little later extended to make use of the old soft paste porcelain and manufacture hard paste porcelain *so long as he did not trench upon the privileges of Sèvres.* "Maurin des Aubiez" may have been a name assumed by Hannong or it may have been the name of a silent partner. At any rate, in a document of 1771, Hannong is mentioned as director of the establishment.

In 1772 Hannong left Vincennes to take charge of the porcelain works belonging to the Comte d'Artois. The next indication of the continuance of the Vincennes hard paste porcelain factory was in 1784, when the Sieur Lemaire, evidently making porcelain there at that time, made a protest against the restrictive edicts. When King Louis Philippe visited the Sèvres factory, many years after, he said that while he was still Duc de Chartres he had given his protection to Hannong in setting up the establishment at Vincennes. No mention of the factory occurs after 1786.

THE BODY. The body of the porcelain attributed to this obscure Vincennes venture is a very vitreous hard paste with a slight yellowish tinge, and it somewhat resembles several of the earlier soft paste products.

THE GLAZE. The glaze is often uneven and defective.

ARTICLES MADE AND CONTOUR. The articles made seem to have been chiefly tableware of a purely utilitarian character. The contours had no particular individuality beyond reflecting the trend of contemporary taste in such matters.

TYPES OF DECORATION. Little painted flowers in polychrome formed the usual decoration. The rose and violet colourings are apt to be faded from over-firing.

THE MARKS. The marks "H" and "P.H" in underglaze blue indicate origin at this factory. Pieces marked "L P" under a ducal coronet, in underglaze blue, are also supposed to have come from the Vincennes works.

FABRIQUE DU COMTE D'ARTOIS CHINA—1769–1810

HISTORY. This factory, in the faubourg St. Denis or the faubourg St. Lazare, began operations about 1769. Pierre Antoine Hannong, leaving Vincennes, became the director here in 1772. Hannong's direction not proving satisfactory from a business point of view, he was removed, and, at the instance of one of the proprietors, the Marquis d'Osson, Barrachin was made director about 1775. It was then that the factory secured the patronage of Charles-Philippe, Comte d'Artois, the brother of Louis XVI. At the same time it obtained the privilege of using the title "*Manufacture du Comte d'Artois.*" With a capable direction and staff, and under distinguished and powerful patronage, it now entered upon a prosperous career.

In 1782 Bourdon-Desplanches was director and performed the achievement of firing an ovenful of china with coal in the presence of the municipal authorities, the Sèvres chemists, and a gathering of savants. The success of this feat made a deep impression, for it meant the saving of a vast quantity of wood fuel which it was becoming all the time more and more difficult to get. Bourdon-Desplanches was rewarded with a subsidy of 3000 livres in recognition of his important accomplishment.

After the restrictive edict of 1784, the factory sought permission to continue making biscuit pieces, busts and other modelled products as well as to go on painting china in all colours and decorating it with gold, on condition of using coal altogether for firing. The petition was granted, provided the gold decoration did not wholly cover any one piece, and provided the biscuit pieces produced were not more than eighteen inches high.

The factory kept on in prosperous working till about 1793. After the worst of the Revolutionary violence and disorder had passed by, the factory resumed its activities, and, under the successive direction of Huet, Benjamin and Schoelcher, maintained operations until 1810 when it was at last discontinued. It was one of the most important of the independent Paris factories and produced a great deal of porcelain of the highest quality.

THE BODY. The hard paste body for the first few years exhibited a slightly yellowish or amber tinge, similar to the paste of the Vincennes factory while Hannong was its director, and was very vitreous. When Bourdon-Desplanches became director the character of the body changed, shewed a pure milky white colour, and was in every way of admirable quality so that it compared favourably with the hard paste body made at Sèvres. The biscuit pieces, likewise, were of excellent character.

THE GLAZE. Under Hannong's directorship the glaze was pitted and displayed many imperfections. When the quality of the body was improved, the glaze also was perfected so that it was clear, transparent and evenly distributed.

PLATE 64

A. BERLIN TEA CADDY   B, ANSBACH TEAPOT

White paste, clear white glaze; decoration in gold, varying shades of brown, violet, vermilion and dull greens

Moulded ornament at base of spout; cold white paste, white glaze; decoration in light green, vermilion, pale blue, deep and light violet

Courtesy of the Victoria and Albert Museum, South Kensington

PLATE 65

LUDWIGSBURG TUREEN

Paste of greyish tinge, clear white glaze; modelled and applied ornament, and ornament moulded in paste about rim of lid and body; deep coloured flower and insect decoration in blue, yellow, violet, vermilion, red and deep yellowish green

Courtesy of the Victoria and Albert Museum, South Kensington

PLATE 66

A. VIENNA EMPIRE-SHAPED MILK JUG
White paste, clear glaze; decoration in gold, mulberry, pale yellow, grey and flesh colour

B. NYMPHENBURG CUP AND SAUCER
White paste, excellent clear glaze; decoration in vermilion, pink, pale green, dull blue and violet

Courtesy of the British Museum

PLATE 67

A. HEREND TRAY WITH PIERCED RIM
White paste, smooth, clear glaze; deep Indian red border with gold arabesques, light centre with vari-coloured decoration

B. COPENHAGEN TUREEN
White paste, excellent clear glaze; decoration in blue, pink, yellow, vermilion and varied shades of green; modelled and applied flower handles

Courtesy of the Victoria and Albert Museum, South Kensington

ARTICLES MADE AND CONTOUR. From the very beginning of the factory's career it turned out a large quantity of ware which seems at first to have consisted chiefly of table services and similar utilitarian articles. Under the management of Bourdon-Desplanches the scope of the products was broadened so that virtually everything was made for which there could be any demand, including a great number of biscuit pieces both in the form of portrait busts and also the statuettes and groups in the manner of those produced at Sèvres.

The contours in general plainly shewed the influence of Neo-Classic design that marked the reign of Louis XVI and some of the forms closely imitated those of Sèvres which set the fashion in such things.

TYPES OF DECORATION. The decorations of the earlier products were generally more or less scattered polychrome flower subjects in the execution of which a reddish-violet colour was conspicuous, this same colour being employed in a thin line to finish the edges and rims of tableware.

Under Bourdon-Desplanches the types of decoration experienced as marked a change as did the character of the paste and the glaze. Landscapes and Classic figure subjects were freely used. Many of these were executed *en camaïeu*, a soft grey being much employed for that purpose. Arabesques in the Pompeian manner frequently entered into well disposed compositions. Carefully executed bouquets and garlands of small flowers in polychrome also supplied a popular *motif* and the blue cornflower decoration, originated at Sèvres, likewise entered into the schemes. The gilding was excellent and judiciously used, even when it occurred in lavish measure.

The chemist of the works devised a blue porcelain paste that could be advantageously employed for work of a decorative character without the addition of gilding or painting, but the usual methods of producing ornamental effects were commonly followed.

THE MARKS. Pieces produced while Hannong was director shew the mark "P.H." applied in underglaze blue. The later marks, after Charles-Philippe became patron, were either the letters "C P" interwoven, or the same letters standing beneath a crown of a Prince of the Blood. Ordinarily these marks were enclosed in a vignette and were applied in red or some other colour, painted on the glaze.

♕
C P

VAUX CHINA—1770-?

HISTORY. Records regarding the porcelain factory at Vaux, near Meulan, are by no means as full as might be desired. In 1770, an hard paste porcelain factory, managed by Sieur Moreau, was in operation there. It has been said that Hannong had some concern with the founding of this establishment, but apparently there is nothing whatever to warrant such a statement. Certainly the character of the china produced would not tend to confirm such an opinion, for wherever Hannong was in control the porcelain produced seems to have been of inferior quality, while the porcelain of Vaux had a splendid white body, the wares were excellently potted, and the gilding and painting, executed in the prevalent manner of the time, left nothing to be desired. The mark used was two crossed "V's".

FABRIQUE DE LA COURTILLE CHINA—1773-1794

HISTORY. Locré established the Fabrique de la Courtille, in the rue Fontaine-au-Roi, in 1773 with the express intention of imitating the porcelain made in Germany. Almost from the outset this factory made a large quantity of china, including tableware, a considerable number of shew pieces such as large and important vases, and a number of biscuit groups and busts.

About 1784 Ruffinger joined forces with Locré and the establishment gained such a conspicuous position that in 1787 it was numbered with the works that were of enough importance to be allowed to operate, although they enjoyed no specific authorisation. It was in this factory, in 1790 or thereabouts, that the process of casting was first employed in France in the making of hard paste porcelain. In 1794, presumably owing to the disturbances of the Revolution, the business came to an end. It seems to have been revived later, but only china of a very commercial type was made.

THE BODY. The body was an excellent and pure white hard paste and the biscuit was of equally good quality with the glazed ware.

THE GLAZE. The glaze was clear and brilliant.

ARTICLES MADE AND CONTOUR. Fine dinner services, tea, coffee and chocolate services, dessert services, candlesticks, sconces and all the usual small articles in common demand at the time were made; also ornamental vases and fine modelling in biscuit ware.

TYPES OF DECORATION. The decorative repertoire embraced arabesques in the Pompeian manner, often on coloured grounds, little flowers and other *motifs* in the style of the period for tableware, and modelled ornament. In connexion with the bases of biscuit ware there were sometimes vermiform applications in white slip, and some of the later porcelain produced was painted like agate.

THE MARKS. The mark was two crossed torches; the biscuit pieces bear the same mark or else the words "Locré à Paris," or "Fabrique de la Courtille."

FABRIQUE DE LA RUE DE REUILLY CHINA— (1774) 1781–1800 (?)

HISTORY. In 1774 a porcelain maker named Lassia sought leave to establish a porcelain works on the rue de Reuilly, in the faubourg St. Antoine, and registered the factory mark "L." Although this date occurs as a possible beginning, there seems to have been no very considerable production of chinaware till somewhere about 1781 when Cadet, Guettard, Lalande and Fontanieu testified to the fire-resisting qualities of Lassia's porcelain. The factory was jointly directed by Lassia and Chanou when it protested against the restrictive edict of 1784. In this same year Chanou left Lassia and set up a factory of his own. Four years later, in 1788, Lassia sought to obtain the exclusive right to make stoves and mantel-pieces of porcelain, but was not successful in his quest. When the factory was discontinued is not definitely known, but it was not in operation in 1800.

THE BODY. The body was of hard paste, hard, white and of excellent quality.

THE GLAZE. The glaze was clear and evenly distributed and compared well with the glaze of other contemporary wares.

ARTICLES MADE AND CONTOUR. From Lassia's application for exclusive right to make porcelain stoves and mantel-pieces, it is evident that the factory essayed unusual things to a certain extent, in addition to the usual articles of manufacture. There were also produced in quantity tableware, tea and coffee services and vases. The contours were of the prevailing Neo-Classic type.

TYPES OF DECORATION. This factory made extensive use of grounds produced with on-glaze enamel colours. A yellow ground of this sort was especially characteristic. Many pieces were also decorated in admirably executed gilding on a white ground. The *motifs* most commonly used were flowers, and arabesques of Classic and Renaissance character and the designs were well adapted to the pieces.

THE MARKS. The mark of this factory was an "L" in underglaze blue or else painted in gold on the glaze. The mark of the independent works started by Chanou, when he left Lassia, was "C.H." in red on the glaze. Pieces of his work are rare, but they are of good quality and the decorations are well painted.

L *L*

FABRIQUE DE MONSIEUR, À CLIGNANCOURT CHINA— 1771 - ?

HISTORY. Pierre Deruelle established an hard paste porcelain factory at Clignancourt in 1771, and apparently carried on work there for three or four years without official authorisation. In 1775 he sought government recognition for his enterprise and gave the required notification to the authorities at Sèvres. At this time he likewise secured the interest of Monsieur, the King's brother, as patron along with the right to style his factory "Fabrique de Monsieur."

De Moitte became the director of the works and a very considerable output of excellent chinaware was made, the factory continuing in active operation until after the Revolution. Indeed, so admirable was the quality of the porcelain in body and glaze, and of such superior character were the gilding and the painted decorations, that the wares could well hold their own in comparison with the work of Sèvres. As a matter of fact, a number of pieces were decorated in the fashions reserved by royal edict to Sèvres, and marked with the crossed and interwoven L's of Sèvres beneath a prince's coronet.

This led to a police investigation, the seizure and confiscation of the pieces so decorated and marked, and the imposition of an heavy fine upon Deruelle. The authorities had no inclination to mitigate the rigours of the law, for the pieces in question were so good that they could readily be mistaken for the work of the royal factory. The contours, the decorations and the gilding of all the chinaware made at the Fabrique de Monsieur were in the Neo-Classic style that dominated the period.

The mark borne by the earliest china produced by this factory was a windmill. After Monsieur became patron, a monogram composed of his initials, L.S.X., was painted in red on the glaze, sometimes with the addition of a prince's coronet above it. Other marks also occur—

the interwoven initials of Monsieur including a D, a D beneath a prince's coronet, and an M beneath a coronet, all three were used and applied in red or gold on the glaze.

FABRIQUE DE LA REINE, RUE THIROUX CHINA—1778-?

HISTORY. Andrè-Marie Leboeuf established an hard paste porcelain factory in the rue Thiroux in 1778. His wares immediately met with such phenomenal success that in the following year he was heavily fined for trenching upon the privileges reserved to Sèvres in the matter of certain processes and the style of decoration. Of all the factories that may be considered as competitors with Sèvres, Leboeuf's was the one of which the Sèvres management had most cause to be jealous and apprehensive. If Leboeuf's work is closely compared with that of Sèvres, it can be seen at a glance why the authorities of the latter establishment were greatly disquieted.

After his uncomfortable experience with Sèvres and the police authorities, Leboeuf secured the protecting patronage of the Queen, who gave him the right to mark his china with her monogram or initial. She gave him further encouragement by ordering from him some of the china for her dairy at Versailles, and also various choice pieces which she gave to her friends as presents. From this royal patronage and the great popularity his work enjoyed, Leboeuf's china came to be known as "Porcelaine à la Reine." After the Revolution the works passed into other hands.

Both the letter A, in underglaze blue, and A beneath the Queen's crown, in either red or gold on-glaze, appear as marks on this truly beautiful china.

FABRIQUE DU DUC D'ANGOULÊME, RUE DE BONDY CHINA—1780- ?

HISTORY. Under the protection and patronage of Louis-Antoine, Duc d'Angoulême, Guerhard and Dihl opened an hard paste porcelain factory, in 1780, in the rue de Bondy. Dihl, a man of broad scientific attainments, is credited with being the first to establish a complete palette of colours that could be used for the decoration of hard paste porcelain.

This factory successfully reproduced all the underglaze coloured grounds used at Sèvres and all the colours for on-glaze painting. In addition to tableware, vases and ornaments of exquisite quality and enriched with the most elaborate decorations, there were made a great many excellent biscuit pieces.

Previous to the Revolution the pieces were marked G.A., occasionally set in an oval vignette with a coronet above it, in red or gold on the glaze. After the Revolution the pieces were signed "Dihl" or "Guerhard and Dihl, Paris," the mark being applied in various ways.

FABRIQUE DE LA RUE POPINCOURT CHINA—1760-?

HISTORY. About 1760 Lemaire established an hard paste porcelain factory in the rue des Amandiers, Popincourt. Nast, the elder, bought the factory in 1783 and it afterwards passed to his sons. Both beautiful tableware and ornaments were produced in considerable quantity, and there were also modelled some exceedingly creditable biscuit pieces. The body and glaze were the same as those of the other hard paste factories operating in and near Paris at the time. The contours and the decorations were all in the Neo-Classic manner of the period. When the pieces are marked they bear the word "Nast" in red on the glaze.

FABRIQUE DU DUC D'ORLÉANS CHINA—1784-1806

HISTORY. This hard paste porcelain factory, established in the faubourg St. Antoine in 1784, in 1786 secured the patronage of Louis-Philippe, Duc d'Orléans and was hence known as the Fabrique du Duc d'Orléans. Not a little good porcelain, well decorated and of some variety, was made there, comparing very favourably with the chinaware produced at the other independent factories in the neighbourhood of Paris. There seem to have been two marks, either one of which might be used—the letters L.J., interlaced, or the letters O.M. In contour and decoration this chinaware followed first the fashions of the reign of Louis XVI, and later the more severe manner of the Directoire period and the Empire.

LAURAGUAIS CHINA—1758- ?

HISTORY. The Comte de Brancas-Lauraguais was deeply interested in hard paste porcelain experimentation and, having made successful trials with the kaolin and felspar found near Alençon, began to make porcelain in the west of France about 1758. The paste was at first coarse and brownish in colour and the glaze was very defective. Later, however, the quality of his porcelain was improved although biscuit pieces shewed a somewhat grey hue. The ware was rather simply decorated in blue. The mark was "B L" interlaced and applied in underglaze blue. The factory was chiefly important on account of its early date and the part it played in the experimental period of French hard paste.

ℬ

STRASBURG CHINA—1745-1754; 1766-c.1780

HISTORY. The making of hard paste porcelain at Strasburg was carried on at several different periods. Paul Antoine Hannong, a faïence maker, early in the eighteenth century pursued experiments in making hard paste and, in 1726, is said to have presented the Strasburg Corporation with a service of plates, salad dishes and platters of fine white porcelain of his own production. When he died in 1739 he was reputed the first person to have made true hard paste porcelain in France. Whence he obtained the necessary kaolin and felspar is not known, but he got enough to establish material evidence that he could make what he claimed. The one indubitable piece of his making is of a greyish paste with a good white glaze and decorations painted in pale rose.

His son, Paul Hannong, who continued to operate the faïence factory, began to make hard paste porcelain in 1745, believing that the ancient privileges guaranteed Strasburg when it was joined to the Kingdom of France would protect him against any action that might be brought by the porcelain makers of Saint Cloud and Vincennes. Several experienced porcelain makers, one a refugee from Meissen and the other lately come from the china factory at Höchst, joined forces with Hannong and before long the Strasburg factory was putting forth a goodly quantity of tableware, flower-pots, and numbers of the little painted groups and statuettes for which eighteenth century people had such a passion.

This venture at Strasburg aroused the fears and animosity of the management at the Vincennes factory who tried to enforce the privileges that had been granted them. Hannong therefore applied for letters-patent, but his petition producing no result, he went to Paris and, in his anxiety, appealed to Boileau the director of the Vincennes factory, offering to treat for the sale of his secrets. The negotiations came to naught, partly because the materials required by the processes were not then believed to be obtainable in France, partly because Hannong demanded a cash payment and an annuity which the Vincennes factory was not prepared to pay.

But Boileau had succeeded in getting possession of Hannong's secrets, and having done so he treated him abominably, securing an order inhibiting Hannong from manufacturing any more porcelain at Strasburg and requiring him to dismantle his oven within a fortnight. Only through the good offices of the Maréchal de Noailles did Hannong gain permission to finish the work he had actually on hand. It was after this episode that Hannong, with the support and encouragement of the Archduke Charles Théodore, established the hard paste porcelain works at Frankenthal.

The second active manufacture of hard paste porcelain at Strasburg began in 1766 under Joseph Adam Hannong, the son of Paul, who had remained in charge of the faïence factory when his father went to Frankenthal. His main object was a large commercial output rather than the making of ornamental wares. In this policy he was successful up to 1780 when the manufacture was discontinued.

THE BODY. The hard paste produced at Strasburg under Paul Hannong, in the 1745–1754 period, was very white but only moderately translucent; the paste of the second period, under Joseph Adam Hannong (1766–1780) was a somewhat heavy, thick substance of a slightly tawny or yellowish tone.

THE GLAZE. The glaze of the first period was apt to be imperfect, unevenly distributed, and exhibited a pitted or spotted surface; the glaze of the second period was also defective and irregular in surface.

ARTICLES MADE AND CONTOUR. In the first period the articles chiefly made were tea, coffee and chocolate services, dinner sets and ornamental flower-pots, with a certain number of the popular polychrome statuettes and figure groups; in the second period the output embraced articles of the same sort, with the addition of some pieces in biscuit.

The contours in general followed the simpler contemporary shapes of Dresden, with a trend towards Neo-Classic forms during the second period.

TYPES OF DECORATION. In the first period the manner of decoration resembled that of the flowered Strasburg faïence, and to hide the glaze defects little flowers and insects were disposed seemingly at random. The colours most used were rose, purple and bluish green, without gilding. In the second period, the same *motifs* of scattered flowers and insects were often used to conceal defects of glaze. There were also Chinese *motifs*, flowers, and small country scenes or figures with an entourage of vegetation. Besides purple, carmine, indigo blue, green, yellow and pale rose, a characteristic bright red was used. Edges and mouldings were often lined with violet carmine. Gilding was rarely used.

THE MARKS. The mark of the first period, under Paul Hannong, was "P.H." either in capitals or cursive letters, in underglaze blue or, occasionally, in rose or brown on-glaze colour; the mark of the second period, under Joseph Hannong's directorship, was "JH" in underglaze blue, often accompanied by figures indicating special patterns. The biscuit pieces bore "H" in the paste.

PH

NIDERVILLER CHINA—1765–c.1850

HISTORY. The manufacture of hard paste porcelain was begun in 1765 at Niderviller by the Baron Jean Louis de Beyerlé, one of the King's Counsellors. The porcelain enterprise grew out of the faïence works that Baron de

Beyerlé had established in 1754. Kaolin was brought from Germany until Baron de Beyerlé bought some of the first kaolin mines at St. Yrieix.

In 1780 General the Comte de Custine acquired the works and François Lanfrey became manager. The sculptor Lemire, who had worked at Lunéville with Cyfflé, came to Niderviller and modelled exquisite vases, shepherdesses, children, cupids and sundry other figures in the Louis XVI manner. Many of them were made in biscuit and materially contributed to the profit and reputation of the works. Lemire conceived the notion of creating in connexion with the factory a school of modelling and design for apprentices, a scheme attended with most admirable subsequent results. When the Comte de Custine died, Lanfrey continued as director and eventually became the owner. After Lanfrey's death, a M. Dryander became director. The factory continued working till the middle of the nineteenth century.

THE BODY. The paste at first, under Baron de Beyerlé, was white and highly translucent; afterwards, under the ownership of Comte de Custine, it was less vitreous but of an equally pure white.

THE GLAZE. The glaze of the Niderviller factory was of the best quality and brilliant, closely resembling the contemporary glaze used at Sèvres.

ARTICLES MADE AND CONTOUR. Besides a great quantity of beautiful tableware, tea and coffee services, vases and all the other items of usual demand, there were produced the numerous biscuit pieces that gave Niderviller a special fame. The contours of the chinaware were at first reminiscent of the manner of Dresden; later, the forms were more typically French and the Neo-Classic contours of the reign of Louis XVI were followed by the Neo-Grec shapes of the Empire period.

TYPES OF DECORATION. The earliest Niderviller china was decorated very much in the styles current at Dresden. There were numerous flower subjects, landscapes, polychrome or *en camaïeu* (Plate 59, A), figures, and oftentimes scenes were drawn from La Fontaine's fables, the composition being enclosed within a geometrical frame or border while scattered flowers adorned the out-lying ground of the porcelain. Purple, carmine and rose were colours much in favour and there was comparatively little gilding. Later, the styles current in France were more freely followed and many of the favourite flower subjects were painted with great delicacy. The cornflower *motif*, introduced at Sèvres, supplied the basis for much exquisite decoration. Porcelain flowers were likewise made in the Niderviller establishment and admirably coloured. Gilding was more largely used in the later work.

THE MARKS. There were no regular marks during the years of Baron de Beyerlé's ownership, although a "B" or "A and N" interlaced, and impressed in the paste, are said sometimes to have been used. Under the Comte de Custine, the mark was first the letters C and N interlaced, and later it appeared as two C's crossed beneath a count's coronet. In 1792 occurs the mark "N", or the words "Nider" or "Niderviller" in underglaze blue. Lanfrey's mark was C.F.L. interlaced, in underglaze blue. When the biscuit pieces and statuettes are marked, it is with "Niderviller" impressed.

MARSEILLES CHINA—1778-?

HISTORY. Experiments in the making of hard paste porcelain began at Marseilles in 1765. The actual manufacture on a commercial basis seems to have started about 1775 or, perhaps, earlier in the faïence works of J. G. Robert. The earlier ware is generally thick and heavy, with a body and glaze of yellowish grey tinge. This china was commonly decorated *en camaïeu* in a burnt siena colour, the decorations being done rather crudely.

The later ware exhibits a whiter body and the monochrome decorations are of much better character. Later still, the Marseilles china had a white body and good, clear glaze, and was well decorated with flowers in the manner of Mennecy and Sèvres. The colours especially favoured were rose, blue, and a greenish blue, the last of which was decidedly characteristic of the factory.

The marks of this factory were R., J. R. and, occasionally, F. R., in underglaze blue.

R R̈ JR

LIMOGES CHINA—1783 TO PRESENT DAY

HISTORY. The Limoges chinaware of modern fame started from a not very brilliant beginning. By an edict of 1783 Massié, Fourniers and Grellet were authorised to manufacture hard paste porcelain, the registered mark of the establishment being C. D. In May 1784 Louis XVI purchased the factory to be used as a branch of Sèvres and the son of M. Grellet, one of the three promoters of the first undertaking, became the director, continuing in that post till 1788 when he was succeeded by M. Alluaud.

PLATE 68

A. BOW BLUE AND WHITE PLATE IN CHINESE MANNER
Creamy paste, slightly bluish glaze; decoration in deep, dull blue

B. BOW BLUE AND WHITE SAUCEBOAT IN CHINESE MANNER
Same paste, glaze and colouring

C. BOW SAUCEBOAT, FRENCH ROCOCO MANNER
Creamy paste, slightly yellowish glaze; moulded ornament impressed in paste, decoration pink, yellow, light blue and bluish green

D. BOW SAUCEBOAT WITHOUT COLOUR DECORATION
Prunus blossoms in relief on sides; moulded feet and handle; creamy paste, glaze of yellowish tinge

Courtesy of the Victoria and Albert Museum, South Kensington

PLATE 69

A. BOW MUG WITH BULGING BASE

Creamy paste, slightly bluish glaze; flower decoration in mulberry, dark bluish green, light yellow and cobalt blue

B. BOW GLOBULAR TEAPOT

Same paste, glaze and colour characteristics as A

Courtesy of the Victoria and Albert Museum, South Kensington

PLATE 70

A. BOW PERFORATED FRUIT DISH
Creamy paste and glaze; decoration in vermilion, cobalt blue, gold and bluish green

B. BOW PLATE
Creamy paste, slightly yellowish glaze; prunus blossoms, without colour, moulded in relief on rim, Chinese peony decoration in green, deep pink, pale blue and bright yellow

Courtesy of the Victoria and Albert Museum, South Kensington

PLATE 71

A. BOW VASE IN THE WHITE
Creamy paste, greyish glaze; modelled and applied, moulded and perforated ornament

B. BOW VASE WITH DEEP COBALT GROUND
Creamy paste, greyish glaze; modelled and applied, moulded and perforated ornament; decoration in reserved panel on cobalt ground colour, in gold, mulberry, yellow, green and vermilion

C. BOW CANDLESTICK WITH MODELLED FIGURE
Creamy paste, greyish glaze; modelled flowers and moulded ornament; decoration in deep rose, green, vermilion, blue, yellow and gold

Courtesy of the Victoria and Albert Museum South Kensington

FRENCH CHINAWARE

The work done at this factory was not very important. During the eighteenth century the paste was of an ivory colour and the decorations usually consisted of little flowers whose colouring was not particularly distinguished although the ware was agreeable enough in its way.

The scheme of a branch factory for the establishment at Sèvres seems not to have worked very well and the factory was afterwards sold. The works are still in operation and producing excellent ware.

The fame of Limoges china is really due to M. Charles Haviland who established works in 1840 to make porcelain for the American market. By his energy and well-directed enterprise he developed the industry to the highest state of perfection in manufacture and the reputation of Limoges china is eminently well deserved. As the chinaware of the period after 1840, however, does not come within the scope of this volume, the subject cannot be dealt with here.

When the branch establishment was disposed of by Sèvres, it was continued by M. Alluaud and is still in existence under the name of Pouyat and Alluaud. The paste and glaze were perfected, the body being a pure white, and a full palette of on-glaze colours was used. Much of this improvement was effected by the end of the eighteenth century.

$$C \cdot D \qquad c : \partial$$

VALENCIENNES CHINA—1785-1797

HISTORY. In 1785 Sieur Fauquez and M. Lamoniary obtained authorisation from the Council of State to open a factory at Valenciennes for the making of common or fine porcelain, after the manner of the porcelain of the Indies, and a local monopoly of manufacture was granted them for ten years, provided they fired their ovens with coal. The paste was pure white and the body and glaze of the best quality. The contours and decorations reflected the styles current at the period. The decorations were executed in a manner consistent with the quality of the china (Plate 59, B). In addition to the tableware and ornamental articles, there were produced some good groups in biscuit.

There was also a common and cheaper grade of porcelain made and decorated in blue after the fashion of the commoner wares of Tournay. The works were finally closed in 1797.

The mark on the pieces of the fine ware consisted of the letters L. V. interlaced. The commoner wares were marked with the name "Valenciennes" or some abbreviation of it.

CAEN CHINA—1798–1808

HISTORY. The hard paste porcelain factory of Caen was founded in 1798 and, with the kaolin and felspar obtained from the neighbourhood of Limoges, produced chinaware of excellent quality in both body and glaze. The Caen chinaware enjoyed great and well deserved popularity, but the disturbed economic conditions of France in the early nineteenth century compelled the factory to close in 1808.

The contours of Caen china were those characteristic

of the Directoire and Empire periods, and many of the shapes shewed much elegance and grace. The decoration was of the highest order in point of design, painting and gilding. A pleasant yellow ground colour was especially characteristic. The beauty and general type of this china may be judged from the jug illustrated (Plate 58, A).

The mark was "Caen" printed in red within a cartouche.

caen

SPANISH AND PORTUGUESE CHINAWARE

MADRID (BUEN RETIRO) CHINA—1759-1808 (1812)

HISTORY. The royal porcelain factory of Buen Retiro, at Madrid, was established in 1759 by Charles III, when he became King of Spain. This establishment was an offshoot, or, perhaps, it might be better to call it a transference of the porcelain industry undertaken at Capo di Monte by Charles when he was King of Naples. As we have previously seen, in the story of Italian china, porcelain making was a darling project of Charles, upon which he spent great sums of money. When he inherited the kingdom of Spain and left Naples, he brought with him most of the skilled workmen and much of the equipment from Capo di Monte, and the inauguration of the new industry in Spain was a matter of the greatest solicitude to the royal patron.

For the first thirty years the porcelain produced was reserved for royal use and disposal, and even after 1789, when a part of the china was allowed to be sold to the public, the sale was not large because of the high price asked for the wares which were nearly all extremely elaborate. Consequently, even in Spain, the Buen Retiro china is exceedingly rare. Outside of Spain it is scarcely known at all.

At Buen Retiro both soft paste and hard paste porcelains were made in great diversity of forms and the fashions of Capo di Monte or Naples, Sèvres, Dresden, and

Wedgwood were extensively followed, often with added elaboration and magnificence according to the Spanish taste of the day.

When the French entered Madrid in 1808 they took possession of the china factory and did much damage. After that, although some porcelain was produced in a desultory way, nothing of note was achieved and the factory, which the French had converted into a fortification, was destroyed by Wellington in 1812.

Various marks were employed, amongst them *fleur-de-lys* and crowns used either by themselves or in conjunction with letters and monograms.

. . . .

At different times, subsequent to the establishment of the Buen Retiro factory, china of a simpler but pleasing character was made at Alcora, Moncloa and Gerona, but these factories were small and their output was very limited. Nor did they endure any length of time.

. . . .

In the latter part of the eighteenth century a small quantity of porcelain was also made in Portugal, both at Oporto and Lisbon. Specimens of Portuguese china are of even rarer occurrence than Spanish china. Buen Retiro was the one important establishment in the whole Peninsula, and both Spanish and Portuguese china are so infrequently met with that specimens need scarcely be considered by the collector as possibilities of acquisition.

GERMAN CHINAWARE

DRESDEN (MEISSEN) CHINA—1710 TO PRESENT DAY

HISTORY. To Johann Friedrich Böttger, erstwhile Berlin apothecary's prentice, belongs the credit of discovering in Europe the secret of making hard paste porcelain.

From childhood Böttger had shewn such interest in chemistry and aptitude for experiment that he was destined for the pursuit of medicine. Accordingly when he was sixteen years old, he was set apprentice to a Berlin apothecary. He straightway plunged into all manner of alchemistic studies, and soon his proficiency in that mysterious lore was bruited about. The impecunious King of Prussia, we are told, hoping and believing that Böttger might have mastered the secret of the philosopher's stone and so be able to transmute the baser metals into gold, was about to seize him and make use of his knowledge. Getting wind of the King's design, Böttger fled to Saxony and, as it turned out, "jumped from the frying pan into the fire."

Augustus the Strong, King of Poland and Elector of Saxony, was quite as much in need of funds as the King of Prussia, and here was a gold-maker fallen into his very lap. He seized Böttger and set him at work to make gold, with the help of a good laboratory, capable assistants and ample working funds. Of course the task ended in failure, as it needs must, but the chemist Tschirnhausen suggested to the King that Böttger's services and knowledge of chemistry, along with the laboratory and apparatus, might be used to better purpose in the cause of industry.

More gold was to be got by promoting manufactures in Saxony than by the fantastic chasing of moonbeams. Faïence factories were rising and prospering in other parts of Germany; why should there not be a faïence factory in Saxony, and why should it not be a source of substantial profit?

The King hearkened readily to this suggestion. Böttger and Tschirnhausen were permitted to change the object of their work and, instead of labouring to metamorphose iron into gold, they examined and experimented with clays and earths. As a result, in 1708 Böttger succeeded in producing the famous red stoneware that was so hard it could be polished on the lapidary's wheel.

The manufacture of the stoneware proved profitable and satisfied the King, at any rate for the nonce, but by this time Böttger had set his mind on solving the riddle of Oriental porcelain which had hitherto baffled its European admirers and he pursued his experiments with unremitting zeal. At last, in 1709, after the death of his collaborator Tschirnhausen, he was able to shew the King a few specimens of what was indubitably true porcelain. As yet, it was unglazed, but Böttger very soon devised the glaze, so that 1709 may be regarded as the dawn of hard paste porcelain making in the Western World.

In January 1710 the Meissen porcelain factory was established by Royal Patent. The works were equipped in the castle of Albrechtsburg overlooking the town of Meissen, a few miles west of Dresden. There the secret processes of manufacture could not be spied upon by prying eyes. These processes were most jealously guarded and for long afterwards the workmen employed were virtually prisoners. In the castle of Albrechtsburg the works remained until 1863, when they were removed to ampler quarters.

At the Leipzig Easter Fair, in 1710, were exhibited some specimens of the new porcelain, and a few weeks later Böttger shewed the King the first painted pieces. But though the factory was established by Royal Writ in 1710, there was still much necessary experimental work to be carried on, and it was not until some years later that the manufacture of porcelain was put on a commercial footing. From 1710 to 1713 at Meissen only the red stoneware was produced for sale. At the Leipzig Easter Fair, in 1713, the Meissen china was first exposed for public sale, and from that time onward its repute increased with amazing rapidity. By 1716 the manufacture, as a commercial enterprise, was well on its way.

Böttger died in 1719. Notwithstanding the repute already acquired by the porcelain of Meissen and the rapidly increasing sale of the wares, the financial affairs of the factory were in great disorder and a royal commission was set to deal with the situation. The difficulties were soon adjusted and, in 1720, Johann G. Herold, the painter, who had worked in the Vienna factory under du Pacquier, came to direct the work at Meissen. He was one of the greatest masters of his time, and under his influence the products soon shewed amazing improvement. Some years later, Johann Kändler, the modeller, joined the Meissen staff, and through the work done and the inspiration supplied by these two men the china of Meissen reached the height of its glory.

In 1759 and 1761 Frederick the Great looted the Meissen factory when he occupied Dresden, and carried off a great quantity of the best moulds and models to Berlin,

PLATE 72

A. BOW PERFORATED FRUIT DISH AND STAND
Creamy paste, slightly greyish glaze; modelled and applied, moulded and pierced ornament; decoration in mauve, yellow, yellowish green, light blue and vermilion

B. BARREL-SHAPED CHELSEA MUG
Creamy paste, slightly greyish glaze; scattered flower decoration in Dresden manner in the same colours as noted for A

Courtesy of the Victoria and Albert Museum, South Kensington

PLATE 73

CHELSEA OBLONG OCTAGONAL PLATTER

Creamy paste, clear white glaze; moulded rim; scattered flower, butterfly and insect decoration in pale yellow, several shades of mauve and mulberry, two shades of green, dull blue and dead vermilion

Courtesy of the Victoria and Albert Museum, South Kensington

PLATE 74

A. CHELSEA FLUTED CHOCOLATE POT
Creamy paste, slightly greenish glaze; moulded fluting; decoration pale yellow, dull vermilion, mulberry and several shades of green

B. CHELSEA EIGHT-SIDED VASE
Creamy paste, clear white glaze; semi-Kakiyemon decoration in cobalt blue, turquoise blue, pale yellow, deep vermilion and gold

Courtesy of the Victoria and Albert Museum, South Kensington

PLATE 75

A. CHELSEA FLOWER HOLDER WITH SCALLOPED FLARE TOP

Creamy paste, clear white glaze; moulded bands and shape; decoration in violet, light blue, pale yellow, green, vermilion and biscuit colour

Courtesy of the Victoria and Albert Museum, South Kensington

B. LATE CHELSEA COVERED SUGAR BASON

Creamy paste, clear white glaze; claret coloured ground with reserved white panels; decoration in gold, green, blue, pale Venetian red and deep mulberry

Courtesy of the Victoria and Albert Museum, South Kensington

whither as well he transported many of the experienced workmen. This interruption marked the end of the most distinctive, and perhaps the finest, period of Meissen porcelain.

When work was ultimately resumed, new influences that eventually became dominant were already beginning to make themselves felt, and the old creative spontaneity and enthusiasm were gone. About 1764 the painter Dietrich introduced the nascent Neo-Classic spirit into Meissen design, and as this influence became more and more manifest in both contour and decoration, the products of Meissen lost much of their erstwhile individuality, displayed an increasing likeness to the creations of other factories, and betrayed a tendency to follow rather than to lead, with a perceptible bias for the ways of Sèvres.

When Count Marcolini became director in 1774, the Neo-Classic style became paramount in all the new creations of Meissen and continued to dominate shapes and decoration alike until what have been called the "frigidities" of the Empire style succeeded at the dawn of the nineteenth century.

In 1814 Kühn became director and numerous technical improvements were introduced, the firing was done with coal, and the composition of the body was simplified. The earlier wares had grown valuable by this time and were largely reproduced, which was fortunate, as all power of fresh creation had apparently become dormant. The factory was moved from the old fortress of Albrechtsburg in 1863. In its new environment it has made great advances commercially, but "has added little or nothing to the progress of art."

THE BODY. The body, at first, was thick and clumsy and the pieces were often warped or fire-cracked. The paste exhibited a slightly yellowish tinge, "which Böttger himself regarded as a fault, but which most people nowadays would doubtless prefer to a colder and over-white tint." Owing to lack of quartz or felspar in the composition—alabaster was used instead—the early paste is not particularly translucent. By a series of experiments and modifications, the paste was brought to a pure, hard white at an early date and the translucency was increased.

THE GLAZE. The early glaze produced by Böttger was thick but of even distribution, and it was clear, transparent, and ordinarily free from flaws. The later glaze was of thinner body and more brilliant in its general appearance.

ARTICLES MADE AND CONTOUR. It was only during the initial or experimental period under Böttger that the output of Meissen was at all restricted in variety. Even then, there was considerable diversity in the tea, coffee and breakfast services, the cups and saucers, the small vases and flower pots, and the less ambitious sorts of tableware and decorative accessories. The factory was still young when it began to put forth all kinds of tableware, vases, and every sort of decorative accessory, as well as the figures that were originated there, the modelled flowers, and the busts, figures and groups both glazed and in biscuit (Plate 62, A).

The contours, at first, were more or less experimental. Shapes were adopted from Chinese models, from metal forms, from faïence, and from whatever source seemed likely to yield material for adaptation. But through all this initial stage, the plastic quality of the material was

GERMAN CHINAWARE

never for one moment lost sight of, and when Kändler came to Meissen he had only to carry on and amplify a tradition already firmly rooted.

Under his direction the shapes, from whatever source they had been derived in the first instance, began to display both local individuality and an unmistakably European character. He was imbued with the Rococo conceptions of his day and delighted in embodying in porcelain forms the subtle curves and moulded scrolls so characteristic of the manner. Both the bodies of the pieces and the decorations modelled and applied to them responded to this impulse. He developed the Rococo schemes to such a degree of exuberance that he has sometimes been regarded, though wrongly, as the originator of the mode. He was, nevertheless, an ardent exponent. He also introduced shapes with well defined architectural mouldings, which was a departure from Chinese precedent.

From 1764 onward, the Rococo contours more and more yielded place to the restrained Neo-Classic shapes, and these, in due order, at the turn of the century, gave way before the modes of the Empire.

TYPES OF DECORATION. The very early types of decoration practised at Meissen included moulding in low relief (Plate 62, B), modelling in high relief; piercings and fretwork, in the latter of which Böttger and his modellers displayed the greatest daring and dexterity alike; painting in enamel colours with a rather limited palette; and painting in gold alone, which meant arabesques and "gold Chinamen" on a flat surface, or Chinese and floral gilt reliefs raised from the flat ground of the white porcelain. The "gold Chinamen," as they were called, were Chinese figures and attendant *motifs* painted in gold in silhouette on the white porcelain, and made a very interesting and effective decoration. Underglaze painting in blue was employed, but in Böttger's time the results were not at all satisfactory. The blue pigment ran and occasionally formed bubbles, behaviour due probably to impurities in the cobalt. Nevertheless, persistent efforts were made to overcome the difficulty, and eventually the trouble was altogether eliminated and underglaze blue decoration became one of the customary processes. China decorated in underglaze blue with the "Strohblumen" and "onion" patterns (Plate 60, A), was exceedingly popular and was made in large quantities. These patterns—especially the former—were so much admired in Denmark and so much copied at Copenhagen that in time they came to be known as "Copenhagen" patterns, although they really originated at Dresden.

With Herold's name are associated the introduction of the Japanese Kakiyemon decoration (Plate 76, B), which was afterwards widely copied all over Europe and was known in England and America as the "old Japan" pattern; the introduction of armorial services; and the popularisation of naturalistic flowers, arranged either in organised compositions or else scattered at random in sprays and single blossoms (Plates 61, B and 60, B), sometimes with the addition of insects here and there in the intervals between them. Flowers and insects thus arranged had the advantage of concealing any chance flaws in body or glaze. This type of decoration, also, was almost universally copied and has always been regarded as peculiarly characteristic of Dresden (Plate 60, B). It was not long *needed* at Dresden for purposes of concealment, but was continued on account of its beauty; many other factories, however, found it not only attractive but most useful in hiding imperfections. The draperies of the figures were often pyed with minute blossoms (Plate 62, A), after the manner of the East India printed cottons, a fashion of decoration akin to the "scattered flower" *motif*.

During Herold's time likewise the "brocaded" Japanese Imari ware, with its strong reds, blues and gold, furnished a popular decorative theme, while dragons and other distinctly Chinese subjects afforded a wealth of material of which the china painters fully availed themselves. Despite the use of these Oriental themes, however, the tendency towards purely European methods of decoration (Baroque gold pattern, Plate 61, A), was constantly growing stronger. The "German flowers" rendered in naturalistic manner were followed by landscapes with ornate borders; by Rococo scrolls and other characteristic Rococo forms, expressed either in colour and gilding or by moulded reliefs accentuated with colour and gold; by modelled flowers, birds and other objects, used as knobs and handles and realistically coloured; by Watteau-like panels and arabesques; by landscapes in monochrome (Plate 61, A); by diapered borders borrowed from Oriental china; and by ground colours with reserved panels in which appeared naturalistic flowers, birds of brilliant plumage, figures, landscapes and pastoral scenes.

Although the trend was away from the employment of Chinese themes, sometimes the reserved panels in coloured grounds, instead of containing the *motifs* just enumerated, were quatrefoil or lobate-shaped and enclosed Chinese subjects in polychrome.

The usual ground colours were pale violet, light blue,

purple, brick-red, apple-green and sea-green, while a yellow which varied from straw colour to deep lemon was particularly successful. Some success attended the experiments in coloured bodies, and grey, blue, mauve, cream and grey-brown were produced. A "dead-leaf" brown coloured glaze was also occasionally used.

By the time the Dresden factory suffered pillage at the hands of Frederick the Great, the Rococo influence, both in contour and decoration, had not only crowded out almost every trace of Oriental elements but, in many directions, had reached the most extravagant developments.

After the resumption of work, the Sèvres influence became steadily more perceptible in the manner of decoration, and the usual complement of Neo-Classic forms and *motifs*—already noted in connexion with the products of the French factories—dominated the day until they were ousted by the more aggressive expressions of the Empire mode. Much of the china made at Dresden during the period of Neo-Classic supremacy was very beautiful, but it was no longer distinctive of the place in its decoration as the earlier wares had been.

THE MARKS. The early Dresden china was marked with the letters K. P. M.—meaning *Königliche Porzellan Manufactur*—with occasional variations to K. P. F. and M. P. M. These marks date from about 1719; much of the earliest ware was altogether unmarked. About the second quarter of the century the crossed swords from the Saxon arms appeared as the mark; they were at first painted in on-glaze blue and afterwards, when they had learned better how to manage it, in underglaze blue. Concurrently with the crossed swords the royal cypher, composed of the letters A. R. in monogram, was used on the royal porcelain. About this time, too, appeared the staff of Æsculapius. After the Seven Years' War and the resumption of work at Meissen, a dot was placed between the crossed swords. With the period of Count Marcolini's directorship, which began in 1774, a star was set between the crossed swords.

BERLIN CHINA—1750 TO PRESENT DAY

HISTORY. With the help of runaway workmen from Höchst, the hard paste porcelain factory at Berlin was started under Wilhelm Caspar Wegeli in 1750. Some excellent tableware and also figures inspired by those of Meissen were made here, but business difficulties and lack of sufficient interest on the part of the King, who seemed to feel that Wegeli's china was not distinguished enough in character to suit his ambitions, drove Wegeli to give up the works in 1757. Under Reichard, who succeeded him, little advance was made. In 1761 Gotzkowski took the works which then acquired all the loot from Meissen and a number of Dresden workmen. It was Frederick the Great's ambition that the Berlin china should equal or excel the products of Meissen and Gotzkowski's management becoming involved in financial embarrassment, in 1763 the King himself took over the establishment and became sole owner. Thereafter the factory continued as a royal enterprise.

Frederick had no intention of keeping the factory merely as an expensive plaything. He was determined it should pay for itself, and not only pay for itself but make a profit. He accordingly adopted some drastic measures towards this end. The Berlin lotteries were compelled to distribute 10,000 thalers' worth of china annually, no Jew could obtain a marriage certificate till he had bought a set of Berlin china, and in various other ways the sales were assiduously pushed. These methods put the factory on its feet as a business concern and it entered upon a course of prosperity that has continued to the present day.

The Body. At first the Berlin china was made of materials from Passau and, owing to impurities, the paste shewed a yellowish-grey tinge, but about 1771 with materials from Silesia and Halle a paste was produced that was very hard, dense of texture and a cold white in colour. These qualities have been maintained ever since.

The Glaze. The glaze was hard, clear, brilliant and technically perfect, but the "severe" character of both paste and glaze made it impossible to secure the bright, glowing colour that could be secured with the less refractory glaze of soft paste porcelain.

Articles Made and Contour. For some time the wares produced consisted chiefly of dinner services, tea, coffee and chocolate equipages, and breakfast sets, along with a few figures, glazed and decorated. Later the wares shewed more variety and elaboration and a number of ornate vases and other decorative accessories were produced, as well as figures in biscuit.

Although the methods of Meissen manufacture were followed and Meissen workmen and decorators employed, Frederick's admiration for French art dictated the following of French forms and the Rococo style consequently flourished at the Berlin factory in a most pronounced manner, although not with quite the same extravagance sometimes displayed under Kändler's inspiration at Meissen. Nevertheless, some trivial grotesqueries were indulged in, such as making lace decoration by coating lace with porcelain slip, the lace being burned out in the firing and leaving the pattern behind it. Late in the century the Neo-Classic mode made itself felt in contour as well as decoration and, in due time, the Empire manner succeeded.

TYPES OF DECORATION. Underglaze blue decoration was much used in the early days of the factory, and moulded low reliefs in the form of ribbing, scrolls and basket-work patterns were exceedingly favoured. The early colour schemes were simple and the palette limited. Often enough a scheme was carried out with only rose colour and grey, red, black and gold or red, green and gold. The palette was subsequently enlarged. The rose-colour of the Berlin china was highly characteristic as Frederick the Great was very partial to it, but the paste and glaze used were of too "severe" a type ever to get the same beautiful *rose Pompadour* that appeared on the soft paste porcelain of Sèvres. Landscapes, figures and floral subjects (Plate 64, A), were frequently painted in monochrome, and for these rose-colour was much used as well as in the combinations with other colours. Diaper borders, often in the form of a small scale pattern which the Germans called "*mosaik*" were freely employed and for these, again, the characteristic rose-colour was favoured. Small scattered flowers, or small flowers in garlands, wreaths and festoons furnished much of the decoration in connexion with these diapered rose borders; likewise, larger flowers in organised composition were not seldom seen. There were also a number of coloured grounds with reserved panels in which appeared flowers, birds, landscapes and figures. The fashions of Sèvres were by no means without their visible influence, especially in the latter part of the eighteenth century when the Neo-Classic mode was paramount. Transfer printing made its appearance about the end of the eighteenth century.

THE MARKS. The mark during the factory's initial period under Wegeli's direction was a W in underglaze blue, with the strokes of the letter crossed. Under Gotzkowski the mark was a crudely formed G. When the factory became a royal possession the mark was a sceptre, adopted in allusion to the sceptre borne by the Electors of Brandenburg as Grand Chamberlains of the Empire. Later, the two sceptres of the Hohenzollerns were used, crossed saltire-wise, thus resembling the crossed swords of Saxony.

HÖCHST CHINA—1746–1796

HISTORY. At the faïence factory of Höchst, a town governed by the Archbishop-Elector of Mainz, attempts to produce hard paste porcelain were made as early as 1720 but no success attended these efforts until 1746 when A. F. von Löwenfinck, a painter who had left Meissen, brought thither the secrets of porcelain manufacture. For a number of years the Höchst porcelain venture had a chequered career. Until about 1760 it seems to have been as much engaged in making faïence as in producing porcelain. Although some progress had been made and some creditable porcelain products achieved, the undertaking was hampered by financial difficulties, and it was not until 1778, when the Prince-Bishop himself took over the factory that satisfactory conditions prevailed. Most of the work produced at Höchst closely echoed the traditions and practices of Meissen, but in two particulars the factory may claim distinction—the quality of the figures modelled by Johann Peter Melchior and others, which gave the establishment great repute, and the characteristic use of two very beautiful enamel colours made from gold, a light transparent rose largely employed in figure painting and a rich carmine extensively affected in rendering monochrome landscapes and scenes. Political conditions about the end of the century had a disastrous effect upon the fortunes of the factory and it was closed in 1796.

THE BODY. The paste of the early porcelain made at Höchst had a greyish tone. It was not long, however, before the body was brought to the chalky white colour common to most German porcelains.

THE GLAZE. The glaze at first was greyish and marked by some flaws. This, too, was soon improved and made clear and brilliant.

ARTICLES MADE AND CONTOUR. Apart from the making of tableware and the other usual items of decorative requirement, Höchst is famous for its admirable figures, groups and portrait medallions, both glazed and in biscuit, modelled by Melchior and a succession of other capable artists.

Following the lead of Dresden, the shapes of the chinaware for some time were preponderantly in the Rococo manner, although the Neo-Classic impulse was manifest in the later productions.

TYPES OF DECORATION. Besides the use of the two distinctive colours already mentioned, and their application in the manner pointed out, the types of decoration practised at Höchst included most of the Dresden repertoire with its moulded ribbings, basket-work, Rococo scrolls and other low-relief ornament (Plate 63, B) raised in the paste; fretwork and piercings; "German flowers," "Indian flowers," scattered flowers and flowers in compositions, garlands, wreaths and festoons; diapered or "*mosaik*" borders; Chinese *motifs* of different sorts; landscapes, figures and scenes; ground colours and reserved panels with birds and flowers; and the later complement of arabesques and Classic elements.

THE MARKS. The mark was a wheel of six spokes, a device derived from the arms of the Archbishop-Elector, often topped with a crown or the Electoral hat, and frequently accompanied by a monogram or initials. Occasionally the wheel has only five spokes. Up to about 1770 the mark was impressed in the paste, or else painted in black, brown, purple, iron-red, or gold. After 1770 the mark almost always appeared in underglaze blue. For the most part, the biscuit pieces are unmarked.

NYMPHENBURG CHINA—1747–1862
(SINCE 1862 CONTINUED IN PRIVATE HANDS)

HISTORY. Under the Elector of Bavaria, Max Joseph III, an hard paste porcelain factory was established as a State enterprise at Naudeck, in 1747, with the aid of the expert, Joseph Jacob Ringler, from Vienna.

Ringler left before the work of establishment was fully accomplished and the factory did not get into thorough working order, capable of satisfactory and continuous production, until 1753. In 1761 the factory was transferred from Naudeck to quarters that had been especially prepared for it adjacent to the Palace of Nymphenburg near Munich, and by the name of Nymphenburg it has always been known. Under the patronage of the Elector Max Joseph, the royal factory flourished exceedingly and, in 1765, employed two hundred workmen. The next Elector, however, felt no especial interest in the making of porcelain and from 1777 to 1799 the manufacture languished and the working force of the factory was cut down so that it can scarcely be said to have done more than barely exist. In 1799 the succeeding Elector determined to restore porcelain making to its former importance and new life was infused into the establishment. In 1800 some of the best workmen from Frankenthal were employed and the output of the factory was greatly increased. In 1862 the establishment ceased to be a royal factory and passed into private hands. The manufacture is still carried on.

The Body. The body is a paste of excellent quality, white, hard and of dense, smooth texture.

The Glaze. The glaze, likewise, is of unexceptionable quality, perfectly distributed, clear and brilliant.

Articles Made and Contour. The articles made include all the customary "useful" tableware and the usual decorative adjuncts, but the making of such chinaware was thrown somewhat into the background by the stress laid upon figures and groups which were of the greatest excellence. The sculptor Melchior came to Nymphenburg and remained there till his death, producing some of his finest figures which contributed much to the factory's fame. Apart from the figures, glazed and in the biscuit, the only special feature of Nymphenburg manufacture is to be found in the food warmers made there.

In the matter of contour the Nymphenburg china followed fairly closely the fashions current at Dresden.

TYPES OF DECORATION. Underglaze blue painting was little, if at all, practised at Nymphenburg and was virtually unknown. Moulding and modelling in high relief were both employed and the raised and modelled parts were accented with colour. Flowers (Plate 63, A), birds and landscapes supplied the usual *motifs*, as elsewhere. Landscapes and peasant scenes were often painted in monochrome and for this purpose copper green was a rather favourite colour. The Nymphenburg decoration is marked by great naturalism and delicacy of painting. From about 1800 it is also characterised by elaborate and well-executed figure painting. It then became a practice to decorate the chinaware, and especially vases, with minutely finished copies of famous pictures in the Munich galleries and although this sort of ornamentation was exquisitely rendered, the taste that dictated the practice is decidedly questionable. Much Nymphenburg china of the period is certainly over-decorated. After 1815 not a little of the painted decoration was performed in Munich.

THE MARKS. The usual mark was some form of the Bavarian coat of arms, although the six-pointed "seal of Solomon" now and then occurred with letters or figures at the points. Initial letters were also used in conjunction with the marks just mentioned.

FÜRSTENBERG CHINA—1746-1753-1888

HISTORY. The hard paste porcelain factory of Fürstenberg was established by the Duke of Brunswick in the castle of Fürstenberg on the Weser. The factory was organised in 1746 by Baron von Langen with the aid of the "arcanist" Glaser from Bayreuth, but nothing of any moment was accomplished until Bengraf, an expert from Höchst arrived in 1753, so that manufacture may really be said to have begun at that date. The factory flourished and produced a large output, but its best period really began about 1770. Fürstenberg was the one German factory that ever used any of the English china as models. The work of Bow and Chelsea furnished not a little inspiration. This connexion was doubtless due to the close family ties existing between the royal family of England and the Dukes of Brunswick. After a period of decline during the Napoleonic wars, the factory gained renewed life and was continued in operation till 1888.

THE BODY. The early paste of the Fürstenberg china was greyish or yellowish in tone owing to impurities in the materials, which came from Passau. Later, this tone was eliminated and the paste was of the same cold white colour and density of texture as the Dresden china.

THE GLAZE. The early glaze was greyish and full of small black specks. The later glaze was clarified, ridded of its imperfections, and rendered clear and brilliant

ARTICLES MADE AND CONTOUR. Tableware, decorative accessories such as vases, sconces, candlesticks and the like were made in large quantity at Fürstenberg, and also a great many figures, groups and statuettes, both glazed and in the biscuit.

It seems to have been the policy at Fürstenberg to use the wares of nearly all other factories as models so that little of a distinctive nature in contour can be ascribed to Fürstenberg china. The chronological succession of Rococo forms, Neo-Classic forms and Empire forms can be traced concurrently with the vogue each commanded in other places.

TYPES OF DECORATION. Accessory to decoration, great use was made at Fürstenberg of moulded raised patterns, such as basket-work, ribbing, fluting, and "webs of Rococo scrollwork in low relief." Perhaps to conceal the imperfections of paste and glaze in the early ware, moulded excrescences from the surface were often greatly exaggerated, and this exaggeration was characteristic. Piercing, fretwork and modelling in high relief were also practised, the modelled and applied reliefs which served as knobs and handles being coloured and gilt.

Sea-green and underglaze blue were probably the only two ground colours used. A great deal of purple or rose-carmine appeared in the painting, both monochrome and polychrome. Iron-red was also a favourite monochrome colour. All manner of subjects supplied *motifs* for decoration, but the drawing of flowers, birds, figures and even of landscapes appeared to have been copied from portfolios of engravings rather than to have been inspired more directly by nature. The smooth surfaces customary during the Neo-Classic period, when there was more austerity of form and some renunciation of brilliant colour, fostered an improvement in the painted decoration. During this period there was an observable tendency to make use of Wedgwood models, just as there had been an earlier following of Bow and Chelsea, and also to pattern after the manner of Sèvres.

THE MARKS. The mark was a capital F in script, painted in underglaze blue. The biscuit pieces were marked with the running horse of Brunswick impressed in the paste.

LUDWIGSBURG CHINA—1758-1824

HISTORY. With the assistance of the "arcanist" Ringler, who has already appeared on several other occasions, Carl Eugen, Duke of Würtemberg, established the hard paste porcelain factory at Ludwigsburg in 1758. The factory was maintained by liberal subsidies and highly creditable work was produced, but after the death of Duke Charles in 1793 a decline set in and the manufacture was finally given up in 1824.

THE BODY. The Ludwigsburg paste was made of impure materials from Passau and, in consequence, always had a yellowish-grey tinge very different from the glistering, strident white of the Dresden body. Incidentally, though not considered so technically perfect, it is much mellower and more pleasant to look at.

THE GLAZE. The glaze was of fine quality, transparent and clear.

ARTICLES MADE AND CONTOUR. All the usual kinds of tableware and decorative accessories were made, and likewise groups, figures and statuettes both glazed and in biscuit. The contours ranged from those prevalent in the Rococo age to the later Neo-Classic and Empire forms.

TYPES OF DECORATION. Patterns moulded in low relief, in the usual devices previously mentioned in connexion with the wares of other German factories, played an important part in Ludwigsburg decoration, and likewise modelling in high relief, the attached reliefs being coloured and gilt. The painted decoration was of excellent quality and the *motifs* embraced landscapes, figures, flowers (Plate 65), wreaths, garlands, birds and butterflies, and occasionally exquisitely painted beetles were also introduced. Lilac was a favourite monochrome colour and sometimes small scattered flowers were thus presented. The modelling and decoration of the figures were of rather exceptional merit.

THE MARKS. The usual mark was the cypher of the reigning duke surmounted by a ducal crown. The cypher of Duke Charles was two C's, back to back and interlaced, in monogram. Sometimes the Würtemberg shield charged with three antlers appears as a mark. The presence of a crown has led to the erroneous name "Kronenberg" sometimes applied to this ware.

FRANKENTHAL CHINA—1755-1795

HISTORY. The hard paste porcelain factory of Frankenthal was established in 1755 by Paul Antoine Hannong, under the patronage of the Elector Palatine, Carl Theodor. In the account of French Chinaware we have already noted the circumstances that led to Hannong's removal from Strasburg where he had previously made hard paste porcelain.

Excellent china was made at Frankenthal, but there were financial difficulties and in 1762 the Elector bought the factory and continued the work under capable directors. Despite the high character of the products, the manufacture was not a success from a commercial point of view and the factory was at last closed in 1795.

THE BODY. The body at first shewed a slightly greyish tinge, but the paste was soon brought to a state of technical perfection in its whiteness and in all the other qualities that enter into the question.

THE GLAZE. The glaze likewise was technically perfect and of brilliant quality.

ARTICLES MADE AND CONTOUR. Table services of all sorts, tea, coffee and chocolate services, and all manner of decorative accessories were produced, and great stress was laid upon making the finest groups, figures and statuettes, glazed and in biscuit.

The work of Sèvres and Vienna to a great extent furnished models for emulation and the sequence of Rococo and Neo-Classic contours disclosed more or less resemblance to the individual interpretations of those factories.

TYPES OF DECORATION. Both the painted decoration and the gilding were of exceptionally fine character, and there was a remarkably full palette of colours in use. A deep royal blue ground colour, in imitation of the Sèvres *bleu du roi*, was highly favoured, and raised gilding, in the manner of Vienna, was successfully executed. A good underglaze black was also employed. Landscapes, figures, cameo subjects in medallions, landscapes in monochrome and polychrome, Classic subjects, birds and flowers in many manners supplied the *motifs*.

THE MARKS. The earlier pieces are marked with the crowned lion rampant of the Palatinate and the initials of Hannong (*J. A. H.*) in monogram. Later pieces bear the cypher of Carl Theodor surmounted by a crown.

THE LESSER GERMAN FACTORIES

The lesser German hard paste porcelain factories, such as Fulda, Cassel, Bayreuth, Ansbach, Wallendorf, Limbach and Kloster-Veilsdorf made some creditable china, but for the most part their wares exhibit no particular individuality. The factory at Fulda, in Hesse, patronised by the Prince-Bishop, was a notable exception and produced work of the greatest distinction, both in the way of table services and figures. The greater part of the work, however, put forth by these factories was of commonplace character and some of them indulged in the vicious practice of buying slightly decorated ware and revamping it with vulgar and over-loaded decoration.

AUSTRIAN CHINAWARE

VIENNA CHINA—1718-1864

History. The hard paste porcelain factory at Vienna was founded by a Dutchman, Claude du Pacquier, in 1718. This undertaking he accomplished with the aid of two runaway employees from Meissen, Samuel Stölzel an "arcanist" or expert in mixtures and mechanical processes, and Christoph Conrad Hunger, an enameller and gilder.

The factory produced work of admirable quality but du Pacquier was embarrassed by financial difficulties and eventually, in 1744, the factory with all its recipes was bought by the Empress Maria Theresa and thereafter conducted as a royal enterprise. The factory remained in the control of the State until 1864 when it was discontinued.

The Body. The paste of the early ware lacked the brilliance and whiteness of the Meissen body owing to the materials used, but after a supply of better material from Bohemia the body was brought to technical perfection according to the accepted standards of hard paste porcelain.

The Glaze. The glaze from the start was good and was soon brought to parallel quality with the Dresden glaze.

Articles Made and Contour. Besides the customary table services and objects of decorative purport, the Vienna factory produced a great quantity of the most elaborate vases and other ornaments and a large number of figures, groups and statuettes, glazed and in biscuit.

In the matter of contour, Dresden models and precedents appear to have supplied most of the impulse until the time when the Neo-Classic spirit began to assert itself, and consequently the Rococo forms flourished in florid exuberance. Even when the Neo-Classic influence became dominant, the Vienna factory without achieving any particular individuality in so doing managed to impart an ornate quality that often verged upon inconsistency. The advent of Empire forms gave greater scope for the display of sheer splendour and intricate enrichment.

TYPES OF DECORATION. Modelling in high relief, moulded ornaments in low relief impressed in the paste, piercing, fretwork, painting and gilding—all these decorative processes were freely employed. The subjects for painted decoration included polychrome Chinese *motifs;* Japanese birds and flowers; Imari red, blue and gold patterns; figures and landscapes; polychrome leafy scrolls with flowers, fruit, canopies, and figures, landscapes or scenes in cartouches; similar *motifs* painted in black with touches of gold; "German flowers," "Indian flowers," Sèvres "chintz" patterns, and hybrid flower forms; painting done over low reliefs; mythological subjects, battle scenes, and *putti* with their attendant embellishments. A number of good ground colours were also in use. In the latter part of the eighteenth century the practice of copying famous paintings as china decorations was followed to excess and many of the pieces of this time are terribly over-decorated.

In addition to the too lavish painted decorations, there was the further enrichment of raised gilding (Plate 66, A), which required several coats of gold, each successive coat being fired and burnished. Further ornament was engraved on this elaborate gilding. The chemist Leithner devised a palette of enamel colours more extensive than was used by any other contemporary factory; he produced an underglaze black; and he also introduced the use of platinum as well as rich gilding. Altogether, the late eighteenth century was a period of the amplest technical resources at the Vienna factory, but while some of the china then produced commands admiration, not a little of it is characterised by vulgar ostentation and indicates unpleasantly decadent taste.

THE MARKS. During the period of du Pacquier's control most of the china was unmarked. After 1744, when the factory became Crown property, the Austrian shield was painted in underglaze blue. After 1827 it was stamped in underglaze blue with a wood block. From 1784 onward the pieces were dated by the last two figures of the year impressed in the paste.

HEREND CHINA (HUNGARY)—c.1830 TO PRESENT DAY

HISTORY. About 1830, Moritz Fischer established an hard paste porcelain factory at Herend, in Hungary. He produced a very fine ware, anticipating Sèvres and Dresden in securing a full range of brilliant colours (Plate 67, A) on hard paste.

Most of the product of this factory was in the form of clever copies of the finest pieces of Sèvres and Capo di Monte porcelain of earlier date and the later enamelled ware of China. Fischer's most brilliant triumph was with the jewel-like enamelled decoration of cups for the Oriental market. The Herend china is marked with the name "Herend" in very small letters and the Hungarian arms are sometimes applied over the glaze. The marks subjoined also appear on Herend china.

SWISS CHINAWARE

NYON CHINA

HISTORY. During the latter part of the eighteenth century, or at the very beginning of the nineteenth, a soft paste porcelain factory was established at Nyon, on the lake of Geneva. It was founded by a Frenchman named Maubrée and during at least a part of its career was directed by Robillard, who had previously worked at Sèvres. The factory was conducted according to French notions and French ideals prevailed, both in the fashion of the ware produced and in the matter of decoration. The influence of Sèvres was predominant.

The paste was white and translucent.

Only tableware and such small pieces as trays, candlesticks and inkstands were made at this factory.

Some of the earlier decoration, with landscapes, birds and tulips, shews a German influence, but most of the china was decorated with violets, roses, cornflowers and other small blossoms in a dainty and thoroughly French manner. Maubrée was himself at one time a flower painter at Sèvres. Some of the decoration was executed in Geneva.

The mark of the factory was a fish in underglaze blue. Manufacture was discontinued early in the nineteenth century, probably about 1813.

ZURICH CHINA—1763-1791

HISTORY. In 1763 an hard paste porcelain factory was established at Zurich by Heidegger and Korrodi who employed Spengler, an expert porcelain maker, along with some workmen, from Höchst to assist them in the undertaking. The traditions of the Höchst factory were followed.

The paste had a greyish tone. For a short period soft paste was tried, but was soon given up. The chief product consisted of tableware and some few decorative accessories, and a modeller from Ludwigsburg, Sonnenschein by name, modelled a certain number of figures.

The decorations were largely landscapes and flowers, the landscapes usually being of Swiss inspiration. Some of them were painted by the Swiss poet, Solomon Gessner. The best work of the factory was produced between 1775 and 1790.

The mark was a capital German Z in underglaze blue. The manufacture was not very profitable and the factory was discontinued in 1791.

DUTCH AND BELGIAN CHINAWARE

"AMSTEL" CHINA—1764–1810
WEESP—1764–1771
OUDE LOOSDRECHT—1771–1784
OUDE AMSTEL—1784–1799
NIEUWE AMSTEL—1799–1810

HISTORY. There are only two establishments to be taken account of in considering the china made in Holland. One of them began at Weesp and had a continuous existence under three other names and in three other places. The second was at The Hague.

Dutch china has always been overshadowed by the importance and sufficiency of Dutch Delft and, consequently, the wares produced during the eighteenth century never had the necessary stimulus to develope any distinctively national characteristics. Nevertheless, a considerable amount of very good china was made and much of it possesses a certain homely charm of "pleasant bourgeois character."

In 1764 Count Gronsfeldt-Diepenbrock acquired the plant of a bankrupt faïence factory at Amsterdam, removed it to Weesp, a little town nearby, and established an hard paste porcelain works with workmen from Dresden, closely following Dresden tradition and practices.

The porcelain produced was of such excellent character that Count Gronsfeldt-Diepenbrock had no hesitation in proposing to Sèvres a scheme of amalgamation, since Sèvres was anxious to make hard paste porcelain and had not yet reached success in the experiments carried on there. The proposal was considered but not concluded as the management of Sèvres saw the many possibilities of international complications.

Then followed embarrassing difficulties for the factory at Weesp. Holland was flooded with Japanese porcelain at the time, thus affecting the market for native wares, and the German workmen were leaving and going home again. In the meantime, however, a Calvinist minister, by name de Mol, had become much interested in the factory at Weesp, regarded it as an opportunity and bought the works in 1771.

He thereupon transferred the establishment to Oude Loosdrecht and continued the manufacture of porcelain, devoting most effort to the production of "useful" ware. Under de Mol's direction the enterprise seems to have prospered and there was a very considerable output of china. After de Mol's death, in 1782, the business was carried on at Oude Loosdrecht by a limited company until 1784.

In 1784 the company removed the works to Oude Amstel and there continued to make the same quality of chinaware until 1799 when the ownership passed to another company.

The new company again moved the works, this time to Nieuwe Amstel, and at that place went on making porcelain until 1810 when the establishment was finally discontinued.

THE BODY. From the very outset, thanks to the experienced Dresden workmen who knew and followed the tried Dresden processes, the hard paste body was technically beyond all cavil, pure white and of the best quality, closely resembling the body of Dresden china.

THE GLAZE. The glaze was of the same, even, transparent brilliant quality as the Dresden glaze.

ARTICLES MADE AND CONTOUR. The china made consisted chiefly of tableware, breakfast sets, "useful" objects of various sorts, small boxes, pots and vases. Later a few more ambitious vases with intricate perforations were made and towards the end of the Oude Loosdrecht phase some busts in biscuit were produced.

The contours, for the most part, were borrowed from German and French sources. The shapes were partly Rococo in style but changed to Neo-Classic forms concurrently with the march of fashion. The leaning to French precedents and models became more pronounced towards the latter part of the Oude Loosdrecht period.

TYPES OF DECORATION. The types of decoration were as heterogeneous as the contours. All manner of *motifs* were used. Some of the china was wholly white with festoons, sprays, or other ornamental *motifs* in slight relief; the piercings of fruit baskets were often picked out with blue; there were moulded *motifs* with a sparing use of colour; cartouches contained small landscapes, birds, and polychrome flowers; sometimes there were Watteau-like subjects and scenes from Italian comedy; modelled fruits, leaves and birds, duly coloured, served as knobs or handles; landscapes and cupids were rendered *en camaïeu;* the cornflowers of Sèvres were frequent; and polychrome landscapes, birds and flowers were especially in favour.

THE MARKS. The Weesp mark consisted of the crossed swords of Dresden with two flanking dots. The Oude Loosdrecht mark was M:O:L:, rendered in a variety of forms. The Oude Amstel mark was the name "Oude

210 THE PRACTICAL BOOK OF CHINAWARE

Amstel" or the letter A. The wares of all the four stages of this factory were so much alike that it is difficult to distinguish them.

THE HAGUE CHINA—1775–1785 (?)

HISTORY. The hard paste porcelain factory established at The Hague in 1775 by the Viennese Anton Leichner had only a short life, but during its career produced some very excellent work. Not only did this factory decorate its own ware, but it also decorated a great deal of the soft paste porcelain made at Tournai. This circumstance has sometimes led to the impression that The Hague factory made both hard and soft paste. Only hard paste was made at The Hague. The factory was given up at the end of about ten years.

THE BODY. The body was a fine, white hard paste of unexceptionable quality, produced according to the traditions of Dresden and Vienna and was virtually identical with them in character.

THE GLAZE. The glaze was also clear, even and brilliant like the glazes of Dresden and Vienna.

ARTICLES MADE AND CONTOUR. The preponderance of china produced consisted of tableware and the more usual objects of household adornment. There were, however, some elaborate vases made. There was no figure modelling and very little moulding in low relief was done, the china commonly presenting a perfectly plain, smooth surface. Energies were chiefly concentrated upon painted decoration which was of an high order. There were some late Rococo contours but most of the shapes were those of the Neo-Classic type.

TYPES OF DECORATION. Flowers in polychrome were, perhaps, the most usual decorative *motifs* employed at The Hague, but there were also "Boucher" children and cupids, with surrounding foliage and attributes, *en camaïeu;* birds of multi-coloured plumage; monochrome landscapes, sometimes in *grisaille;* and antique heads in profile, set in medallions with a pale pink ground. This last form of decoration was rendered with peculiar success.

THE MARKS. The mark was the city emblem—a stork holding a fish in its beak. This mark was painted in underglaze blue on the hard paste china made at The Hague; it was painted in on-glaze blue on the soft paste china made at Tournai but decorated at The Hague.

BRUSSELS CHINA
SCHAERBEEK, NEAR BRUSSELS—1784–1791
ETTERBEEK, NEAR BRUSSELS—1775–1803

HISTORY. The hard paste porcelain factory at Schaerbeek, near Brussels, was founded in 1784 by J. S. Vaume and continued in operation for only seven years.

The products consisted mostly of tableware and "useful" objects. It is possible that figures also may have been made. The Schaerbeek china was moderately decorated—landscapes like fine India ink drawings, small scattered flowers, landscapes in green, and scattered sprigs in conjunction with friezes and festoons of foliage formed the usual *motifs*.

The mark was a "B", with or without a crown, and sometimes with the words "Monplaisir près Bruxelles," in underglaze blue. The mark also occasionally occurred in other colours on-glaze.

The hard paste factory at Etterbeek, also near Brussels, was founded by Chrétien Kühne, from Saxony, in 1775. It made tableware, articles of household embellishment, and groups and single figures, both glazed and in biscuit. The decorations were of heterogeneous types, but birds, flowers and *genre* scenes predominated. The mark was E. B. in monogram. Little is known of the doings of this factory and it is said to have closed in 1803.

SWEDISH AND DANISH CHINAWARE

MARIEBERG CHINA—1758–1788

HISTORY. The porcelain factory of Marieberg, near Stockholm, is the only establishment in Sweden we have occasion to consider. It began its existence in 1758 under the management of a certain Ehrenreich, but succeeded in producing nothing save faïence until Pierre Berthevin became director in 1766. At one time or another various Frenchmen of talent were employed and, in nearly every instance, contributed materially to the improvement of the china produced. The factory passed through a number of vicissitudes and made numerous experiments with paste. Some of the china made was exceedingly beautiful, but the product was limited and the Marieberg ware is not plentiful. The manufacture came to an end in 1788.

THE BODY. The paste of Marieberg was an exceedingly variable quantity. Under Berthevin the body was a soft paste akin in composition to the French soft pastes. It was highly translucent, of a greenish yellow tone, and was sometimes marred by flaws. Between this and the white hard paste of fine, smooth texture, made for only two years, 1777 and 1778, under the Frenchman Dartou, there were many variations, but the most constant form was a semi-hard paste, white, slightly translucent, with a chalky or limy texture, and of uneven surface. The pieces made from this body are those that exhibit a peculiarly individual charm. The ware is attractive in appearance and highly prized, especially in Sweden, but it is very brittle.

THE GLAZE. The usual glaze, except the brilliant glaze on the hard paste that was made for two years, was soft and mellow and very like to that of Mennecy, which seems to have been regarded as a model.

ARTICLES MADE AND CONTOUR. The output at first consisted largely of custard cups. Other articles of tableware and sundry decorative accessories were gradually added until, at a comparatively late date, figures were included in the list of products.

The contours were almost wholly French and, for a great part of the time, were fashioned in a moderate Rococo manner. Towards the latter part of the factory's career the Neo-Classic trend became evident. Some of the early pieces were patterned so closely after the wares of Mennecy that they might almost be considered replicas.

TYPES OF DECORATION. As with the shapes of the early Marieberg china, so also was it with the manner of decoration. The methods of Mennecy decoration were so closely copied at the beginning that, without rigid scrutiny and an examination of the marks, it would be difficult to distinguish between the pieces.

Besides the Mennecy flowers and the Mennecy manner, other *motifs* of decoration employed included polychrome flowers of a more general character and diverse rendering, armorial bearings with garlands, medallions with wreaths and festoons, landscapes and *genre* subjects, coloured rims for plates with flowers in the centre, fretwork, piercings and modelled flowers that were naturalistically coloured, moulded low reliefs such as basket-work, foliage and ribbings, flowers in monochrome, small landscapes in iron-red, reddish purple or copper green, enclosed within panels, often of quatrefoil shape and, very frequently, only a few gilded lines on an otherwise undecorated body. Decoration with polychrome flowers was, perhaps, the most commonly used. The monochrome flowers were often painted in pure blue, in a strong bluish green, and in a full rich purple. The last named colour was especially characteristic of the factory.

THE MARKS. There are many variations in the Marieberg marks but the most usual mark is some form of the three crowns of Sweden, with or without MB. Occasionally the fleur-de-lys from the royal arms is added. The mark occurs in underglaze blue or in red on-glaze. Many pieces are altogether unmarked.

MB

COPENHAGEN CHINA—1756 TO PRESENT DAY

HISTORY. About 1756 a porcelain factory was opened at Copenhagen with J. G. Mehlhorn, a former Dresden modeller, as director. Mehlhorn's directorship seems to have produced no tangible results in the shape of porcelain and only experiments were made. It was not until 1759, when a Frenchman, Louis Fournier, who had worked at both Sèvres and Chantilly, came to Copenhagen and succeeded Mehlhorn that a soft paste porcelain was made. This soft paste porcelain, whose body somewhat resembled that of Saint Cloud and Chantilly, was of pleasant quality and continued to be made till the end of 1765, when Fournier was succeeded by Frantz Müller. Although Müller continued for a while to make soft paste porcelain, he was experimenting with hard pastes of which he produced a sort by 1772 or 1773. This body was much improved by 1776 and perfected by 1780.

Under private management the establishment was beset by financial difficulties so that, in 1779, it was taken over by the King and then began an highly successful career.

THE BODY. The soft paste body made during Fournier's management was translucent and of a creamy or more or less yellowish tinge while the soft paste made under the first part of Müller's *régime* had a greyish tone. The first hard paste made by Müller was darkish and somewhat grey. It was improved until, by 1780, it was hard, translucent and pure white.

THE GLAZE. The glaze of the first soft paste had a soft, lustrous brilliance and felt soapy to the touch. Müller's early glaze was imperfect and had a yellowish tinge. The final glaze for the hard paste body was smooth, perfectly transparent and brilliant.

ARTICLES MADE AND CONTOUR. Under Fournier the pieces produced were, for the most part, of small size and included bowls, powder-boxes, cups, custard cups, cream jugs, sugar-basons, breakfast sets and small vases. The list was gradually increased to include full sets of tableware, tea services, flower pots, tankards, tureens, punch bowls and a number of decorative accessories. From 1780 onward much larger, more "important" and elaborate vases, clock cases, mirror frames and sconces were added to the list, along with numerous figures, both glazed and in biscuit.

Although certain German influences in contour could be traced from time to time, the French influence was clearly predominant. The more restrained Rococo shapes were at first prevalent but were gradually supplanted by Neo-Classic forms. From 1780 onward the Neo-Classic types were universal and were later followed by the Neo-Grec shapes.

TYPES OF DECORATION. Polychrome flowers (Plate 67, B), in the manner of Chantilly, supplied one of the earliest *motifs* and always remained in favour. Besides these, the decorative scope included modelling in high relief, fretwork, moulded ornamentation in low relief such as ribbings, flutings and foliage patterns, the use of ground colours, wreaths, garlands, landscapes, flowers and landscapes *en camaïeu* or in two colours such as purple and copper green, Classic heads in wreathed and garlanded medallions, contemporary portrait medallions, landscapes and heads in *grisaille*, Chinese subjects, a few comics and battle scenes, and the minute later flowers such as the cornflower *motif* popularised by Sèvres. The gilding was good and used in moderate amount. There was always a fondness for decorations in blue and white and the *Strohblumen* and "onion" patterns borrowed from Dresden were always great favourites and have remained so to the present day. They are commonly known as "Copenhagen" patterns.

THE MARKS. The Copenhagen mark is three wavy lines in underglaze blue. Many of the earlier pieces are unmarked, but from Müller's time onward this mark has appeared and is still well known on the modern wares of the Copenhagen factory which it would be a pleasure to discuss did they fall within the scope of this book.

RUSSIAN AND POLISH CHINAWARE

ST. PETERSBURG CHINA—1744

HISTORY. The Imperial Russian china factory was established in 1744 under Christoph Conrad Hunger who had managed the Vezzi factory in Venice for five years and had also gained his experience at Meissen, Vienna and elsewhere. Under his *régime* little was produced and he was soon succeeded by other directors. Until 1753 little was produced but small articles such as cups, saucers, jugs, and snuff boxes which were used as presents from the Court, although some statuettes were made as early as 1752.

A great change took place about 1763 when the products became partly commercial. The factory was continued under Imperial control.

There were two grades of ware made, the body of one being pure white and of the finest hard paste quality, the other being not pure white and of somewhat variable tinge. The glaze was good. Besides tableware and splendid vases, figures were produced both glazed and in biscuit. At first all the decoration was in the Dresden manner with "gold Chinamen," and monochrome landscapes and flowers in purple or green with gold or black. Later the range of colours increased and there were scenes from daily life, landscapes, animals, and multi-coloured birds and flowers. Most of the decoration was in a very gorgeous manner and highly elaborate, the best manners of Dresden and Sèvres being closely followed.

RUSSIAN AND POLISH CHINAWARE

The china was marked with the Imperial Russian eagle and with the initials or monograms of the rulers, either impressed in the paste or painted in black or gold.

There were also china factories in Moscow and at Korzec in Poland where not a little good china was made and decorated in an acceptable and highly characteristic manner.

ENGLISH CHINAWARE
BOW CHINA—1745-1776

HISTORY. Up to almost the middle of the eighteenth century, whatever experiments in porcelain making may have been conducted previously, there was no established china factory in England. For her chinaware England had been dependent upon the Orient or else upon either the soft paste products of France or the hard paste china of Germany. Of all three kinds she had had abundant experience, and all three kinds were sufficiently represented throughout the length and breadth of the Kingdom. The people knew and admired chinaware, and there was no danger of its being confounded with Delft earthenware imitations, no matter how cleverly they were made.

About the middle of the century there was a determined effort to establish china factories in England and to make wares for home consumption. There are fugitive notices of sundry ventures in this direction and some of them, in all likelihood, succeeded in producing tangible results of a more or less satisfactory nature, though scanty in quantity, before coming to an untimely and unrecorded end. The two earliest china factories to achieve an enduring foothold and put forth a substantial volume of finished wares of recognised commercial and artistic worth were Bow and Chelsea.

The early history of the Bow factory is wrapped in obscurity. It was at Stratford-le-Bow, in Essex, and at some early stage of its career—perhaps from the very outset—it was called "New Canton." In December 1744 a patent was issued to Edward Heylyn and Thomas Frye empowering them to engage in the manufacture of chinaware. A second patent was issued to Frye alone in 1749. What had been going on in the meantime is not certainly known, but it is not unreasonable to assume that attempts at china production had been made and rewarded with some measure of success. We shall probably not be far wrong in assigning 1745 as the date for the inception of the factory, and in regarding the years between then and 1750 as the period of small beginnings inevitable for a private enterprise of the sort, unaided by any princely patronage or royal subsidy, as were so many undertakings of a similar nature on the Continent.

At all events, by 1750 the mist of uncertainty clears away somewhat and we reach our first definite, authentic information which shews that the works then belonged to the Messrs. Crowther and Weatherby who had entered into partnership in that year. It was in 1750 that the first *known* piece of Bow china was made, although it was doubtless not the first fruit of the factory's existence. Thomas Frye, one of the original patentees, appears as manager, and in that capacity he continued till 1759, when he retired because of ill health. Much of our information regarding the Bow factory is gathered from the notebooks, diaries and memorandum books of John Bowcocke who was the commercial manager and traveller for the works.

The policy of the Bow factory seems to have been to place its chief reliance upon products of a distinctly commercial nature and to devote its efforts mostly to making and selling "useful" wares. In the announcement of the first auction sale of Bow china, held in 1757, is duly advertised "a large assortment of the most useful china in Lots, for the use of Gentlemen's kitchens, Private families, Taverns, etc."

It was customary in the eighteenth century for the china factories in England, besides maintaining shops or warehouses for the sale of their goods, to hold auction sales in London at certain intervals in order to dispose of any surplus stock they might have on hand, to popularise further their products, and to introduce any new creations they might have devised since the preceding sale. These sales sometimes covered a period of a fortnight or even longer.

The first London warehouse for the sale of Bow chinaware was opened in 1753 in Cornhill, near the Royal Exchange. Just after the first auction, in 1757, which took place at the rooms of Cock & Co., "in Spring Gardens, leading into St. James's Park," an advertisement announces the opening of a second warehouse:

"For the convenience of the nobility and gentry, their warehouse on the Terrace in St. James's Street is constantly supplied with everything new, where it is sold as at Cornhill, with the real Price marked on each piece without Abatement."

This west-end venture, however, seems not to have met with the measure of success its promoters had hoped for it, and it was given up the following year, its stock of china being disposed of by auction.

From his memoranda and accounts, we learn that Bowcocke made journeys throughout the country to further the sales of the chinaware and, in 1758, the records shew that he was eight months in Dublin on the same errand, receiving frequent consignments of chinaware from

PLATE 76

A. BRISTOL TRAY
Shaped edge and slightly moulded rim; garland and scattered flower decoration

B. LOWESTOFT CUP AND SAUCER
Moulded flutings and small flower decoration

Courtesy of the Victoria and Albert Museum, South Kensington

the works and disposing of it by auction. The policy of relying mainly upon china of a more or less commercial description for profit seems to have brought success, for a period at least. Bowcocke's account book shews £10,000 cash receipts in 1753, and from the statement of T. Craft, a former employee, we learn that the works kept between two and three hundred people busy.

Frye's retirement from the works, it appears, marked the first stage in the course of decline. Weatherby died in 1762, and in 1763 Crowther, the remaining partner, became bankrupt. In May, 1764, the stock in trade of the Bow factory was sold by auction, but in some way, and probably on a greatly reduced scale, Crowther managed to carry on the business for some years afterwards. The London Directory for 1770–1775 records the warehouse of John Crowther, of Bow China Works, at number 28, St. Paul's Churchyard. In 1776 the entire business was sold for an inconsiderable sum to William Duesbury of Derby, the moulds, models and all other effects were removed, and thus ended the existence of the Bow factory. In 1777 Crowther was admitted an inmate of Morden College, Blackheath, and in that safe haven he spent the residue of his days free, let us hope, from carking business anxieties.

From the emphasis laid by its owners upon the commercial purveying of "useful" wares by the factory, it must not be inferred that Bow china was lacking in artistic merit, nor that the makers were at all blind to either the desirability or necessity of combining excellence of quality, grace of contour, and beauty and variety of decoration in the porcelain they put forth. While stressing the fact that their products were primarily useful as well as beautiful, they made not a few excursions into the realm of the purely ornamental, as the many statuettes and groups that issued from the Bow factory bear witness. In all likelihood these were made at Bow throughout the greater part, if not the whole, of the factory's career. If they could not be placed in the "useful" category, they had all the same a definite commercial value for they were most popular chimney-piece and table adornments, from the cottage and farmhouse to the manor and hall.

While some of the pieces made at Bow were not such as to commend themselves to the taste of every china-lover, and others would unquestionably be treated by nearly everybody with scant respect if they had been made only yesterday and not an hundred and seventy-five years ago, nevertheless the great bulk of chinaware that issued from "New Canton" was of a quality to command hearty admiration. All manner of articles were made, and they were made with great diversity of contour and decorated with a rich variety of patterns.

THE BODY. The body or paste of the Bow china was a variable quantity. Mr. Burton pertinently observes that "much trouble will . . . be saved collectors and others if they will look upon the Bow body as varying from time to time within fairly wide limits." The very early Bow paste was neither particularly white nor particularly translucent. It is obviously not a bone-ash body but the rich paste of glassy or soft paste porcelain, of similar quality with that of Chelsea. It has a distinctly warm, creamy tint and is translucent enough where the ware is thin, but quite opaque where it is thick. When fractured, it shews the dry, gritty or granular texture of other soft paste china and the break never exhibits the glossiness of partial vitrification characteristic of hard paste. It seems highly probable that the formulas for the early paste of both Bow and Chelsea were derived from a common source, and that the common source was someone well acquainted with the processes followed at Saint Cloud, Chantilly and Mennecy-Villeroy. It was in such a way that the knowledge of porcelain making usually travelled.

Much of the Bow paste, especially the later paste, is exceptionally hard, a quality perhaps to be accounted for by the presence of the bone-ash or some of the other ingredients subsequently used in the course of experimentation. It was doubtless to this continued experimentation, in the effort to achieve hard paste or its nearest approximate, that the differences in the Bow body were due. The late pieces are better potted than those of early make, thinner and of much whiter body, but they are poorer in substance; the pieces of the middle period are intermediate in quality.

THE GLAZE. The early Bow glaze, which is rich in lead, shews a slightly yellowish tinge and is apt to gather in the hollows of embossed patterns and at the base of the pieces. It is peculiarly soft, mellow and satin-like both to sight and touch. The glaze of the later ware is quite different in appearance, being perceptibly harder and more brilliant. For the blue and white ware the glaze was often slightly tinted with blue, a device adopted from the Chinese so as to bring the blue of the decoration and the colour of the body more harmoniously together and avoid any harshness of tone.

ARTICLES MADE AND CONTOUR. Besides the "useful" articles of chinaware made at the Bow factory, a category which included every description of tableware for all occasions and every accompaniment of tea tackle, there were vases, flower pots, candlesticks, sconces, "Girandoles and Branches for Chimney Pieces," inkstands, patchboxes and all the usual accessories for writing and dressing tables. There were also large numbers of the modelled figures and statuettes always in great demand.

The contours of the earlier china were perceptibly influenced by Chinese (Plates 68, B and 69, B) and Dresden prototypes, but often displayed a good deal of independent interpretation. The figure work, of course, was in the first instance of Dresden inspiration but soon assumed a thoroughly English character. While the Oriental and Saxon influences were still strong in the expression of contours, the Rococo influence of Sèvres made a profound impression and Rococo shapes enjoyed marked popularity for a long time. The factory was discontinued before Neo-Classic tendencies became dominant.

Types of Decoration. The types of decoration employed at Bow were exceedingly varied and were inspired by both Chinese (Plates 68, A and B; 70, A and B), and Japanese examples, on the Oriental side, and by Dresden, Chantilly, Mennecy and Sèvres (Plate 68, C) precedents, from the Continental angle.

The decorative processes included moulding, piercing (Plate 70, A), modelling in relief, painting, transfer printing and gilding. The white Fuchien ware of China supplied the inspiration for the white pieces decorated with sprigs of "prunus" (Plates 68, D and 70, B) or plum blossoms in relief, of which many were made. Other types, too, of relief floral ornament were moulded and luted on to the surface of the pieces (Plate 71) they were meant to adorn. Much use, also, was made of moulded patterns impressed on rims of plates and other parts of table china.

The prunus blossom supplied a frequent *motif* for this purpose as well as divers other floral items, and this moulded ornament, though left uncoloured itself (Plate 70, B), was not seldom used in conjunction with painted decoration immediately beside it.

In surveying the coloured decoration, first of all must be mentioned the blue and white ware, painted in underglaze blue, obviously inspired by the blue and white K'ang Hsi porcelain of China (Plate 68, A and B). If not made from the inception of the factory, its production began soon after and was continued in large quantities. The account books shew it was highly popular and constantly in demand. While the decorative inspiration of this ware was unmistakably Chinese—and many of the contours were Chinese, too—the execution was patently English. Powder blue ware was also imitated, with shaped white panels in reserve on which appeared various Chinese *motifs* either in blue or else with polychrome flowers, birds and butterflies. Some of the Chinese ware with solid dark blue glaze was imitated to a certain degree. A few of the *motifs* on the blue and white Bow china suggest a Delft origin.

Probably the most popular type of polychrome decoration, and one of the earliest produced, was the Kakiyemon mode or, as it was commonly called, the "old Japan" pattern. Even when it was not literally rendered, all sorts of adaptations from it made their appearance. Pieces painted in the Kakiyemon manner were frequently enriched with points of old dull gilding. The Japanese Imari decoration was also reproduced, though to a less extent.

Other Oriental *motifs* followed were the Chinese peonies (Plate 70, B) and chrysanthemums in polychrome, Chinese diapered borders for the rims of plates and edges of dishes, Chinese fighting cocks and other birds, and figures in the manner of the "Mandarin" china so esteemed about the middle of the eighteenth century.

Flowers scattered at random in the so-called Dresden manner, and flowers gathered in bouquets and bunches (Plates 69, A and B), after the fashion of Chantilly and Mennecy, were common *motifs* of polychrome ornament, as also were small flowers gathered in garlands, wreaths and festoons, and likewise larger groupings of a few flowers or fruits painted with great naturalistic precision. The rims of dishes and plates that were adorned with this last-named sort of decoration were sometimes painted with a broad band of brownish grey. Other edges, especially on early pieces made before gilding was extensively practised, were often painted with a narrow line of reddish brown. There were, furthermore, plates and dishes moulded in the form of leaves; these were coloured according to nature.

Some of the china was enriched with heraldic bearings and further decked with little scattered multi-coloured flowers and diapered rims, much in the manner called "Lowestoft." Amongst the later wares were pieces with ground colours and reserved panels in which appeared figures, flowers, gaily-coloured birds, or Watteau-like groups in polychrome, very much in the manner of Sèvres. Occasionally decorations were executed altogether in gold on the white porcelain ground.

Still further, there were pieces decorated with landscapes, groups of figures, and country scenes, in grey, rose-violet or red *en camaïeu*, in the manner of Mennecy, Vincennes or Sèvres. These latter were not painted but printed with transfer designs. In some cases, where there

PLATE 77

A. WORCESTER TEAPOT
White paste, excellent clear glaze; decoration adapted from the Japanese Imari brocade patterns in red, gold, green and blue

B. WORCESTER PLATE
White paste, clear glaze; decoration inspired by Japanese Imari patterns, in red, deep blue and gold

Courtesy of the British Museum

PLATE 78

LATE WORCESTER PLATE
White paste, clear glaze; Empire style decorations in gold on ground-coloured rim, naturalistically coloured landscape in centre.

Courtesy of the Museum, Royal Worcester Pottery

PLATE 79

A. WORCESTER BLUE AND WHITE BOWL
Decoration in deep blue in the Chinese manner; white paste, clear glaze

B. WORCESTER PLATE WITH DEEP BLUE GROUND
Paste white, clear glaze; shaped white panels reserved in deep blue ground colour, reserved panels containing multi-coloured *motifs*; remote Japanese Imari influence

Courtesy of the Museum, Royal Worcester Pottery

PLATE 80

WORCESTER CHOCOLATE POT WITH SWELLING BASE
White paste, clear glaze; attenuated Mandarin figures in pale but varied colours

Courtesy of the Museum, Royal Worcester Pottery

was not so much elaborate detail, the outlines were printed in transfer and filled in with different colours painted on. The printing of transfer designs seems to have been done at Battersea. Oftentimes, where the centre of a plate or platter is filled with a transfer design, the border surrounding the rim is painted, thus indicating an early stage of the printing process.

Although in old sales lists and advertisements it is sometimes noted that the "old Japan" pieces were "most beautifully painted by several of the first masters from Dresden," it is much more likely that they were executed wholly by English hands. Thomas Frye, the manager, was an artist of no mean capacity and whether he himself did some of the painting or not, he was quite competent to direct all the operations without foreign assistance. Designs were gathered from all manner of sources and either adopted outright or else adapted to suit the circumstances. It was not an unusual thing for patrons to lend choice pieces of Oriental or Continental china in their possession to serve as models. As only one instance of this sort, may be quoted a memorandum in the factory records of 1756: "Patterns received from Lady Cavendish: a Japan octagon cup and saucer, lady pattern; a rib'd and scollop'd cup and saucer, image pattern; a basket bordered dessart plate; a Japan bread and butter plate."

The little Bow figures or statuettes, many of which are full of charm, were painted in bright colours in a manner appropriate to the subjects represented, although it is generally considered that their colouring was less satisfactory than the colouring done at the rival Chelsea works.

THE MARKS. A very large quantity of Bow china was unmarked. On the pieces marked, various devices occur. Of these, the anchor and dagger, usually painted in red or a reddish brown, it is important to remember. There is also sometimes found an arrow, with or without an annulet; likewise the monogram F. The caduceus and the bow and arrow marks are considered of doubtful import. Divers other marks, often mentioned in connexion with Bow, are of doubtful attribution.

CHELSEA CHINA—1745–1770

HISTORY. Like the early history of Bow, the earliest chapter of Chelsea's history is scant and involved in uncertainty.

What we *know* is that the Chelsea factory was working in, or slightly before, 1745 and that in that year were produced the celebrated "goat and bee" cream jugs with the legend "Chelsea, 1745" scratched in the paste before it was fired—sufficient evidence that the establishment was in existence and functioning. It is also recorded that a group of Staffordshire potters went to work in 1747 at the Chelsea China Manufactory. Becoming disgruntled, they left and returned to Staffordshire, an event which seems not to have affected the Chelsea works in the least for it went blithely on in its course of progress.

What we *believe* to be likely is that the factory was established by or, at least, managed by one Charles Gouyn, who is said to have been either a Fleming or a Frenchman, and that his skilled workmen came from France and Germany. Gouyn's identity and personality are largely conjectural. In his exhaustive book on Chelsea china, William King points out that "the strong resemblance between early Chelsea porcelain and that produced by the French soft paste factories renders it highly possible that Chelsea was started by some refugee from St. Cloud, Chantilly or Mennecy, and if this be so, Gouyn may well have been the individual in question " It is also likely that Sir Everard Fawkener was deeply concerned in the inception of the Chelsea factory and may have been responsible for financing and establishing it. He was at first a merchant and accumulated a comfortable fortune. Upon being knighted, about 1735, he was sent as ambassador to Constantinople; in 1744 he was made secretary to the Duke of Cumberland, and, in 1745, was given a lucrative post as joint postmaster-general. We shall meet with Sir Everard again further on.

Be all these things as they may, about 1749 Nicholas Sprimont appears on the scene and Charles Gouyn disappears shortly thereafter. Hence onward, the main facts of the factory's career are no longer obscure. Nicholas Sprimont, said to have been a Frenchman, but certainly some time a silversmith by trade with a shop in Compton Street, Soho, becomes manager and directs affairs so capably that the enterprise grows and prospers apace.

Sprimont directed the concerns of the factory with energy and discretion, and displayed great good taste in determining the character of the wares put forth. While not despising the manufacture of things of common use for which there was necessarily a constant demand, it must be confessed that Sprimont's efforts seem to have been more keenly bent in the direction of making elegant and elaborate articles and in multiplying the variety of products. Nevertheless, such was the distinction and charm of

Chelsea china that the greater stress upon decorative considerations seemed not to prejudice financial returns.

Every conceivable thing that could be made of porcelain was made at Chelsea. Advertisements of sales and sales catalogues—some of the old sales catalogues have fortunately been preserved—acquaint us that "Epargnes and Srvices for Deserts, beautiful Groupes of Figures, etc., complete Table Sets of round and Oval Dishes, Tureens and Plates, with the greatest Variety of other useful and ornamental Pieces" are to be disposed of; that "a large and beautiful Lustre, richly ornamented with flowers and a fine figure of Fame sounding a trumpet," "a most significant Lustre in the Chinese taste," and "a most grand Lustre . . . with Flora and Cupids in the middle" are all within the reach of an eager public; that there are "several very curious Deserts, used at the most elegant and great Entertainments and now divided into proper Lots: Consisting of Domes, Temples, Triumphal Arches, Epargnes, etc., embellished with Trees, Arbors, Flowers, China Figures, Vauses, Girandols, Candlesticks, Branches and other Ornaments used at Desarts, with several sets of China Dishes, Plates and Tureens," awaiting purchasers; and that desirous customers may be accommodated with the "greatest choice of Branches with the best Flowers, such as were on the Chandelier at the last Sale; and upward of three thousand of those Flowers to be sold by themselves so that Ladies and Gentlemen may make use of them in Grottos, Branches, Epargnes, Flower-pots, etc., agreeable to their own taste." Nor were the foregoing by any means all. The catalogues include many other diverting conceits.

By 1754 the business was in a flourishing condition.

There was a warehouse for the sale of Chelsea china in Pall Mall, as well as the shop at the factory. Also, in the spring of that year occurred the first sale by auction of surplus and special stock and this sale lasted fourteen days. Again, in 1755 and 1756, sales were held lasting sixteen days. Then came a period when Sprimont was ill and the production of the factory was diminished. By 1757 the warehouse seems to have been moved to Piccadilly. After Sprimont's recovery, or partial recovery, the Chelsea factory took on a new lease of life, many new and rarely beautiful decorations were put forth, and the annual sales were resumed. Sir Everard Fawkener died in 1758 and, about that time, Sprimont became owner of the works.

But Sprimont's health was failing. At the end of the advertisement for the sale of 1761 appeared this notice:

"The Proprietor, *N. Sprimont*, after many Years intense Application, has brought this Manufactory to its present Perfection; but as his Indisposition will not permit him to carry it on much longer, he takes the Liberty to assure the Nobility, Gentry, and others, that next Year will be the last Sale he will offer to the Public."

As a matter of fact, there were other sales for some years. Sprimont continued to make periodic farewells, like a *prima donna*, for eight years longer and did not retire till the summer of 1769, during all which time the beautiful Chelsea wares appeared for sale. Finally, in August 1769, he sold the factory and all its equipment to James Cox, and in February, 1770, Cox sold it to William Duesbury and John Heath of Derby. Thus ends the story of the Chelsea factory as an independent organisation.

Some years before this disposal of the Chelsea plant, despite the outward appearances of prosperity and the maintenance of brilliant achievement in the wares produced, it became evident that the financial affairs of the factory were going from bad to worse and that there was little likelihood of improvement. This was partly due, no doubt, to the keen competition of other china factories that had been established, partly to Sprimont's failing health. Consequently, he was glad to relinquish the business and, after the disposal of stock by the 1769 sale, Cox got "the kilns, mills, models in wax or lead, all the manufactured or unmanufactured porcelain," and "all the materials and utensils," as well as the lease, for £600.

Although the factory had ceased to be a profitable concern, Sprimont retired in comfortable circumstances. He had an house in town and a country place in Dorset, and kept his own carriage. But he was not long to enjoy release from the anxieties of the porcelain works. He died in 1770.

Duesbury continued work at the Chelsea factory, using it as a branch of the works he had established at Derby in 1756. Upon this status the Chelsea works were kept in operation until 1783, when Duesbury decided to concentrate all his activities at Derby. The china made during this period of close association is known as Chelsea-Derby china. When the factory in Chelsea was finally given up, all the skilled workmen, along with the moulds, models and other trade appliances, were transferred to Derby. The kilns were demolished in 1784 and everything not deemed worth the cost of removal was destroyed.

THE BODY. The Chelsea body exhibited three distinct phases, the first from the beginning of the factory to about 1750, when Sprimont deemed it expedient to harden the paste. This second period lasted till about 1759, when renewed energy was manifested after Sprimont's illness. Then it was that the body was brought into closer conformity with the body produced at the other English factories.

The paste of the first period was soft, very translucent, of fine granular texture, warm creamy colour, and closely resembled the paste of Saint Cloud and Chantilly. The paste of the second period, introduced about 1750, was harder, less translucent, of a sandy, granular texture, but still of a mellow creamy tone. The earlier pieces of this period are apt to be heavy and thick and are occasionally warped in the firing; the surface, also, is sometimes uneven. It has been suggested that the change may have been due to introducing finely ground Oriental porcelain into the composition of the mixture. Whether this was the case or not, the so-called "moons" in the body are characteristic of this period—small, moon-like discs, more translucent than the rest of the paste, visible if the piece is examined by transmitted light. The paste of the third period was modified by the addition of bone-ash, of which a large percentage was introduced into the composition. This bone china paste was still harder, of smoother and closer texture, white, and easier to manage in the firing.

THE GLAZE. The glaze of the first period was rich, soft, unctuous, mellow, and waxy to the touch. It often shewed minute pinhole flaws. The glaze of the second period was much more perfect in distribution, soft, mellow, and of pleasant waxy aspect. The glaze of the third period was harder and more brilliant.

ARTICLES MADE AND CONTOUR. As already mentioned, the articles made at Chelsea were of manifold diversity. Besides the table services, tea, coffee and chocolate services, the figures, the usual articles of household adornment, and the items mentioned in the catalogues quoted in the foregoing *History*, there were sundry pretty trifles such as buttons, bottle stoppers, trinkets for watch-chains, knobs for walking-sticks, thimbles, smelling bottles, snuff-boxes, patch-boxes, inkstands and divers other objects suggested by active inventive faculties.

In general, the contours of the articles produced were influenced by three chief sources of inspiration—Oriental forms (Plate 74, B), types characteristic of Dresden manufactures, and the shapes in use at Sèvres. Just how and when these types were manifested, we shall see in the section on *Types of Decoration*. The Rococo influence, as might be imagined from the date of Chelsea manufacture, was most conspicuously in evidence.

TYPES OF DECORATION. While the types of decoration followed at Chelsea plainly point to the Orient, Dresden (Plates 72, B; 73; 74, A and 75, A), and Sèvres as the three main springs of influence, the themes drawn thence were either imitated outright or else used as a basis for adaptation. Models of all three were carefully studied whenever the Chelsea designers could gain access to them. Pieces were sometimes borrowed from friends and patrons, as pointed out in the account of Bow, or sometimes the factory tried to buy good things outright for its own permanent collection. Of the latter course we have an instance on record in a letter written by Sir Charles Hanbury Williams, June 9th, 1751, to Henry Fox. Sir Charles Williams was then British Plenipotentiary at Dresden and while he was absent from England Fox was keeping his china at Holland House. This enlightening bit of correspondence was published in the *Burlington Magazine*.

PLATE 81

WORCESTER VASE OF LATE PERIOD
White paste, clear glaze; moulded ornament; gold decorations with figures in naturalistically coloured landscape with panel reserved in ground colour

Courtesy of the Museum, Royal Worcester Pottery

PLATE 82

WORCESTER CHOCOLATE POT WITH DOMED LID
White paste, excellent clear glaze; decoration in semi-Imari manner with red,
deep blue and gold predominating

Courtesy of the Museum, Royal Worcester Pottery

PLATE 83

WORCESTER SOUP PLATE
White paste, clear, smooth glaze; engraved and transfer printed design in dull green monochrome
Courtesy of the Museum, Royal Worcester Pottery

PLATE 84

EARLY WORCESTER MUG OF DR. WALL PERIOD
Creamy white paste, clear transparent glaze; bright apple green ground colour with shaped and reserved white panel bearing polychrome flower decoration

Courtesy of the Museum, Royal Worcester Pottery

The writer of the letter says:

"I received a letter about ten days ago from Sr. Everard Fawkner who is I believe concerned in the manufacture of China at Chelsea. He desired me to send over models for different Pieces from hence in order to furnish the undertakers with good designs; and would have me send over fifty or three-score pounds worth. But I thought it better and cheaper for the manufacturers to give them leave to take any of my China from Holland House and to copy what they like. I have therefore told Sr. Everard that if he will go to your house you will permit him and anybody he brings with him to see my China and to take away such pieces as they may have a mind to copy."

This letter not only indicates clearly the manner in which many of the best Chelsea designs were obtained, but also throws valuable light on Sir Everard's close connexion with the Chelsea factory. Sir Charles Williams had a valuable collection of china and that part of it to which his letter doubtless had special reference was a dinner set presented to him in 1748 by Augustus III, Elector of Saxony. It included "a dessert service with sweetmeat dishes in the form of artichokes, laurel leaves, sunflowers and double leaves, as well as tea and coffee sets, spoons and knife and fork dishes."

Vegetable-shaped dishes, leaf-shaped dishes and dishes made in the semblance of animals and birds were common in Dresden china of the period and the strong Dresden influence can be seen in such articles produced at Chelsea as well as in the figures and groups—some of which were direct copies—and in the extensive use of patterns moulded or impressed in low relief upon the paste in the form of basket-work, ribbing (Plate 74, A), flowers, Rococo scrolls and other ornaments.

The direct Oriental influence was not extensive and,

with few exceptions, was Japanese rather than Chinese. The most conspicuous Japanese influence is seen in the Kakiyemon and Imari designs of which much use was made. There is constant reference to the Kakiyemon styles under such names as "tyger and rock" pattern, "old Japan," "wheatsheaf and pheasant," "pheasant and border," and "lady pattern."

The Sèvres influence came later and was clearly indicated by the florid Rococo shapes, especially in the case of vases and other decorative pieces, the use of ground colours and reserved panels, the manner of gilding, and the *motifs* employed for the painted decoration.

The ground colours included a rich Mazarine blue, turquoise blue, pea-green, sea-green, red, yellow and a rich claret colour (Plate 75, B), the last being quite distinctive of Chelsea and never produced anywhere else. With these ground colours there were reserved panels in which appeared well painted naturalistic flowers, birds with gay plumage, fruits, landscapes, figures, pastoral scenes and scenes of gallantry after the manner of Watteau and Boucher. Besides these painted decorations in reserved panels, there were endless flower *motifs*—scattered flowers, flowers in organised compositions, garlands, wreaths and festoons.

There were also landscapes detached from any panel setting and to some extent both landscapes and flowers were rendered in monochrome, at a certain period a green *camaïeu* being much favoured for this purpose.

After William Duesbury bought the Chelsea factory and all its equipment in 1770 the Chelsea manner of decoration was continued, but certain changes became evident in this Chelsea-Derby period. For one thing, the elaborate Rococo shapes of vases and ornamental jars were discontinued and in their place appeared the more austere and simpler shapes inspired by Neo-Classic taste. *Motifs* from the "antique" were employed and all the painted decoration became much "tighter" and laboured. Also there was a tendency to over-decorate and load ornament on to excess. The rich claret-coloured ground, so distinctive of Chelsea, was discontinued, or when attempts were made to produce it it appeared diluted and washed out. The beautiful pea-green and turquoise grounds also experienced much the same sort of dilution.

THE MARKS. A very early mark, seldom met with, is an incised triangle. The usual early Chelsea mark is an embossed oval with an anchor in low relief. Occasionally the embossed anchor was touched with red enamel colour. Later it was customary for the anchor to be drawn by the painter or gilder when he had finished the decoration, and although it sometimes occurs in blue, it is generally to be found in red or a reddish brown. The gold anchor is generally found on the later pieces when very elaborate gilding was in fashion at the works. In a few cases, two gold anchors are found side by side.

In the Chelsea-Derby period, from 1770 to 1784, the mark consisted of the anchor of Chelsea in conjunction with the D of Derby. This combination of marks seems to have been used indifferently for the pieces produced both at Chelsea and at Derby during this period when both establishments were under the same ownership.

WORCESTER CHINA—1751 TO PRESENT DAY

HISTORY. About the middle of the eighteenth century, some prominent residents of Worcester were deeply concerned at the languishing industrial condition of the city. At the instance of Doctor John Wall, who had conceived the plan of establishing china manufacture as one means of remedy for the stagnation, in 1751 fifteen gentlemen incorporated a company entitled "The Worcester Tonkin Manufacture" to put the scheme into immediate operation.

The capital subscribed was apportioned in forty-five shares of £100 each, and five of these shares were presented to Doctor Wall and William Davis, apothecary, in recognition of "their discovery of the art and secrets of porcelain making" which they were making over to the company.

Whence these "secrets" were obtained is not recorded, but the actual working knowledge of formulas and processes was doubtless supplied by some experienced workmen who had gained that knowledge in another factory. It was only such intimate knowledge that could ensure immediate and satisfactory results and avoid a long period of costly experiments. A paragraph in the deed of incorporation named R. Podmore and J. Lyes, two skilled workmen, to whom special considerations were promised in the shape of occasional gratuities and a small percentage of profits in order "to ensure their fidelity." It is plain, therefore, that these two were to supply the technical experience.

In July, 1751, Warmstry House, an old mansion near the Cathedral, was leased and adapted to the purposes of a factory. Kilns were constructed and a staff of workmen got together.

In the *Gentleman's Magazine* of August, 1752, a sale of the newly made wares was advertised to commence on the 20th of September next following. Only small articles were made at first, for the kiln capacity was limited. But these small articles were of a useful sort, and the stock was soon increased to include the whole range of tableware. While aiming to produce chinaware of engaging appearance, the directors also endeavoured to put forth wares that would be thoroughly serviceable for table use and general domestic purposes. They were well aware that the china of Chelsea and Bow, however beautiful it might be, often came to disaster when brought into sudden contact with hot water. They knew that this shortcoming hindered its popularity and caused a preference for Oriental china that was not affected by sudden changes of temperature. They therefore tried to make a denser, harder body with better heat-resisting qualities and, at the same time, to follow Oriental models of shape and decoration that would compare favourably with the Chinese porcelain that was admittedly the standard.

Working to this double purpose, they succeeded in obtaining a paste that met the requirements of durability and resistance to heat, and also produced tableware so closely identical with the chinaware imported from the East that they advertised in the *Oxford Journal* in 1763 to inform the public that "services of Chinese porcelain can be made up with Worcester porcelain, so that the difference cannot be discovered." And what they promised, they were able to perform.

About 1768 a number of Chelsea decorators were

employed on the staff at Worcester, and with their advent on the scene larger and more elaborate pieces were made and the scope of decoration was considerably broadened. Nevertheless, with all the improvements and beautiful as the Worcester china undoubtedly was, the sales did not come up to justifiable expectations and there seems to have been some radical defect in the business management.

Dissensions arose amongst the proprietors and there was a reorganisation in 1772 as a result of which the factory passed into the control of a smaller number of partners. After Doctor Wall's death, in 1776, the affairs of the factory sank into a discouraging state and, in 1783, Thomas Flight, who had been for a long time the company's London agent at their warehouse in Cheapside, bought the whole establishment for £3000 and his sons, Joseph and John, assumed the management of the works.

Very soon after the change of ownership, Robert Chamberlain, who had been the first apprentice of the Company in 1751 and had risen to the post of head decorator, left and with his son set up an independent china decorating establishment nearby in Worcester, obtaining his undecorated china from the Caughley factory.

He was so successful in this venture that in 1788–89 he built kilns at Diglis, in Worcester, and began to manufacture porcelain on his own account in opposition to the original factory at Warmstry House. Needless to say, there was keen rivalry and intensely bitter feeling between the two establishments, especially as they were both making virtually the same kinds of china.

In 1793 Martin Barr was taken into partnership with the Flights, the firm then being known as Flight & Barr. In 1807 Martin Barr the younger was admitted to partnership and the firm then became Barr, Flight and Barr. In 1829 the last of the Flights died and the factory was carried on by the Barrs.

Meantime, the rival factory of the Chamberlains had prospered and grown firmly established. New partners had been taken into the business from time to time, and there was no sign of abatement in the ruinous competition between the two concerns. Finally, in 1840, the two factories were amalgamated and, after several subsequent readjustments of partnership, the establishment was vested in a joint stock company under the name of the Worcester Royal Porcelain Company, which has continued in operation to the present day.

THE BODY. In all likelihood, the first paste was closely analogous to that first used at Bow and Chelsea—a fritted soft paste rich in glassy constituents. Very soon, almost from the first in fact, soapstone or steatite was used, a much harder and more infusible but less translucent paste resulting. The soapstone body continued in use till well towards the end of the century. Bone-ash may have been used in small quantities as early as 1760. Between 1800 and 1810 numerous experiments were made to improve the paste, and about 1810 the bone porcelain body, composed of china clay, china stone and bone-ash, was finally adopted.

The earliest body was creamy in colour; the soapstone body was less creamy though mellow and not dead white; the bone-ash body was whiter, but not the dead, cold, glittering white of German porcelain.

THE GLAZE. The earliest glaze, rich in lead, had a soft luscious quality of surface; the glaze of the soapstone body was less fusible and had a certain amount of ground

Oriental porcelain in its composition and some oxide of tin, which rendered it slightly opalescent or pearly and contributed to the Chinese-like quality of the blue and white ware; the final glaze was harder and more brilliant.

ARTICLES MADE AND CONTOUR. From the first, stress was laid upon the manufacture of useful articles rather than cabinet pieces. For a long time tableware was the chief product and elaborate vases and ornamental pieces were rarely made. Even as late as 1769, the catalogue of the auction sale in London, a sale that lasted for five days, mentions only four or five sets of covered jars and beakers.

After the coming of the Chelsea painters in 1768, however, there began a new development at Worcester and larger and more elaborate pieces began to be made, while even the ordinary tableware reflected the new influence in the manner of its decoration. Eventually, a certain number of large and ornate vases (Plate 81), covered jars, beakers, candelabra and the like were made, but the main emphasis of the factory was always placed on tableware and allied adjuncts.

At the very outset, Chinese types (Plate 80) often served as models of contour, for Chinese porcelain was regarded as the standard to be emulated. At a later stage the shapes made at Sèvres exerted an appreciable influence, but there was never any approach to the exaggerated Rococo forms in use at that factory. Worcester Rococo was Rococo under restraint. From about 1770 onward the contours shew perceptibly the Neo-Classic trend and about 1800 and immediately afterwards the Neo-Grec influence was visible. Worcester never ran to

PLATE 85

A. DERBY OVAL BUTTER DISH WITH SHAPED LID
Creamy paste, clear glaze; gilded feet, handles and bandings; ground colour bluish grey, festooned flowers in burnt orange, yellow, pale green, and rose colour for the ribbons

B. DERBY VASE
White paste, clear glaze; deep blue ground colour with elaborate gilt decorations and reserved naturalistic landscape panels on the sides

Courtesy of the Victoria and Albert Museum, South Kensington

PLATE 86

A. DERBY PLATE WITH FLOWERED BORDER
Creamy paste, glaze slightly greenish; spirally divided rim, with decoration in vermilion, deep blue, gold and light green

B. DERBY PLATE WITH IMARI DECORATION
Creamy paste, glaze slightly greenish; Japanese Imari inspiration modified with pattern carried out in light and dark blue, pale greenish yellow and pale yellowish green, deep Venetian red, deep violet and gold

Courtesy of the Victoria and Albert Museum, South Kensington

PLATE 87

A. DERBY CUP AND SAUCER B. DERBY BOWL

Paste white, clear colourless glaze; arabesque decoration in gold, deep yellow, deep vermilion, light green and violet

Paste white, faint greenish tinge in glaze; decoration in bright rose, yellow, light green, blue, burnt Siena and gold

Courtesy of the Victoria and Albert Museum, South Kensington

PLATE 88

PLYMOUTH COVERED GARNITURE JAR OF CHINESE SHAPE
White paste, glaze slightly greyish or smoked; decoration in yellow, green, mulberry, purple and deep Venetian red

Courtesy of the Victoria and Albert Museum, South Kensington

ENGLISH CHINAWARE

extremes of contour, however, and Rococo, Neo-Classic and Neo-Grec interpretations were always moderate.

TYPES OF DECORATION. A very few of the earliest known Worcester pieces are in white, but they are so rare that it is hardly worth while enumerating them under Types of Decoration. Moulded decoration in low relief was largely employed in the shape of basket-work, ribbing, fluting, flowers, scrolls, and the favourite embossed pine-cone or imbricated pattern. Modelling in high relief was little resorted to. Piercing and fretwork for such articles as fruit baskets were freely used. The moulded pieces also included such articles as the cabbage-leaf jugs with masques under the spouts, pickle dishes, artichoke cups in the form of leaves, and rockwork and shell stands for sweetmeats.

Chinese porcelain was more imitated (Plates 77, A and B; 79, A and 80) at Worcester than anywhere else and nowhere else were the imitations so successful. During the first fifteen or twenty years all the best pieces of blue and white ware were (Plate 79, A) produced, the designs being mostly Chinese. Transfer printed decoration was first used about 1757 and the designs were engraved by R. Hancock. The printed pieces, as well as those bearing landscapes, figures and fanciful scenes, often displayed the portraits of popular heroes, such as the Marquis of Granby or the elder Pitt. These transfer designs (Plate 83) were admirably wrought and appeared in black, blue, purple and red. The underglaze blue printing was not used before 1770.

After the coming of the Chelsea painters in 1768 the underglaze blue for the blue and white ware continued to be used but, in addition, we find underglaze blue in the form of powder-blue grounds and scale blue, with panels reserved for "plants, exotic birds, fruit and flowers in brilliant enamel colours" (Plate 1). Besides the blue grounds there were apple-green (Plate 84), pea-green, bright canary yellow, sea-green, French green, turquoise blue and a purplish crimson somewhat approximating the wonderful Chelsea claret colour. There were also radiating trellis and vine patterns, rose sprays, landscapes, Watteau pastorals and woodland scenes, patterns wholly in blue and gold, scattered flowers, flowers in bouquets, garlands and wreaths, designs adapted from the Japanese Imari ware (Plates 77, 79, B and 82), and, from 1790 onward Classic figures executed in bat printing which gives a delicate stippled effect, and designs taken from the work of Angelica Kauffmann, Cosway and Bartolozzi. During the Flight and Barr period the decorations were more precisely painted (Plate 78) and gave an impression of "tightness;" there was also a tendency to over-decorate the pieces at this time. The so-called "dress services" with armorial bearings enclosed by overly ornate borders were good examples of this unfortunate trend.

THE MARKS. The earliest mark was a W in script. The usual mark was a crescent which may occur simply in outline, in solid colour, or with shaded lines. It is usually in underglaze blue, but is sometimes found in on-glaze red or gold. The early printed pieces had not these factory marks but generally had the inscription "R. H. Worcester" minutely engraved amidst the ornamental scrolls or on the groundwork. This mark was commonly accompanied by an anchor. "R. Hancock fecit" is likewise found on a few of the early pieces printed in black.

During the later periods from 1783 to 1840 the names

or initials of the firm are impressed in the paste, painted in underglaze blue, and painted or printed in red on-glaze, thus: "FLIGHTS" or "FLIGHT," "FLIGHT & BARR," "FLIGHT, BARR & BARR," "BARR, FLIGHT & BARR," "F. B. B.," and "B. F. B." The earlier of these are occasionally accompanied by the crescent. After 1788 the mark is surmounted by a crown.

Chamberlain's factory generally marked their china with "Chamberlain's" in script, or with "Chamberlain's, Worcester," with or without the address of the London agency. The later Chamberlain marks are often printed.

DERBY CHINA—1755 TO 1848; 1848 TO PRESENT DAY

HISTORY. The Derby china factory was established by William Duesbury in 1755. Duesbury was the son of a Longton potter and for some years prior to the establishment of the porcelain factory he had been a china painter in London, executing commissions for Chelsea and Bow, now and again, purchasing undecorated wares and painting them, or painting special pieces to the order of private customers. About 1754 he seems to have been at Longton Hall helping Littler with his porcelain factory.

In 1755, with the financial aid of John Heath, he started the factory at Derby, converting a few cottages into workshops and erecting kilns. Comparatively little is known of the factory and its work until 1770 when Duesbury bought the Chelsea factory. As we have already seen, he kept both factories in operation until 1784, in the meantime buying out the establishment at Bow when it was offered for sale. After 1784 all the work was conducted at the Derby factory.

William Duesbury, who was apparently a clever business man and an able manager, died in 1786 and was succeeded in the conduct of the works by his son, the younger William Duesbury who carried on the business until 1795. In 1795, during the minority of the third William Duesbury the factory was conducted by his stepfather, Mr. Kean and the firm was known as Duesbury & Kean. This partnership was dissolved in 1811, owing to family dissensions, and the business was sold to Robert Bloor who had been a clerk and salesman during the former partnership.

Bloor was altogether commercially minded and forsook the standards that had previously prevailed. For a while the factory was highly prosperous, but the cheapened wares and the lowered standard of decoration brought the inevitable nemesis and the business fell off sadly. In 1828 Bloor became deranged and the factory was carried on under a managing clerk, its fortunes sinking lower and lower until it was finally closed in 1848.

A small factory was then started by a group of the old Derby workmen with a Mr. Locker, formerly chief clerk, as the manager. From this nucleus a business grew up which has been carried on to the present day. In 1876 a new and altogether distinct company was formed which is known as the Royal Crown Derby Porcelain Company.

THE BODY. While there is no definite information to be obtained respecting the body and glaze of the earliest Derby ware, it was almost certainly a glassy or soft paste like the body first in use at Bow and Chelsea. By 1764 experiments had evidently been in progress for improving the composition of the body. It was then that Richard Holdship, one of the partners of the Worcester company, in a most unprincipled and dishonest manner, betrayed the interest of his own organisation and engaged "to impart in writing to Duesbury and Heath his secret process for making china according to the proofs already made by him, and to supply them with all sufficient quantities of soapy rock at fair prices." Presumably the Derby body was improved and hardened as a result of this underhand deal. There seems also to have been a change about 1770 for one of the first things Duesbury did on buying the Chelsea factory was to send ten bags of bone-ash from there to the plant at Derby. About the end of the century the regular bone porcelain composition, comprising, china clay, china-stone and bone-ash, was adopted. The early body had a mellow creamy tone, and this mellowness was never wholly lost, although in the later, harder body it was not so noticeable.

THE GLAZE. From the first the Derby glaze was good. The early glaze was soft and velvet-like; the later glaze was harder and more brilliant but not obtrusively so.

ARTICLES MADE AND CONTOUR. In the early days of the factory, besides the making of tableware and all the other distinctly "useful" items of chinaware, small figures were produced in large quantities and the establishment seems to have done a particularly thriving business in that direction. Before the absorption of Chelsea, figures and groups in biscuit were made. With the acquisition of the Chelsea works and Chelsea traditions, the Derby establishment continued to make all the diversity of wares produced under Sprimont. These have already been enumerated in the Chelsea section.

In the matter of contour, however, as already pointed out, Duesbury made a change and supplanted the exuberant Rococo forms by the soberer contours dictated by the Neo-Classic mode (Plate 85, B). At a later date still, the Neo-Grec forms had their vogue in the Derby chinaware.

TYPES OF DECORATION. Under the Chelsea-Derby *régime* the Chelsea methods of decoration were continued so that, save for the evidence of marks, it would often be difficult to say whether a piece was Chelsea or Chelsea-Derby. Attention, however, has been called to the growing tendency to load on too much decoration (Plate 85, A), and to a somewhat "tighter" and less spontaneous character in the painting. It is unnecessary to recapitulate all the characteristic forms of Chelsea decoration, but it must be pointed out in addition to these that a very rich and ornate adaptation of the Japanese Imari patterns (Plate 86, B) was characteristic of the Derby factory and that, in the late period, a great use was made of flowing gold scrolls (Plate 87) in conjunction with one or two rich colours to complete the scheme of arabesques. Under the second William Duesbury both the flower painting and the other painted decorations (Plates 87 and 86, A) reached the height of excellence. At this time, too, not only figures and statuettes in biscuit were produced, but likewise very excellent portrait medallions in biscuit.

THE MARKS. The earliest mark of Derby was a script D, but it is of the rarest occurrence. The usual mark is a D beneath a crown and this was used down to about 1782. It was usually applied in underglaze blue, but is found also in purple, green, and rose. The Chelsea-Derby marks have already been given. Not long after 1782 crossed batons and six dots accompanied the crowned D. This mark is generally in purple or mauve, though it may occur in blue or in gold. While Kean was a partner the letter K occasionally appears in company with the D. When Bloor bought the works the pieces were marked "Bloor, Derby," with or without the crown. The Bloor marks were generally printed. A Gothic D crowned and printed in red belongs to the Bloor period, when the marks were commonly in red. Forged Dresden and Sèvres marks in underglaze blue are not uncommon on Derby pieces.

LONGTON HALL CHINA—1752–1758

HISTORY. The china factory at Longton Hall in Staffordshire was a short-lived enterprise. It was established about 1752 by William Littler, the son of a Burslem potter, and came to an untimely end amidst financial difficulties in 1758. Littler and Aaron Wedgwood, who had entered into partnership with him, launched their business with insufficient capital and always suffered from this handicap until the end came. Their aim was to make china like that of Bow and Chelsea, but to produce it at a lower cost and sell it cheaper. During the few years of its limited production, Longton Hall china had a moderate sale in the Midlands. An auction sale in London, in 1757, failed to realise the proceeds expected. The entire stock was sold by auction in London and Birmingham, in 1758, and the factory was abandoned.

THE BODY. The Longton Hall body was a soft paste, granular in texture, full of specks and of a dingy, greyish white tinge. It has been called "the worst china ever produced in England."

THE GLAZE. The glaze was harder than the glaze of Bow and Chelsea; it was also thinner in its distribution and less likely to crackle and craze.

ARTICLES MADE AND CONTOUR. Tableware formed the principal output of the Longton Hall factory. Elaborate vases were never undertaken, but there were a few beakers, small vases and pomatum pots made. The figures mentioned in the sales advertisements were merely the table accompaniments of fruit baskets and similar dessert pieces. The shapes coincided with the Rococo phases (Plate 110, B), interpreted at Bow and Chelsea.

TYPES OF DECORATION. Flowers, birds, and country or pastoral scenes with a few figures were *motifs* much employed. A bright underglaze cobalt blue was frequently used, either as a ground colour or in heavy masses. Reserved panels for bird or flower *motifs* were commonly enclosed with scrolled borders in raised white. In modelled ornament, acanthus leaves were especially favoured. There was little gilding.

THE MARKS. Longton Hall china was seldom marked and may easily be mistaken for inferior Bow or Chelsea ware. When marked, it had two L's crossed, or a device evolved from two L's.

PLATE 89

PLYMOUTH MUG WITH SWELLING BASE
Paste white, glaze slightly greyish or smoked; decorated with Chinese *motifs* in brilliant colours, green, vermilion, dull blue, bright yellow and mulberry

Courtesy of the Victoria and Albert Museum, South Kensington

PLATE 90

A. PLYMOUTH MUG WITH SWELLING BASE

White paste, glaze slightly bluish grey or smoky; flower bouquet and spray decoration in gold, violet, vermilion, blue, green, and yellow

B. PLYMOUTH SAUCEBOAT OF ROCOCO SHAPE

Paste white, glaze slightly bluish grey or smoky; moulded ornament in paste; colour decoration in black, Venetian red, mulberry and grey green

Courtesy of the Victoria and Albert Museum, South Kensington

PLATE 91

BRISTOL CHOCOLATE POT WITH DOMED LID
Hard white paste, clear, colourless glaze; bright marbleised or stippled cobalt ground, rather harsh; elaborate scroll and band gilding of excellent quality; reserved white panels with polychrome flowers in green, mulberry, yellow, purple and deep Venetian red

Courtesy of the Victoria and Albert Museum, South Kensington

PLATE 92

A. BRISTOL PEAR-SHAPED CHOCOLATE POT
Creamy paste, clear glaze; flowered decoration in Dresden manner in pale pink, yellow, deep cold green, smoky violet, Venetian red and gold

B. BRISTOL FIGURE OF *AUTUMN*
Creamy paste, clear, colourless glaze; decoration in green, yellow, vermilion, dull blue, pale mulberry and gold

Courtesy of the Victoria and Albert Museum, South Kensington

LIVERPOOL CHINA—1800-1841

HISTORY. Although Liverpool was at one time an important centre of the ceramic industry, the quantity and quality of porcelain made there during the eighteenth century seems very problematical, despite the contention that four potters were engaged in making china, to wit, Richard Chaffers, Seth Pennington, Philip Christian and Reid & Company. It seems scarcely likely that there would be so few traces remaining had real china ever been manufactured at Liverpool in the eighteenth century in any appreciable quantity. Dillon suggests that some eighteenth century soft paste porcelain that may have been made at Liverpool has been classified as Worcester or Salopian.

Further difficulties arise when one considers the readiness displayed by eighteenth century manufacturers to label as porcelain articles whose composition is nearly identical with that of pottery. Much of the Delft ware made at Liverpool went by the name of porcelain, whereas its only actual resemblance to porcelain was its white colour.

Nevertheless, there are in the Liverpool Museum specimens, purporting to be of Liverpool manufacture, that shew a good quality of paste and glaze as well as creditable decoration. There are examples of transfer printing, chiefly in black and brown, but also in green, deep purple, rose and red. Likewise there are Chinese designs, landscapes, rustic scenes, butterflies, red grounds, and also patterns in underglaze blue. Instances of bat-printing, too, occur.

Perhaps the most interesting figure connected with the Liverpool ventures at china making was Richard Chaffers. Through the advice of Podmore, of the Worcester factory, Chaffers made an expedition into Cornwall in search of soapstone. The search was ultimately successful and Chaffers returned to Liverpool assured that he would be able to obtain all the soapstone necessary. The ware subsequently manufactured and sold by Chaffers & Co., as advertised in the *Liverpool Advertiser* in December, 1756, undoubtedly contained soapstone, but it seems not to have been a true porcelain.

At a more recent date (1800–1841) the Herculaneum works on the banks of the Mersey manufactured genuine porcelain. There is no difficulty in identifying its wares as they are plainly marked with the full name of the place, occasionally accompanied by the crest of the Liverpool Borough. There was no improvement in quality or decoration (Plate 110, A), to distinguish the Herculaneum china from the products of other factories and while the decorations were pleasing, they were obviously adapted from types then in vogue at Davenport and elsewhere.

LOWESTOFT CHINA—c.1756–c.1802

History. Probably no one kind of china has ever stirred up so much contention or so much hot partisanship —or opposition, as the case may be—as the china that *was* made and the china that was *not* made at Lowestoft. Half the time, a violent Lowestoft partisan will ignore *facts* and claim an unlimited and elaborate production for a very small establishment; the violent opponent grudgingly admits that anything at all was made there. Both of them find the truth unpalatable.

PLATE 94

A. EIGHTEENTH CENTURY CHINESE
POWDER-BLUE VASE
Reserved and shaped panel in white bearing multi-coloured symbols or emblems
Courtesy of the British Museum

B. CAUGHLEY MUG
With scrolls and bands of characteristic deep blue and gold
Courtesy of the Victoria and Albert Museum, South Kensington

As a matter of fact, most of the china that goes by the name of Lowestoft and that a great many people persist in calling Lowestoft, was never anywhere within miles of the place. On the other hand, there unquestionably *was* a porcelain factory at Lowestoft, and some very engaging chinaware was made there. All these facts are known and attested. But fallacies die hard, and it will probably be a long time before the admirers of chinaware will unite in giving the factory and its wares their just due without either addition or subtraction.

The factory was established by Messrs. Walker, Brown, Aldred and Richman and a considerable output of soft paste porcelain was produced so that it was worth while to have a warehouse in London. An advertisement in a London paper of 1770 acquaints the public that "Clark Durnford, Lowestoft China Warehouse, No. 4, Great St. Thomas the Apostle, Cheapside, London" will supply merchants, shopkeepers and others with the china made in Suffolk. There seems also to have been a fairly brisk local trade.

The factory was closed about 1802 or 1803 after having continued in operation for nearly half a century.

THE BODY. The body was a soft paste with a yellowish tinge and is not very translucent.

THE GLAZE. The glaze was often slightly tinged with cobalt and was sometimes imperfectly fired so that it is a little dulled. There are often minute black points or specks in the glaze also. The Lowestoft glaze is strongly characteristic, not only because of this perceptibly bluish tinge that occurs on all pieces decorated in underglaze blue even when other colours in enamel are used with it, but also owing to its frequently thick and uneven distribution which is especially noticeable on the larger pieces. On pieces decorated only in enamel colours over the glaze, the glaze is apt to be more thinly applied and to shew a greenish tinge. The quality of the glaze on Lowestoft china with polychrome decoration contributes to the pearly appearance similar to that of Oriental china with decoration of the same sort.

ARTICLES MADE AND CONTOUR. The articles made at Lowestoft were largely tea-services, punch bowls, cups and saucers, mugs, dishes, small plates, jugs, inkstands, basons, sauce boats, open-work fruit baskets and smaller ware generally. No large services or ambitious articles of a decorative nature seem to have been attempted.

The shapes were either copied from Chinese models or adapted from the wares of other factories such, for instance, as the cabbage-leaf jug of Worcester pattern.

TYPES OF DECORATION. At the beginning there seems to have been some imitation of Delft floral and scroll *motifs* in underglaze blue, but most of the early Lowestoft followed Chinese patterns. For a number of years all the decoration was in underglaze blue (Plate 96, A and B), and it was not until about 1785 or 1790 that decoration in enamel colours began. In addition to the underglaze blue decorations there were moulded low reliefs in the form of ribbing, fluting, basket-work, scrolls (Plate 96, A), rosettes (Plate 96, B), and flowers. Piercing and fretwork also played an important part in the ornamentation.

In the polychrome decoration the favourite *motifs* were either Chinese subjects or else small flowers (Plates 51, A and 95, B) in sprays or singly, and the colouring, though bright, was delicate (Plate 95, A). Constant use was also made of fretwork (Plate 96, C), scale or diapered borders or borders derived from the Chinese cord and tassel *motif*. Rose-colour was evidently much favoured by the Lowestoft china painters (Plate 95, A).

Both Bow and Worcester workmen and decorators seem to have been employed at various times and this would account for some of the similarities in decoration to be found. So far as the blue and white ware is concerned, however, it should be borne in mind that Lowestoft has not the greenish tinge of Bow and Worcester when held against the light, nor has it the thin glaze with a greenish tinge displayed by the Caughley blue and white, but its glaze is thick and of distinctly bluish tinge.

In the blue and white ware also occasionally appear little local views, and in some instances these are set in panels and surrounded by a ground of powder blue which latter the Lowestoft makers seem to have been especially successful in copying from the Chinese. Straight and curved ribbings and flutings were often employed and on the pieces with narrow ribbing there was frequently a blue decoration of lines with minute sprays and flowers resembling the modern Copenhagen china, although the Lowestoft blue is deeper. The Chinese dragon in blue was obviously appropriated from the Worcester pattern. There was also apparently some attempt at transfer printing in blue, in emulation of the Caughley willow pattern. A few black transfers, too, are said to have been made.

Designs prompted by the willow pattern or adapted from other Oriental *motifs* were executed in underglaze blue along with on-glaze red and gold, but the polychrome decorations were chiefly designs derived from the Chinese porcelain of the *famille rose,* or else the minute flower sprays and single blossoms usually associated with the name of Lowestoft, although decorations almost identical with the latter were also employed at New Hall, Wirksworth and elsewhere. The blue cornflower *motif* often appeared, there were occasionally pink or puce monochromes, there were "Mandarin" figures, doubtless inspired by Worcester, now and then cornucopias filled with flowers, while a very few instances of decorations with Classic figures have been attributed to Lowestoft, as well as a few instances of large flowers naturalistically painted. Armorial devices are known to have been executed but, so it seems, not often.

THE MARKS. There seems to have been no regular factory mark on the Lowestoft china and many pieces are altogether innocent of anything resembling a mark. Marks of other factories it appears, however, were now and again copied or approximated.

PLYMOUTH CHINA—1768-1770

HISTORY. The hard paste porcelain factory was established by William Cookworthy at Plymouth in 1768. Cookworthy was a plymouth chemist who for years had been deeply interested in the subject of porcelain manufacture. He was persuaded that the materials requisite for making true hard paste porcelain, similar in the nature of its body to the porcelain of China or the hard paste porcelain of Dresden, could be found in England. He furthermore believed that those materials existed in abundant quantity in Cornwall. For a number of years he experimented with Cornish kaolin and felspar, or china clay and china stone, as they are usually called, and after discovering the most satisfactory sorts and the proper proportions for the composition, he established the Plymouth china factory with the aid and backing of Thomas Pitt of Boconnoc (afterwards Lord Camelford), having first secured a patent granting him exclusive right to the use of his composition for a term of years.

Cookworthy was sixty-three years old when he obtained his patent and founded the factory and he utterly lacked all experience in directing the mechanical processes and the details of management. The obstacles to be overcome were too great to admit of even moderate success for the venture and, in 1770, the Plymouth factory was abandoned and the business transferred to Bristol where Richard Champion, a young, capable and energetic man developed the enterprise into the famous Bristol china works.

The Body. The body of the Plymouth china was a true hard paste, the first that had been made in England. It was extremely hard, and was pure white and translucent, possessing all the qualities that good hard paste porcelain should have.

The Glaze. The glaze of the Plymouth china was often very imperfect, a circumstance due to imperfect firing. It was frequently thick and uneven in patches and apt to be full of bubbles. In many cases it had a distinctly greyish tone from the smoke. This smoke stain was technically an imperfection, of course, but as a matter of fact it not seldom added to the charm of the china.

Articles Made and Contour. Much of the product consisted of the smaller sorts of tableware and tea services, although a number of excellent figures and groups and some admirable vases were also made. The shapes were more or less of a moderate Rococo fashion although a number of Chinese forms (Plates 88 and 89), also were employed.

TYPES OF DECORATION. Modelling or moulding in low relief in the form of scrolls and leaf *motifs* (Plate 90, B) formed part of the decorative system; also the modelling of shell-shaped salt-cellars, figures and other items in fuller relief or in the round contributed its share. A number of pieces appear in the white. Many pieces were decorated altogether in underglaze blue, but the blue was rather blackish where it had been thickly applied and was also apt to be streaky. The polychrome pieces shew brilliant and beautiful colouring (Plates 88, 89 and 90, A), and the enamel-painted decoration is always in the form of sprays of flowers and detached birds and butterflies (Plates 88 and 90, A). Ground colours were not used until after the business had been transferred to Bristol.

THE MARKS. When the pieces are marked they bear the alchemical symbol for tin which looks like a combination of the two Arabic numerals, 2 and 4. On the blue and white pieces the mark is in underglaze blue; on the polychrome pieces it is in red or reddish brown. On a few of the pieces where there is much gilding, the mark is in gold but it is not unlikely that some of these pieces may have been made at the Bristol factory.

BRISTOL CHINA—1770-1781

HISTORY. In 1770, when Cookworthy joined forces with Richard Champion and transferred the Plymouth factory to Bristol, the business was established in a building on Castle Green. From 1770 to 1773 this business was

PLATE 93

A. BRISTOL PLATE WITH SHAPED AND MOULDED RIM

Hard white paste, faint bluish tinge in glaze; decoration in green, rose, brown, blue shading to purple, vermilion, yellow and gold

B. BRISTOL PLATE WITH SHAPED AND MOULDED RIM

Hard white paste, faint bluish tinge in glaze; interlaced blue ribbon border, flower spray decoration in blue, violet, pink, green, greenish yellow, vermilion and gold

Courtesy of the Victoria and Albert Museum, South Kensington

PLATE 95

A. LOWESTOFT SMALL BOWL

Soft white paste, clear glaze; red border inside rim, flowers in mulberry, yellow, dull blue, vermilion and green

B. "TRIFLE FROM LOWESTOFT" MUG WITH CORN-FLOWER DECORATION

Soft white paste, glaze faintly bluish; decoration in blue, mulberry, bluish green and touches of vermilion, green border

Courtesy of the Victoria and Albert Museum, South Kensington

PLATE 96

A. LOWESTOFT BUTTER BOAT
Soft white paste, distinctly bluish glaze; moulded ornament impressed in paste; decoration in deep dull blue

B. LOWESTOFT CREAM PITCHER
Soft white paste, bluish glaze; moulded ornament impressed in paste; decoration in deep dull blue

C. LOWESTOFT PIERCED FRUIT BASKET
Soft white paste, very bluish glaze; moulded ornament; decoration deep blue

Courtesy of the Victoria and Albert Museum, South Kensington

PLATE 97

A. CAUGHLEY SAUCER
Creamy paste, clear glaze; decoration in gold and very deep blue

B. CAUGHLEY COVERED CUP WITH TWO HANDLES
Creamy paste, clear glaze; characteristic decoration in gold and very deep blue

Courtesy of the Victoria and Albert Museum, South Kensington

carried on under the firm name of Wm. Cookworthy & Co. In 1773 Champion bought Cookworthy's interest and patent rights and the firm then became Richard Champion & Company.

Champion was a merchant in the American trade and also an ardent supporter of Burke, and when the troubles incident to the American Revolution arose he sustained serious losses. In 1775, with Burke's support, he tried to obtain an extension of Cookworthy's patent, but the most he could secure was the sole right to use the china stone and china clay in making porcelain; others might employ the same materials so long as they did not manufacture porcelain within the time limit of the patent. Even though aided by Burke and other powerful friends in Parliament, litigation cost Champion dear for Josiah Wedgwood and the Staffordshire potters created a strong opposition to the renewal of the patent in any form. These charges and the losses occasioned by the war with the Colonies crippled Champion financially and he sought to extend the capital of the business but the times were not favourable.

A London warehouse, at 17 Salisbury Court, Fleet Street, was opened in 1776 and the best period of the enterprise seems to have been from 1776 to 1778, but at the end of that time Champion entertained the thought of selling the factory and his patent rights. A sale was effected in 1781 to a company of seven Staffordshire potters and Champion retired from the field of manufacture, going not long after to South Carolina where he died in 1791. The Bristol works were closed and the new company transferred the scene of their activity first to Tunstall and then to New Hall, at Shelton.

THE BODY. The paste was white, intensely hard, dense of texture, and translucent. In hardness and infusibility the Bristol body excels both Chinese and Dresden porcelain. Bristol china sometimes shews "wreathing," slight spiral ridges running round the piece from bottom to top, caused by imperfect manipulation in "throwing" and moulding the clay on the potter's wheel. When fractured or chipped the surface is more or less conchoidal with a waxy lustre.

THE GLAZE. The imperfections of the Plymouth glaze have already been noted. At Bristol the difficulties were overcome and an evenly distributed, clear, brilliant glaze was perfected. The simpler ware was glazed and fired at one operation, in the Chinese manner; the more elaborate pieces were first fired to a partial biscuit state, then dipped in the glaze and fully fired.

ARTICLES MADE AND CONTOUR. There were two grades of ware made at the Bristol factory—the "Cottage China" and the finer and more elaborate pieces. The cottage china included the ordinary "useful" tableware and a few small figures that were not carefully modelled. The shapes and decoration of the cottage china were simple. The finer tableware and the vases, jars and beakers were admittedly inspired by the Dresden manner. Figures (Plate 92, B), and groups, excellently modelled, were made both glazed and in biscuit, and there were also in biscuit portrait medallions and plaques with armorial bearings, often surrounded by the most delicately fashioned wreaths of flowers. The fine tableware and tea and coffee equipages never displayed the exaggerated Rococo shapes of Dresden but rather tended to conservative Chinese shapes and the more sober forms of Neo-Classic derivation. The catalogue of the 1780 sale of Bristol china notes "elegant patterns in Desert Services, Tea and Coffee Equipages, Cabinet and Caudle cups," and the contours of many of these articles distinctly bear the Neo-Classic impress.

TYPES OF DECORATION. The cottage china was simply decorated, generally with multi-coloured sprigs and sprays of flowers or with festooned ribbon borders. Very little of it was decorated with underglaze blue. Gilding was not used, and the glaze was applied before firing, in the usual Chinese manner. In the general output and finer sorts of Bristol china, ribbing, fluting, the embossed pine-cone or scale pattern, scrolls and other moulded low reliefs were employed and some of the vases display considerable ornament modelled in high relief and applied. A brilliant on-glaze blue ground (Plate 91) was used with reserved panels for multi-coloured flowers and birds, but the on-glaze blue usually has a mottled, smeary appearance. Yellow and various other ground colours were more successful. Festoons and wreaths of green leaves afforded a characteristic *motif* and these wreaths sometimes enclosed medallions with a chocolate ground on which appeared Classic figures in *grisaille*. The Bristol gilding was rich (Plate 91), and often beautifully effective. The finer glazed figures were well decorated in enamel colours. The most successful and satisfying of the Bristol decorations were generally the multi-coloured flowers (Plates 76, A; 92, A and 93, A and B), grouped in compositions, scattered, or disposed in garlands and festoons with or without ribbons. Champion was peculiarly successful with the green that appears in laurel leaves and festoons.

THE MARKS. While the factory belonged to Cookworthy & Co. the mark seems to have been the alchemist symbol for tin, the same as the Plymouth mark, painted in gold. The regular Bristol mark after Cookworthy's withdrawal, was a cross, incised in the paste, painted in blue underglaze or, more usually on-glaze, or in gold. The mark "B" was also used. When numerals occur they are the decorator's mark. The Dresden mark in underglaze blue was sometimes employed.

NEW HALL CHINA—1781–1825

HISTORY. When Richard Champion brought the Bristol china works to an end, he transferred his patent rights to a group of experienced potters who, in 1781, established a factory at Tunstall. Upon the withdrawal of two of their number, after some disagreement, in 1782 they removed the establishment to New Hall, at Shelton.

The members of the New Hall company seem unfortunately to have lacked the foresight to acquire either the experienced workmen or the invaluable collection of moulds of the Bristol company. Furthermore, although the New Hall organisation had been virtually established by Champion, the directors were unwilling to follow that worthy pioneer's example. Their ends were first and foremost commercial and they had little interest in maintaining the high standards and ideals of Bristol. At first they continued to make hard paste porcelain but soon made a change to a softer body and, eventually, adopted the bone standard. Content as the New Hall manufacturers were with a product, for the most part, inferior in the quality of its paste, mediocre in its ornamentation, and notable principally for its cheapness, it is not to be wondered at that New Hall china, coloured as it often was in gaudy enamels, with patterns of no particular distinction, failed to make either a wide or enduring appeal. The term of the patent ran out in 1796, and although an half-hearted attempt was made to improve the ware by the adoption of new methods in 1812, the end was stayed for only a short time and the factory was permanently closed down in 1825.

The earlier paste was milk white with a glittering glaze; the later paste was white or slightly greyish-white and had a thin glassy glaze with a somewhat greenish tinge.

The Bristol "cottage china" in all likelihood inspired a good deal of the New Hall product. The decorations were simple, sometimes crudely executed, and without gilding. Not a little of the unmarked china made at New Hall seems to have been attributed to Lowestoft, especially the sort embellished with sprays, sprigs or wreaths of small flowers and minute roses, joined together with little ribbons or lines of dots. In the better pieces produced, where the small flower wreaths or baskets of flowers were reasonably well executed (Plate 103, A and B), the confusion with Lowestoft can be readily understood. The basket device appearing on the teapot is rather characteristic of New Hall. Moulded ornament was occasionally used and landscape subjects were now and again employed. Classic figures, too, may be found but are rare. The colours are often thick and heavy;

again they are noticeably thin. In not a few instances the outlines of the design were transfer printed and the colours were afterwards applied with a brush. For the china decorated with small flowers, in what is usually considered the "Lowestoft" manner, diaper patterns in deep pink or puce were often employed for borders. There were likewise adaptations of various sorts from the Chinese *famille rose* porcelain, and Japanese "Imari" patterns, too, were produced, the details of the design being commonly larger than those of the Derby "Imari."

When the New Hall china was marked, the earliest mark was the letter N incised in the paste; the later mark was the name New Hall in italics in a double circle, transfer printed on the glaze.

PINXTON AND TORKSEY CHINA—PINXTON, 1796–1818; TORKSEY, 1803–1808

HISTORY. John Coke, brother of the Lord of the Manor of Pinxton in east Derbyshire, had developed a keen interest in the manufacture of porcelain as it was then conducted, and consequently when he discovered a fine white earth on the estate at Pinxton he was convinced that it could be used to advantage in making porcelain.

The first reports of trial specimens were unsatisfactory, but Coke, still determined, resolved to try his own hand. He secured the services of William Billingsley, a painter from Derby, built a factory at Pinxton in 1796 and set about establishing what he believed would be a prosperous business.

At first, all went well. The ware produced, while inferior in painting to the chief products of the day, was a fairly good commercial ware. It was mostly decorated with flowers rendered in a more or less realistic manner as this was the type of ornament for which Billingsley was famous. To some extent, however, ground colours were used (Plate 104, B), with reserved panels and in these panels appeared either small landscapes or flower subjects.

As time went on, Billingsley paid less and less attention to the works. He took no active part in the painting and scarcely fulfilled John Coke's idea of an efficient manager. Such a state of affairs could not continue very long and finally they parted—Billingsley to wander about the country, engage in an abortive attempt to make china at Mansfield, and then be heard of later at Torksey; John Coke to recover his declining trade as best he could.

The factory was continued under the management of a Mr. Banks and, later, under a Mr. Cutts, but it never achieved any degree of success and the entire establishment was abandoned in 1818.

The Pinxton ware is sometimes marked with a cursive P in red. Occasionally the marks that appear at the end of the section are also found on china made at Pinxton.

After his failure at Mansfield, Billingsley retired to Torksey in Lincolnshire and, in 1803, established a porcelain factory with the help of his daughters who assisted him with the painting. The products of this venture met with even less success than those of Pinxton and the entire business was an utter failure. The year 1808 saw Billingsley fleeing from his creditors, never to be heard of again as an independent porcelain manufacturer. His Torksey wares are almost impossible to identify as they bear no mark.

CHURCH GRESLEY CHINA—1795-1808

HISTORY. Church Gresley must appear amongst the names of porcelain factories, in spite of the fact that no authentic piece of china emanating thence is known to exist.

This factory, started by Sir Nigel Gresley, seems to have had a tragic, and certainly had a brief, career. Sir Nigel, once Lord of the Manor of Burslem, fell upon evil days and had to retire to the family seat, Church Gresley, near Burton-on-Trent in Derbyshire.

Here, in 1795, he sought to recover his fortunes by the manufacture of porcelain, and although he superintended the work himself, employed his daughter as a decorator, and obtained the professional aid of W. T. Coffee, the Derby modeller, the venture was far from successful.

In 1800, Mr. Nadin, a local colliery proprietor, assumed the responsibilities of the concern, and even though he succeeded in obtaining from Queen Charlotte an order for a dinner service at £700, he was unable to execute the more important pieces such as the plates, platters, dishes and tureens which were all spoiled in the firing.

A third and final proprietor, Mr. Burton, of Linton in Derbyshire, met with no better success in the conduct of the works, and the year 1808 saw the factory definitely closed.

CAUGHLEY CHINA—c.1772-1799; 1799-c.1815

HISTORY. Thomas Turner, a man of some independent means and social standing, sometime an engraver at Worcester, went to Caughley in Shropshire about 1772 and there began the making of porcelain at a pottery that had been established near twenty years earlier but had hitherto made only earthenware.

PLATE 98

A. SPODE OBLONG SUGAR BASON
Creamy paste, clear glaze; typical Chinese decoration in shades of brilliant green, pink, yellow, deep blue, biscuit and gold

B. OVAL, SPIRAL FLUTED CAUGHLEY SUGAR BASON
Creamy paste, faintly bluish glaze; moulded flutings; Chinese decoration in pale green, light and bright yellow, vermilion and cobalt

Courtesy of the Victoria and Albert Museum, South Kensington

PLATE 99

A. SPODE COVERED BUTTER DISH
Creamy paste, glaze of faintly greenish tinge; light grey blue ground with rich gilding, flowers in pink, vermilion, cobalt, yellow and green

B. SPODE STONE-CHINA PLATE
White paste, glaze slightly bluish; rose-coloured diapered border, rest of decoration in rose, biscuit, vermilion, green and deep violet

Courtesy of the Victoria and Albert Museum, South Kensington

PLATE 100

SPODE OVAL DISH WITH SHAPED RIM
Creamy paste clear glaze; transfer printed decoration in warm grey, gilded rim and handles
Courtesy of the Victoria and Albert Museum, South Kensington

PLATE 101

A and *B*. SPODE COVERED BUTTER DISH AND TRAY

Cream paste, clear glaze; bright cobalt ground with reserved panels in white, rich gilding, flowers in pink, blue, burnt orange, deep violet and light green

Courtesy of the Victoria and Albert Museum, South Kensington

For a number of years after Turner started the porcelain factory at Caughley, blue and white ware with printed transfer decorations was the chief article of manufacture and probably no establishment ever did more to popularise blue-printed china. Two characteristic patterns emanated from Caughley that have enjoyed vast popularity and are known the world over—the "willow pattern," and the "Broseley dragon." A London warehouse called the "Salopian China Warehouse" for the sale of Caughley chinaware was established in 1780 at number 5 Portugal Street, Lincoln's Inn Fields.

Thomas Turner retired from business in 1799 and sold the works to John Rose who continued to operate them in connexion with the Coalport factory nearby until 1814 or 1815 when they were closed and dismantled.

THE BODY. The Caughley paste was a good body both whiter and more translucent than the paste of the Worcester china.

THE GLAZE. The glaze was clear, perfectly transparent and of perfectly smooth and even distribution.

ARTICLES MADE AND CONTOUR. Tableware, tea and coffee services and all the "useful" items of chinaware were the chief products. Vases were made and a certain number of decorative items, but none of a large and elaborate character. The contours most favoured were either based on Chinese models or else followed the Neo-Classic impulse dominant at the period.

TYPES OF DECORATION. Until after 1780 the decorations consisted almost altogether of blue-printed transfer patterns, chiefly in Chinese designs, "but produced in a manner that no Chinaman ever dreamt of." Nevertheless, they were very good and the patterns were sharply engraved and cleanly executed. The blue was clear and strong and as the body was whiter than the Worcester body and the glaze perfectly transparent, the Caughley blue and white china never had the same mellowness of the Worcester blue and white which closely approximated the Chinese porcelain in quality. The Caughley blue and white china was sometimes painted in underglaze blue, as well as transfer printed, although transfer printing was usual for the willow pattern. In both cases the later Caughley blue and white was often enriched with bands of gilding and appeared not unlike much of the blue and white Chinese porcelain of the period that was made for export. The willow pattern appeared about 1780 and whole dinner services were made with this design which immediately achieved wide popularity. Dinner services were also painted in underglaze blue with "Chantilly sprigs" after the manner of some of the old Chantilly china.

Turner went to France in 1780 and is said to have brought back several French china decorators. After that date there was greater variety in decoration. Small multi-coloured flowers (Plate 94, B) were much used, either scattered or composed in bouquets, festoons or wreaths. One type of decoration that was very characteristic of Caughley consisted altogether of blue and gold (Plate 97, A and B). The blue appears in bands or in flower shapes and all the delicate sprays, fine tracery and other minute details are done in gold. Besides a great variety of flower subjects, landscapes were employed and also birds with bright plumage. The later flower painting in colours quite holds its own with the work of Worcester.

THE MARKS. The earliest Caughley mark was a C, commonly printed in blue, and closely resembling the

Worcester crescent. S, painted or printed in blue, was also an early Caughley mark. Later, the word "SALOPIAN" was impressed in the paste and sometimes the painted S or C marks were used along with it.

COALPORT CHINA—(1780) 1790 TO PRESENT DAY

HISTORY. In 1780, John Rose, who had been trained at Caughley, established a small porcelain factory at Jackfield nearby. In 1790 he moved his establishment to Coalport, a mile farther down the Severn, and in 1799 bought the Caughley factory. The business from the first prospered exceedingly and, after Rose's death in 1841, was continued by his nephew. After 1875 the establishment was acquired by a company and the business was carried on upon the old site by the Coalport China Company.

THE BODY. The body was white and highly translucent and in every way very similar to the Caughley paste.

THE GLAZE. The Coalport glaze was of especially excellent quality. It had a felspathic basis, like the glaze of hard paste porcelain, but fused at a much lower temperature owing to the use of silicate of soda and potash and a large percentage of borax. When the enamel colours were fired on this glaze they readily fused with it and sank into it so that the mellow effect produced was similar to that of the softer lead glazes on the old soft paste porcelain.

ARTICLES MADE AND CONTOUR. The chief product of the Coalport factory was tableware along with the usual decorative accessories of an average type, although to some extent the more ambitious creations of Sèvres, Dresden and Chelsea were copied in the form of vases and other cabinet pieces.

In contour the Coalport productions in large measure followed the Caughley patterns, but also made direct imitations of the pieces produced at Sèvres and Dresden. Neo-Classic and, later, Neo-Grec impulses were plainly reflected in many of the shapes used.

TYPES OF DECORATION. Besides continuing the Caughley manner of decorating, and emulating the manners of Sèvres and Dresden, painters from Worcester, Derby and the Staffordshire potteries were employed and these men brought with them all the current styles of those places. The deep Mazarine blue ground colour, so famous at Derby, was reproduced at Coalport and many other ground colours were also used, especially pink, apple green, claret, a bright canary yellow, and grey, while a fine *rose Pompadour* was particularly esteemed. In the reserved panels with the ground colours, and also on china without ground colours, the widest variety of decorations were employed (Plate 107, A), including all manner of floral subjects (Plate 108, A), garlands, festoons, wreaths, landscapes, figures, gaily feathered birds (Plates 108, B and 109, A), and heraldic devices. Of common occurrence were basket borders with small flowers, birds and insects, in the Dresden manner; "Swansea roses"; the Brosely dragon in green as well as in blue; the "Bourbon sprig" or cornflower; blue underglaze flowers and sprigs in the old Chantilly fashion; the "worm sprig" pattern in underglaze blue; designs drawn from the Chinese *famille rose* porcelain; flowers, fruit, game and fish naturalistically painted; and moulded patterns in low relief as well as flowers modelled in high relief and coloured. After the Nantgarw factory was discontinued Billingsley migrated to Coalport and continued to paint his well-known roses and other exquisite flowers until the time of his death in 1828. During Rose's lifetime the factory was noted for its elaborate vases embellished with well painted pictures set in panels.

THE MARKS. On early pieces occurs the mark "Coalport." Later, the marks vary. We find "*Coalport,*" "JOHN ROSE & CO., COLEBROOKDALE," "C. B. D.," and "C. D." On some later pieces C and S are combined and in the bows are the small letters C, S and N, for Caughley, Swansea and Nantgarw, the factories absorbed by Coalport.

SPODE CHINA—c.1789 TO PRESENT DAY (COPELAND'S)

HISTORY. Not long after the middle of the eighteenth century, Josiah Spode the elder or "Old Spode," to quote the name by which he is often known, established a pottery near Stoke-on-Trent and produced a great variety of earthenware of beautiful quality. He was a man of cultivation, intelligence, initiative and sound business enterprise and, in the latter part of the century, he entered upon experiments in making porcelain. Although it is impossible to say precisely when the first Spode china was produced, there appears to be good reason for believing that it may have been as early as 1789. In any event, the testimony of the old pattern books shews clearly that porcelain of a fine type was being made by 1794.

Josiah the Elder died suddenly in 1797 and his son, Josiah the Second, assumed the direction of the business, a post for which he was peculiarly well fitted both by his intimate knowledge of all the processes involved and by his good taste and ability in the realm of decoration. The business prospered exceedingly, thanks to the wisdom displayed in its conduct and the good judgment evinced in the matter of decoration, and Josiah Spode left it on a firm basis to his son and partners. The same business continues to-day under the name of Copeland.

THE BODY. Although bone-ash had been used in making English china before "Old Spode" entered the field of porcelain manufacture, it was at the Spode factory first that a correctly determined formula of calcined bones in combination with china clay and china stone was used, and this produced a body which, from the late eighteenth century, became the standard for nearly all subsequent English pastes. At one time Josiah Spode the Second made a venture in what he called "Felspar China," adding pure felspar while reducing the proportion of china-stone, but the previously determined bone porcelain remained the standard and the "Felspar China" was ultimately abandoned, even the formula being destroyed or lost.

The Spode body is a paste of rich tone, white and translucent, without being glassy.

THE GLAZE. The glaze is clear and transparent without being cold and glittering like some of the hard German glazes.

ARTICLES MADE AND CONTOUR. The articles produced consisted chiefly of tableware and the usual decorative accessories, although a number of "important" vases and cabinet pieces were made. Nor should we overlook the great variety of smaller objects such as inkstands, wafer boxes, bird baths and dishes, charming miniature sets, open work baskets and small figures.

The contours to a great extent followed the precedent of earlier-established factories and also reflected the Neo-Classic taste that was paramount when the factory was founded.

TYPES OF DECORATION. One of the most distinctive types of decoration employed in the early days of the Spode factory was what is sometimes known as the Crown Derby Japan Pattern, although the evidence of the Spode pattern books shews that Josiah Spode was devising Anglo-Oriental designs of this type (Plate 102) long before the flood of Japanese designs with which the name of the Derby factory became so closely associated. These patterns, with their deep velvety blues and rich gold, were derived, as already pointed out, from the Japanese Imari porcelain.

Josiah Spode the Second was himself an accomplished designer and his well-matured judgment led him to a preference for a preponderance of Chinese design as appropriate for the decoration of china, although he by no means eschewed other types. The purely English type of decoration, and the French type were both represented very fully in the products of the Spode factory. In the interpretation of Spode Oriental designs there is often observable a strongly English flavour.

The decorations employed on Spode china include floral subjects, fruits, birds (Plates 98, A; 99 and 101), landscapes and figures, along with rich gilding, and were used both in connexion with ground colours (Plate 99) and on china without ground colours. Transfer printing was also much used (Plate 100) in black, blue and other colours and bat-printing was likewise employed in black and in colours. In not a few instances outline designs were transfer-printed and then filled in with colour by brush. This was particularly the case with much of the "Stone" china.

The ground colours frequently used on Spode china include dark blue, scale blue, apple-green, yellow, grey, marbled brown, turquoise, striped red and gold, crimson, marbled blue, salmon, green, lavender, canary and blue, solid gold and dotted or stippled gold, and gold scale on a blue ground.

In an enumeration of the types of decoration must be included raised flowers and birds, the willow pattern, flowers in Chinese taste, apple-green grounds with flowers in panels, views, raised fruit in colours on white grounds in the Dresden taste, bouquets of flowers on white stippled grounds, birds in the Chelsea manner, hunting scenes, bouquets and scattered flowers, numerous adaptations from the Chinese *famille rose* and *famille verte*, adaptations from the Japanese Hizen porcelain, landscapes with raised white flowers as accompaniment, medallions, vine leaves and grapes, butterflies, landscapes in *grisaille*, monochromes in sepia with gold borderings or maroon with gold borderings, and monochromes in other colours also, moulded decorations of various sorts amongst which must be mentioned the white flowers and other small *motifs* in low relief against such coloured grounds as pale lavender or green, Persian *motifs*, arabesques and seaweed patterns, blue and white willow designs, gold fruit and foliage on a royal blue ground, Van Hysum flowers

PLATE 102

A. SPODE VASE IN JAPANESE IMARI MANNER   *B.* SPODE SAUCER AND *C.* SPODE CUP AND SAUCER, IN
Creamy paste, clear glaze; decoration in rich gold, biscuit, brilliant   DIFFERENT VERSIONS OF JAPANESE IMARI MANNER
green, very deep blue and vermilion   Creamy paste, clear glaze decoration in gold, very deep rich blue
vermilion and yellowish green

Courtesy of the Victoria and Albert Museum, South Kensington

PLATE 103

A. NEW HALL CUP AND SAUCER

White paste, glaze of faintly bluish tinge; flower spray, festoon and ribbon decoration in pale bluish green, dull Venetian red, deep pink, deep violet and touches of blue

B. NEW HALL STRAIGHT-SIDED TEAPOT

White paste, glaze of slightly bluish tinge; decoration in pale bluish green, deep pink, deep violet and Venetian red

Courtesy of the Victoria and Albert Museum, South Kensington

PLATE 104

A.

B.

A. SWANSEA VASE WITH MODELLED AND APPLIED FLOWERS IN BISCUIT
White paste, glaze transparent; decoration in gold, light blue, pink, black, vermilion and pale yellow

B. PINXTON JARDINIÈRE
White paste, glaze slightly greenish; buff ground colour, decoration in green, sepia, yellow and gold

Courtesy of the Victoria and Albert Museum, South Kensington

PLATE 105

A. NANTGARW PLATE WITH SHAPED RIM   *B*. NANTGARW PLATE, SHAPED RIM

Paste white, clear glaze; brilliant flower decoration in yellow, blue, pink, vermilion, purple, shaded greens and gold   Paste white, clear glaze; light blue ground colour in rim, with rich gilding, panels in green, yellow, brown, mauve, pink, blue and yellow

Courtesy of the Victoria and Albert Museum, South Kensington

and fruit in a salmon and gold setting, Classic figures inspired by the designs found at Pompeii and Herculaneum, clouds and cupids, Capo di Monte figures, "Mandarin" *motifs*, raised flowers, birds and figures in mat gold on coloured grounds, and the inimitable Billingsley roses and other flowers naturalistically painted on stippled gold grounds or plain gold grounds, besides the other forms of decoration before mentioned.

Spode "Stone China" is not porcelain and strictly speaking has no place in this volume but it was so near an approximation to porcelain and from 1805 onwards, when it began to be manufactured in company with the real china, it exercised such a profound influence and was so popular on account of its beautiful decoration, that it would be both unfair and ungracious not to give it at least a passing mention.

Spode's "Iron Stone Ware," as it was usually called, received colours and preserved their brilliance in a manner surpassing all other stone ware. Furthermore, it was a semi-porcelain and frequently translucent. It had a beautiful white body and the superiority of the products and their comparative cheapness built up their popularity on the Continent to such an extent that the French faïence makers were well nigh driven out of business.

To a great extent Chinese designs derived from the *famille rose* were used for the decoration of the "Stone China" (Plate 99, B), and such patterns as the Peacock design, the Parrot design, the Peony design, and others of similar character, all of which were truly remarkable for the beautiful freshness of their colouring and well balanced composition, earned well merited favour and became justly famous.

THE MARKS. The marks on Spode china are plainly displayed and shew the various changes in the constitution of the firm at different dates.

SPODE   (SPODE / Stone-China)

MINTON CHINA—1798 TO PRESENT DAY

HISTORY. The Minton china factory was established at Stoke-on-Trent by Thomas Minton in 1798, and has continued to the present day. As the experimental days of porcelain production were past and the factory was fortunately spared any spectacular vicissitudes during its career, there is little history to chronicle. The best traditions of the day were followed in the making and decorating of the china and there is nothing particularly distinctive to be noted in that connexion. The decoration was always good and the pieces are plainly marked so that it is not difficult to identify them. The mark was an adaptation of the crossed L's of Sèvres with an M between. Tableware has always been the chief product although decorative accessories also have played their part.

DAVENPORT CHINA—c.1793–1887

HISTORY. The Davenport factory at Longport, a suburb of Burslem, was established by John Davenport about 1793; the business was continued by his descendants till 1887. The body, glaze and workmanship of the Davenport china are of the highest order, but the decorations, for the most part, possess no particular distinction and are exactly like those employed at all the contemporary factories. The influence of Derby, in this respect, is more noticeable than that of others. Elaborate dinner services, dessert services, tea and coffee services and vases were extensively produced. Great use was made of ground colours for rich decorations, an apple-green being particularly favoured. The marks were "DAVENPORT," "DAVENPORT, LONGPORT," sometimes alone and sometimes above an anchor. After 1806 the mark was occasionally "DAVENPORT, LONGPORT, STAFFORDSHIRE," surmounted by a crown.

DAVENPORT

WEDGWOOD CHINA—c.1804

HISTORY. There are in existence a few pieces of Wedgwood china, of more or less average design, and marked with the word "WEDGWOOD" stencilled in blue or red over the glaze. These specimens were manufactured at Etruria by Thomas Byerly in the first decade of the nineteenth century.

The Wedgwood china had a fine light body with a brilliant glaze whose surface was remarkably smooth and satin-like in appearance. Decorations occur in both underglaze blue and enamel colours, the underglaze blue displaying a purplish tinge. The designs often consist of flowers and butterflies, either naturalistically painted or in a conventional Chinese manner with lattices. Butterflies and large flowers in colours were sometimes used and a number of blue and white services were made, enriched with heavy gilding.

For the most part they do not exhibit any of the grace of refinement of the early Wedgwood ware and they met with so little success that the venture of making porcelain was abandoned by the Etruria works after a few years of feeble effort.

NANTGARW CHINA—1811–1822

HISTORY. The Nantgarw porcelain factory was established at the little village of Nantgarw, near Cardiff, in 1811 by that vagrant porcelain painter William Billingsley and a little group of associates who had been induced to support the scheme. The early efforts were marked by discouraging failures and by 1814 all the funds were exhausted. Mr. Dillwyn, a pottery manufacturer of Swansea, however, was persuaded that Billingsley could make good china if he had the proper facilities and the scene of operations was transferred to Swansea.

There the work was attended with more success, but the methods of manufacture were uncertain and the ware was often completely spoiled in the firing. In 1817 Dillwyn, exasperated at the loose methods and the constant waste, sent Billingsley and his assistants packing.

They then returned to Nantgarw where some other associates came to the rescue with fresh capital. Better results now rewarded the endeavours and the Nantgarw china achieved a sudden popularity. The leading London dealers engaged to take as much of it as the factory could make and the Prince Regent ordered a dinner service. The production was limited and a great quantity was spoiled in the firing. Finally, in 1819, the business broke down and the plant was sold at auction. W. Weston Young bought the plant and turned over the management to Thomas Pardoe of Bristol. In 1822 the ultimate collapse came and the factory was closed.

THE BODY. The body was a soft paste, very white and of exceptionally mellow appearance, and remarkably translucent—more translucent, in fact, than any of the other English porcelains.

THE GLAZE. The glaze was clear, soft and mellow, with a rich velvety quality.

ARTICLES MADE AND CONTOUR. Dinner services, tea and coffee services and dessert services were the articles chiefly made, although a certain number of small vases, inkstands and other decorative accessories were also fashioned. The contours were those of the Neo-Grec period and, while agreeable enough, shewed no especial distinction.

TYPES OF DECORATION. The most characteristic *motif* of decoration employed at Nantgarw consisted of flowers (Plate 105, A and B). These flowers were painted in the Billingsley manner, so often seen on Derby china, where a number of blossoms grouped in composition are realistically rendered in rich colouring (Plate 107, B), or else they were painted in the Young manner, single flowers being copied most meticulously as though intended to serve as illustrations of botanical specimens. Fruits were also treated in the same manner and, occasionally, birds supplied the theme. The favourite flowers were Billingsley's admirably painted double roses, along with tulips, lilies and other blooms of brilliant and contrasting colours. Very often butterflies and small insects figured in the decorations, and Pardoe painted birds on branches as well as flowers while, in some instances, single birds executed with the exactitude of ornithological coloured illustrations (Plate 106) supplied the theme. The Billingsley roses and other flowers frequently occur massed in panels reserved on gold grounds (Plate 107, B). For rims and borders ground colours were largely used, sometimes with reserved panels (Plate 105, B) and sometimes without. Moulded ornament in low relief was often employed and, in many cases, the relief was left in the white, the coloured decorations occupying the smooth surfaces. A great deal of the Nantgarw china was decorated not at the works but in London, by Mortlock. Gilding was sparingly applied at Nantgarw; the pieces decorated in London are apt to exhibit much fuller gilding.

THE MARKS. The most usual mark was the name NANT-GARW, impressed in the paste, oftentimes accompanied by the letters C. W., also impressed. Any mark or marks other than this, or *not impressed in the paste*, should be regarded with distrust. Very rare marks are the name Nantgarw beneath a crown, name and crown both being painted in puce colour, or NANT-GARW, in capital letters, in gold, enclosed within a line. The name NANTGARW printed in red is a mark to excite suspicion. A great deal of spurious Nantgarw china is to be found.

NANT GARW   *Nantgarw*
    C.W.

SWANSEA CHINA—1814–1823

HISTORY. Ever since 1764 there had been a prosperous little earthenware factory at Swansea and it was to this little plant that L. W. Dillwyn welcomed Billingsley, Walker and the rest of the disconsolate and ill-fated Nantgarw troupe in 1814, immediately after they were obliged to relinquish their first Nantgarw effort. Kilns were built alongside the earlier pottery and work commenced.

The early Swansea china, made on the first arrival of the Billingsley tribe, was the best and was precisely like that of Nantgarw. The great trouble, however, was that about ninety per cent. of it was regularly spoiled in the firing. To overcome this difficulty, Walker modified the composition of the body.

After 1817, when Dillwyn could no longer stand the frightful expense of these wasteful methods and sent the whole Billingsley contingent flying, the china was made of this modified body and the factory was carried on under the direction of Timothy Bevington, one of the shareholders. In 1820 Bevington became owner of the establishment and work was carried on a little longer, but the venture was not profitable and the factory was closed in 1823.

THE BODY. From 1814 to 1817, while the Billingsley *régime* lasted, the body was the same soft paste as used at Nantgarw—granular, exceedingly translucent, and very white, but with a faint greenish tinge when held up against the light. After Billingsley's departure from Swansea, modifications were made in the body in order to render it harder, denser and more durable. The later paste had a yellowish tinge, a more chalky texture, and was less translucent. Some of it, indeed, was opaque.

THE GLAZE. The glaze on the earlier Swansea china was the same as the Nantgarw glaze. The glaze on the modified body seems to have been softer and was distinguished by its peculiar dead whiteness.

ARTICLES MADE AND CONTOUR. Tableware, dessert services, tea services and the smaller decorative accessories were the products of the Swansea factory. The contours shewed all the usual Neo-Grec characteristics of the period.

TYPES OF DECORATION. The most characteristic decoration of Swansea china consisted of "Billingsley" flowers, that is to say, flowers painted in the manner affected by Billingsley whose methods were greatly admired by most of the china decorators of his time and were closely imitated. For each flower he laid a flat ground of colour and then brushed out the high lights and usually juxtaposed light and dark flowers to intensify the effect. These multi-coloured flowers were sometimes small and arranged in bouquets, knots, garlands and festoons. Birds were often employed as decorative themes and, to a certain extent, low reliefs moulded in the paste were used in conjunction with colour and gilding for the enrichment of plate rims. Decorative scrollwork and ribbons, in colour or in gold, were likewise made use of. Incidentally, gilding was much more freely employed at Swansea than at Nantgarw. There were also wild roses, wild strawberries, and Henry Morris introduced elaborate fruit compositions. To a small extent figure subjects, with stippled grounds, and monochrome landscapes are to be included in the decorative catalogue. Ground colours were a good deal used, frequently of delicate tones, but besides these there were deep blue, pink yellow, buff or biscuit colour and green. Oftentimes marbling or mottling appeared instead of a solid ground colour for the borders of plates and dishes, the marbled effect being produced by a network of lines of a deeper shade than the underlying ground colour or else by a network of gold lines. Figures were not made at Swansea but modelled flowers in high relief, not seldom in the biscuit (Plate

PLATE 106

NANTGARW PLATE
Paste creamy, clear glaze and brilliant: richly gilded rim, decoration in bright yellow and orange, shades of yellow, yellowish green and brown

Courtesy of the Victoria and Albert Museum, South Kensington

PLATE 107

A. COALPORT CUP AND SAUCER
Paste white, glaze slightly bluish; gold banding, monochrome decoration in warm grey

B. EMPIRE-SHAPED NANTGARW INKPOT
Paste white, glaze brilliant; highly naturalistic flower panels in yellow, blue, pink, green and rose, heavy brilliant gilding

Courtesy of the Victoria and Albert Museum, South Kensington

PLATE 108

A. COALPORT BUTTER DISH IN TRAY *B.* COALPORT CYLINDRICAL VASE
Paste white, glaze clear and brilliant; decoration in blue, deep pink Paste creamy, glaze brilliant; decoration in gold, light grey-blue
and light green pink and yellow

Courtesy of the Victoria and Albert Museum, South Kensington

PLATE 109

A. ROCKINGHAM SUGAR BASON   *B.* ROCKINGHAM JUG

Paste white, glaze clear and mellow; decoration in green, blue, pink and gold

Paste creamy, glaze clear; biscuit-coloured ground, heavy gilding, flowers in reserved panels in deep orange, light blue, yellow and green

Courtesy of the Victoria and Albert Museum, South Kensington

104, A), were applied to embellish vases and similar objects, in conjunction with colour and gilding on their smooth surfaces.

THE MARKS. In all likelihood, much of the earlier china made at Swansea bore the Nantgarw mark. The Swansea marks were the name SWANSEA impressed in the paste or printed in red, DILLWYN & CO., BEVINGTON & Co., and, after 1817, a trident was often impressed in the paste along with the other marks.

ROCKINGHAM CHINA—1820-1842

HISTORY. The Rockingham china factory, at Swinton in Yorkshire, was established by Thomas Brameld about 1820 as an outgrowth of the potteries that had flourished for some time previously. The work was under the patronage of Earl Fitzwilliam, Marquis of Rockingham and, for this reason, was called Rockingham china. A few years after the start of the enterprise, Brameld was financially embarrassed, but the Marquis of Rockingham came to the rescue and continued generous support as long as the factory lasted. Despite the ambitious designs of Brameld, the excellence of the body and glaze, and the acclaim with which the ware was received, the works did not pay and were closed in 1842.

THE BODY. The body was bone porcelain of the best quality, dense in texture and creamy white in colour.

THE GLAZE. The glaze was clear, transparent, perfectly distributed and brilliant.

ARTICLES MADE AND CONTOUR. Besides the usual production of table services, dessert services, tea services and all the customary smaller decorative accessories, a number of large and exceedingly elaborate vases and cabinet pieces were made and also statuettes in biscuit, in the Derby manner. The contours were those that distinguished the period when a certain diluted remainder of Neo-Grec influence still survived. Although some of the shapes were fairly good, none of them possessed any real distinction. The best were survivals from former periods. Moulded edges were of common occurrence on dessert services.

TYPES OF DECORATION. Although all the technical processes of manufacture and decoration were perfect, and although no expense was spared to secure the services of the best artists and decorators of the period, the prevailing taste of the time was sinking to lower and lower levels, and the only distinction apparently left for Rockingham china to achieve was in the way of gorgeousness.

All the possible decorative processes, enumerated and explained in earlier pages, were understood and employed and all the earlier modes of decoration, as understood and interpreted at that particular time, were made use of. Ground colours with reserved panels (Plate 109, B), in which were flowers, fruits, birds or landscapes, were particularly favoured, and lavish gilding was extensively practised. Elaborate dessert services with landscapes and still life subjects became a speciality of the works. Most of the pieces were very much over-decorated. Rockingham china is famed both for its beautiful ground colours and for the exquisite finish of its painting. Amongst the favourite ground colours were the noted "Rockingham green," popular for dessert and tea services, apple-green, a darker blue-green, deep mazarine blue, bright blue, azure, three grades of pink, the darkest of which closely approached the famous Chelsea "claret," yellow somewhat deeper then the well-known Derby canary, buff or biscuit colour with gold for borders, pale orange, and a cool grey which, in conjunction with a little gilding, was favourably regarded by Quakers and was presumably devised for their use. Diaper patterns were also occasionally employed to good effect.

THE MARKS. The marks that usually occur are the words "Rockingham Works, Brameld," or "Royal Rockingham Works, Brameld," printed or else impressed in the paste, along with a griffin, the crest of the Fitzwilliam family, impressed or painted in red. The crest is said not to have been used till 1826. Sometimes a royal crown also appears.

WIRKSWORTH CHINA—c.1759–1777 (?); c.1804–?

HISTORY. In the second half of the eighteenth century soft paste porcelain was made at the Holland Manor House, at Wirksworth in Derbyshire. Although the history of the factory is obscure, there seems to be reason to believe that it was established about 1759, that one Gill was connected with it, and that it continued in operation till about 1777. It is believed that pottery was first made at Wirksworth and that porcelain making was a subsequent venture; in what year the manufacture of porcelain began, it is impossible to say. From about 1777 till after the beginning of the nineteenth century there was apparently a cessation of work. Then, sometime subsequent to 1804, it is said that Billingsley revived the Wirksworth establishment for a brief period.

The paste, not of the softest variety, was of good quality, fairly translucent, smooth of texture and of a slightly warm-grey tinge. The products appear to have been chiefly tea equipage, dessert services and the usual sorts of tableware.

Bemrose mentions the similarity of the decorations to those in general use at Lowestoft, while the colouring was strong though not crude. A good deal of delicately moulded ornament in low relief was used—daisies, honeysuckle, roses and leaves. The subjects of decoration were chiefly flowers such as roses, pinks, cornflowers and bluebells, in small scattered sprigs and sprays, in knots and garlands attached with bows of ribbon or with rows of dots, and also occasionally in the form of larger blooms. The tasselled ornament to be found on Lowestoft borders was often employed, as well as dots, and the panels or cartouches for borders filled in with scale or diaper designs. The colours most used were crimson, pink, a reddish brown, puce, blue, green and yellow.

MADELEY CHINA—c.1827–1840

HISTORY. The manufacture and decoration of China at Madeley, in Shropshire, seems to have been the immediate outcome of the discontinuance of the Nantgarw and Swansea china. In its general character the Madeley china was virtually the direct successor of these wares.

The china factory at Madeley was established and conducted by Thomas Martin Randall who, prior to engaging in this enterprise, was a member of the firm of Robins and Randall, Burnsbury Street, Islington, china decorators. During the great popularity of Nantgarw and Swansea china, Mortlock, the London china dealer of Orchard Street, was ready to take every bit of it he could get, whether decorated or "in the white." As a matter of fact, a great deal of it was shipped to London in the white and there decorated, as already mentioned in the account of Nantgarw china. One of the firms that executed much of the decoration was that of Robins and Randall. A considerable amount of the Welsh china, when decorated in the Sèvres manner was profitably sold as "Old Sèvres," for its highly translucent, glassy body closely resembled the earlier French paste. Randall was well aware of the lucrative business to be done in both the Welsh and the old French chinaware, and this knowledge doubtless encouraged him to undertake his manufacturing scheme. Being an experienced chemist, as well as a capable decorator, he was thoroughly familiar with all the processes of making soft paste porcelain. When he severed his connexion with the London firm and went to Madeley, in 1825, he was well prepared for the making of soft paste porcelain.

Two kinds of china were made at Madeley and a third kind was decorated there. There was a soft paste china that was very like the porcelain of Nantgarw, Swansea and the earlier Sèvres; there was a china whose body was somewhat harder and this was produced in a more essentially commercial manner; and there was French chinaware imported in the white, or bearing only slight decorations that could be removed with acid, and of this large quantities were decorated.

In 1840 Randall, having acquired a comfortable fortune and being well advanced in years, retired from business and the Madeley factory was closed.

THE BODY. The china dealers considered the Madeley body the nearest approximation to the old Sèvres soft paste ever made. It was just as translucent as the finest Nantgarw porcelain, but more creamy in tone and, therefore, possessed of the mellow quality characteristic of the best old Sèvres. The Nantgarw was often like snow in the whiteness of its tone; the Madeley paste was more like cream or rich milk. The harder paste had much the same appearance. There was no bone-ash used in the composition.

THE GLAZE. The glaze had the same general resemblance to the old French glaze as the body had to the Sèvres paste.

ARTICLES MADE AND CONTOUR. The articles chiefly made at the Madeley works were tea services, sweetmeat dishes, cake trays, wine coolers, candlesticks, spill vases, cabinet cups and covers, dishes, plates and general tableware and decorative accessories. Besides, there were occasional plaques for furniture inlay and a few statuettes and figures. The contours were both those characteristic of the period and those typical of Sèvres and the other Parisian factories in the latter portion of the eighteenth century.

TYPES OF DECORATION. At Madeley the most capable decorators were employed and nearly all the decoration was distinctly in the French eighteenth century manner, especially in the particulars more or less typical of Sèvres. This following of French fashions was so much the case that not a little of the Madeley china was habitually sold by the dealers at high prices as old Sèvres, and some of them were exceedingly annoyed at "the old Quaker," as they called Randall, because he would not forge the Sèvres marks. On both varieties of paste produced at Madeley the decorations included flowers, fruit, birds, *amorini*, delicately executed landscapes and pastoral scenes after the fashion of Watteau and the painters of his school, along with Rococo scrolls and other incidents of embellishment. The gilding was good and was often of an elaborate character. A number of good ground colours were used, the most successful of which were *rose Pompadour*, turquoise blue, apple-green, and pink.

THE MARKS. Neither kind of Madeley paste shews any marks. This absence of marks made it very easy for dealers when they wished to do so—as it seems a number of them did—to forge marks. Whatever marks were on the French china decorated at Madeley were allowed to remain.

LANE DELPH (MASON) CHINA—LATE EIGHTEENTH CENTURY—c.1850

CAULDON (RIDGWAY) CHINA—1813–c.1858

HISTORY. Some time in the latter part of the eighteenth century Miles Mason established a pottery at Lane Delph (now Middle Fenton) in Staffordshire where a considerable quantity of ironstone china was made and well decorated with patterns similar to those used at Derby. In addition to the ironstone china, however, a certain amount of porcelain seems to have been made in the fore part of the nineteenth century. The popular willow pattern and divers other decorations were used, and a number of the Oriental patterns were printed in blue and red, with gilded borders. The "willow pattern" ware of Lane Delph was often printed in a paler shade of blue than was to be found on wares made elsewhere. About the middle of the nineteenth century the factory was sold and passed through various hands subsequently. The Lane Delph or Mason china displayed a variety of marks, all of which were plainly indicative of the origin.

The Cauldon Place Works, at Shelton, were established by Job Ridgway in 1813. These works continued in the control of the Ridgway family until 1858, when John Ridgway retired and sold out his interests. Earthenware of various sorts, stone-china and porcelain were all made at the Cauldon Place Works. The porcelain was of admirable quality and some of it displayed decorations that were both elaborate and rich. All the decorations were well executed, whether the subjects were flowers, fruit, birds, landscapes or figures. Green, deep blue and *rose Pompadour* were favourite ground colours and the gilding was both rich and excellently laid. Various marks were used, but nearly all of them clearly shew the source of manufacture.

PLATE 110

A. LIVERPOOL CUP AND SAUCER *B.* LONGTON HALL VASE
Paste white, glaze cold white; decoration in bright blue, bluish and yellowish greens, light Indian red and dark vermilion and varied browns   Paste white, glaze slightly greyish; decoration in deep mulberry, yellow, pink and green

Courtesy of the Victoria and Albert Museum, South Kensington

PLATE 111

A. TUCKER SHELL-SHAPED DISH
Milky white paste, clear glaze; decoration in deep blue, light green and gold

B. TUCKER JUG OF CHARACTERISTIC SHAPE, c.1830
Milky white paste, glaze slightly bluish; moulded ornament at base, lip and handle; flowers in natural colours, brilliant gilding

Courtesy of the Pennsylvania Museum, Philadelphia

PLATE 112

A. TUCKER SUGAR BOWL, c.1830
Milky white paste, clear glaze; monochrome landscape decoration in dark brown

B. TUCKER COFFEE POT, c.1830
Milky white paste, clear glaze; all decoration in brown

Courtesy of the Pennsylvania Museum, Philadelphia

PLATE 113

LARGE TUCKER WATER JUG OF CHARACTERISTIC SHAPE, c.1835
Paste milky white, clear, brilliant glaze; typical flower decoration in natural colours, brilliant gilding

Courtesy of the Pennsylvania Museum, Philadelphia

PLATE 114

A. SMALL TUCKER PLATE   B. VASE-SHAPED TUCKER JUG
Milky white paste, clear, brilliant glaze; decoration wholly in   Milky white paste, clear, brilliant glaze; moulded ornament in
gold "spider" pattern   body, gold decoration

Courtesy of the Pennsylvania Museum, Philadelphia

PLATE 115

A. FRAGMENT OF SOFT PASTE PORCELAIN, c.1770
Made at Southwark, Philadelphia. Creamy paste and glaze; decoration in blue

Courtesy of the Pennsylvania Museum, Philadelphia

B. SMALL TEAPOT AND TEACUPS OF ORIENTAL CHINA
One of a set from which William Penn drank tea in Philadelphia

Courtesy of Mrs. H. Genet Taylor

PLATE 116

A. BLUE STAFFORDSHIRE PLATE *B.* LIVERPOOL JUG, c. 1800
Transfer printed in underglaze blue; made for the American trade, Transfer printed in black, made for the American trade
view of the old waterworks in Philadelphia

Courtesy of the Pennsylvania Museum, Philadelphia

AMERICAN CHINAWARE

To many it may appear strange that more space has not been devoted to American china. As a matter of actual fact, very little china was made in America prior to 1840, the year up to which this volume treats of china making. Most of the old china in America, with the exception of the products of one exceptional china factory, is either china made at one of the factories already enumerated in England or else china imported from the East. The china of the British factories forms part of the common Anglo-Saxon heritage, along with language, laws and customs.

The plates, platters, dishes tureens jugs and tea services with American buildings, views and public personages printed in blue as decorations, were, almost without exception, made at Liverpool or the Staffordshire potteries for the American market. Comparatively few of them are really chinaware at all. Most of them are an excellent quality of white earthenware or stone china and, therefore, strictly speaking, do not come within the purview of this volume which deals with porcelain of both the soft paste and hard paste types and the bone-porcelain, which stands mid-way between the two.

As pointed out, in the earlier sections, the chinaware of Oriental and English origin can be studied and collected in America just as well as in England, for it was brought to America in the Colonial period and in the early years of the Republic by ship-loads.

THE GLAZE. The glaze was clear, soft and of a velvety quality.

ARTICLES MADE AND CONTOUR. The articles made were of the "useful" sort and included dinner services, dessert services with fretwork fruit baskets, tea services and all the small table accessories. The shapes were those then current in England and were patterned on those of Bow, Chelsea and Worcester.

TYPES OF DECORATION. The types of decoration included moulded devices in low relief and painted flowers and leaves in underglaze blue.

THE MARKS. The mark was a small P in underglaze blue.

In the Pennsylvania Museum (Memorial Hall) there is a piece (Plate 116, A) of this ware, belonging to the Franklin Institute, which once formed part of a dinner and dessert service. It is of good quality and compares favourably with the early work of Bow or Worcester.

BERGEN (NEW JERSEY) CHINA—c.1825

HISTORY. "The Jersey Porcelain and Earthenware Company," was incorporated in the town of Bergen, New Jersey, on the 10th of December, 1825. "In the following year," we are told by Dr. Barber, "the products of the factory were awarded a silver medal at the exhibition of the Franklin Institute, Philadelphia, as being the 'best china from American materials.'" In the Trumbull-Prime Collection in Philadelphia there is a bowl of good body and glaze made at Bergen. The manufacture of porcelain did not continue, however, more than a couple of years and seems never to have produced any appreciable results.

AMERICAN CHINAWARE

NEW YORK CHINA—c.1816

HISTORY. Porcelain is said to have been made in New York City early in the nineteenth century, probably by Dr. Mead, and it is believed that ware of an excellent quality was produced from American materials, but data concerning this venture and authenticated pieces, with one or two exceptions, are lacking. In the Pennsylvania Museum, (Memorial Hall) Philadelphia, there is a vase fifteen inches high, of soft paste body and exceedingly white glaze marked "finished in New York, 1816." There is no gilding and it is without coloured decoration.

PHILADELPHIA (TUCKER) CHINA—1825-1838

HISTORY. From 1816 to 1822, Benjamin Tucker, a Philadelphia Quaker, had a china shop in Market Street. His son, William Ellis Tucker, who had a talent for drawing and painting, often decorated the china and his father built for him a kiln in the back premises wherein to fire it. The younger Tucker was obsessed with the notion of making porcelain and carried on numerous experiments to that end. At length, having satisfied himself that he could achieve his purpose, he established a china factory in 1825, his younger brother Thomas being associated with him. In 1828, Thomas Hulme became a partner and in 1832 Judge Joseph Hemphill became a member of the firm. William Ellis Tucker died in 1832 but the business was carried on with great success until 1838, when it was discontinued.

THE BODY. The body was neither the same as the French soft paste porcelain nor was it the same as the bone porcelain made in England, but it had characteristics common to both. It was, indeed, more nearly allied to the

BIBLIOGRAPHY

BIBLIOGRAPHY

1. "THE NEW CHAFFERS": MARKS AND MONOGRAMS ON EUROPEAN AND ORIENTAL POTTERY AND PORCELAIN, WITH HISTORICAL NOTICES OF EACH MANUFACTORY:* William Chaffers, 13th Edition. Reeves & Turner, London, 1912.

2. ENGLISH PORCELAIN: Arthur Herbert Church, Chapman & Hall, London, 1885.

3. PORCELAIN, ORIENTAL, CONTINENTAL AND BRITISH: R. L. Hobson, E. P. Dutton & Co., New York, 1906.

4. OLD ENGLISH CHINA: Mrs. Willoughby Hodgson, G. Bell & Sons, London, 1913.

5. POTTERY AND PORCELAIN: A HANDBOOK FOR COLLECTORS; Translated from the Danish of Emil Hannover, with notes and appendices, by Bernard Rackham, E. Benn, Ltd., London, 1925.

6. A HISTORY AND DESCRIPTION OF ENGLISH PORCELAIN: William Burton, Cassell & Co., London, 1902.

7. A BRIEF HISTORY OF OLD ENGLISH PORCELAIN AND ITS MANUFACTORIES: M. L. Solon, Bemrose & Sons, London, 1903.

8. CHELSEA PORCELAIN: William King, Benn Bros., London, 1922.

9. CATALOGUE OF THE SCHREIBER COLLECTION OF PORCELAIN: Victoria and Albert Museum, South Kensington; His Majesty's Stationery Office, London, 1915.

10. CATALOGUE OF THE HERBERT ALLEN COLLECTION OF ENGLISH PORCELAIN: the Victoria and Albert Museum, South Kensington, Bernard Rackham, His Majesty's Stationery Office, London, 1917.

---

*This compendious book is veritably the china lovers' and collectors' "Bible", so to speak. It contains an enormous quantity of data regarding every aspect of both pottery and porcelain and is an indispensable source of reference for the student.

BIBLIOGRAPHY

11. CATALOGUE OF THE COLLECTION OF ENGLISH PORCELAIN IN THE DEPARTMENT OF BRITISH AND MEDIAEVAL ANTIQUITIES AND ETHNOGRAPHY OF THE BRITISH MUSEUM: R. L. Hobson, London, 1905.

12. CONTRIBUTIONS TOWARDS THE HISTORY OF EARLY ENGLISH PORCELAIN: J. E. Nightingale, Bennett Bros., Salisbury, 1881.

13. THE CERAMIC ART OF GREAT BRITAIN: Frederick William Llewellynn Jewitt, J. S. Virtue & Co., London, 1883.

14. ENGLISH POTTERY AND PORCELAIN: Edward Andrews Downman, London, 1918.

15. THE FIRST CENTURY OF ENGLISH PORCELAIN: W. Moore Binns, Hurst & Blackett, London, 1906.

16. SPODE AND HIS SUCCESSORS: Arthur Hayden, Cassell & Co., London, 1925.

17. OLD SPODE: T. G. Cannon, F. A. Stokes & Co., New York, 1924.

18. THE CERAMICS OF SWANSEA AND NANTGARW: W. Turner, Bemrose & Sons, London, 1897.

19. WORCESTER PORCELAIN: R. L. Hobson, B. Quaritch, London, 1910.

20. A CENTURY OF POTTING IN THE CITY OF WORCESTER: Richard William Binns, London, 1877.

21. THE CHEYNE BOOK OF CHELSEA CHINA AND POTTERY: Reginald Blunt, London, 1924.

22. THE POTTERY AND PORCELAIN OF DERBYSHIRE: Alfred Wallis and W. Bemrose, Junior, Bemrose & Sons, London, 1870.

23. LONGTON HALL PORCELAIN: William Bemrose, Bemrose & Sons, London 1906.

24. OLD BOW CHINA: Egan Mew, T. C. & E. C. Jack, London, 1909.

25. CHELSEA AND CHELSEA-DERBY CHINA: Egan Mew, T. C. & E. C. Jack, London, 1909.

26. BOW, CHELSEA AND DERBY PORCELAIN: William Bemrose, Bemrose & Sons, London, 1898.

BIBLIOGRAPHY

27. THE OLD DERBY CHINA FACTORY: John Haslem, G. Bell & Sons, London, 1876.
28. CHATS ON ENGLISH CHINA: Arthur Hayden, F. A. Stokes & Co., New York, 1904.
29. THE A. B. C. OF COLLECTING OLD ENGLISH CHINA: J. F. Blacker, G. W. Jacobs & Co., Philadelphia, 1910.
30. THE CHINA COLLECTOR: H. William Lewer, D. McKay, Philadelphia, 1914.
31. A HISTORY AND DESCRIPTION OF FRENCH PORCELAIN: E. S. Anscher, Translated by William Burton, London, 1905.
32. PORCELAIN: William Burton, London, 1906.
33. ROBERT HANCOCK AND HIS WORKS: A. R. Ballantyne, London, 1885.
34. POTTERY AND PORCELAIN IN THE UNITED STATES: Dr. Edwin Atlee Barber, New York, 1901.
35. CHINESE PORCELAIN BEFORE THE PRESENT DYNASTY: S. W. Bushell, Pekin, 1886.
36. CHINESE ART: S. W. Bushell, Handbook, Victoria and Albert Museum, South Kensington, 2 VOLS. 1906.
37. CHINESE POTTERY AND PORCELAIN, BEING A TRANSLATION OF THE T'AO SHUO: S. W. Bushell, Oxford, 1910.
38. LA MANUFACTURE DE PORCELAINE DE CHANTILLY: Paris, 1892.
39. HISTOIRE DES MANUFACTURES FRANÇAISE DE PORCELAINE: Comte de Chavagnac, Paris, 1906.
40. LES ORIGINES DE LA PORCELAINE EN EUROPE: Baron J. C. Davillier, Paris, 1882.
41. PORCELAIN: E. J. Dillon, London, 1904.
42. HISTOIRE DE LA CÉRAMIQUE, POTERIE, FAÏENCES ET PORCELAINS CHEZ TOUS LES PEUPLES: E. Garnier, Tours, 1882.
43. THE SOFT PASTE PORCELAIN OF SÈVRES: E. Garnier, London, 1892.

BIBLIOGRAPHY

44. DICTIONNAIRE DE LA CÉRAMIQUE: E. Garnier, Paris, 1893.

45. DISCORSO SULLA FABBRICA DI PORCELLANA STABILITA IN VINOVO: Vittorio Amadeo Gioanetti, Torino, 1859.

46. CHINESE PORCELAIN AND HARD STONES: Edgar Gorer and J. F. Blacker, London, 1911.

47. LA CÉRAMIQUE CHINOISE: E. Grandidier, Paris, 1894.

48. CHINESE PORCELAIN: W. G. Gulland, London, 4th Edition, 1918.

49. ROYAL COPENHAGEN PORCELAIN: Arthur Hayden, London, 1911.

50. PORCELAIN OF ALL COUNTRIES: R. L. Hobson, London, 1906.

51. HISTOIRE ARTISTIQUE, INDUSTRIELLE ET COMMERCIALE DE LA PORCELAINE: A. Jacquemart et E. Le Blant, Paris, 1862.

52. HISTORY OF THE CERAMIC ART: A. Jacquemart, Translated by Mrs. Bury Palliser, London, 1873.

53. HISTOIRE ET FABRICATION DE LA PORCELAINE CHINOISE: Stanislas Julien, Paris, 1856.

54. HISTORY OF THE COALPORT PORCELAIN WORKS: Frederick William Llewellynn Jewitt, London, 1862.

55. THE GARLAND COLLECTION IN THE METROPOLITAN MUSEUM, NEW YORK: Laffan, New York, 1907.

56. THE SÈVRES PORCELAIN OF BUCKINGHAM PALACE AND WINDSOR CASTLE: Guy Laking, London, 1907.

57. LA MANUFACTURE DE PORCELAINE DE SÈVRES: Gaston de Breton, Paris, 1882.

58. POTTERY AND PORCELAIN: Frederick Litchfield, London, 1912.

59. A HISTORY OF POTTERY AND PORCELAIN: J. Marryat, London, 1868.

60. HISTORY AND DESCRIPTION OF CHINESE PORCELAIN: W. C. Moukhouse, Notes by S. W. Bushell, London, 1901.

61. LA FABBRICAGIONE DELLA PORCELLANA IN NAPOLI E DEI PRODOTTI CERAMICI AFFINI: G. Novi, Napoli, 1879.

BIBLIOGRAPHY

62. RELICS OF WILLIAM COOKWORTHY: Prideaux, 1853.
63. LOWESTOFT CHINA: W. W. R. Spelman, London, 1905.
64. CONTINENTAL CHINA: C. H. Wylde, London, 1907.
65. CHINA COLLECTING IN AMERICA: Alice Morse Earle, New York, 1907.
66. OLD ENGLISH CHINA WITH AMERICAN VIEWS: Edwin Atlee Barber, Indianapolis, 1899.
67. THE OLD CHINA BOOK: N. Hudson Moore, F. A. Stokes & Co., New York, 1903.

INDEX

INDEX

A

Advice, to china student, 30-37
Albrechtsburg, Castle of, 179, 181
Alcora, china, 177
Ale, breakfast beverage, 2
Alençon, kaolin and felspar, 166
Alluaud, M., 172, 173
Atlantic seaboard, 12
America, 12, 13
American, china, 293-299; Colonies, 4
Amstel, china, 207-210
Anglo-Oriental, designs, 275
d'Angoulême, Fabrique du Duc, 164
Ansbach, 200
Antheaume, 112
Antonibon, Pasquale, 100
Applied reliefs, 26
Arabesques, 157, 276; Classic, 161; Renaissance, 161
d'Argenson, Marquis, 121, 135
Arita, 75, 77; china, 79, 80
Armand, 147
Armorial bearings, 52, 148, 228, 246, 258, 262
Arras china, 150
d'Artois, Comte, 154; Fabrique du, china, 155-158
Aubert, 147
Aubiez, Maurin des, 154

Augustus III, Elector of Saxony, 237; the Strong, 178
Austrian china, 201-203

B

Bachelier, 120, 147
Banks, Mr., 267
"Barbary" porcelain, 92
Barber, Dr. E. A., 296
Barbin, François, 115; Jean-Baptiste, 115
Barnegat sands, 12
Baroque, age, 35; contour, 35, 36; manner, 109
Barr, Martin, 242; Flight & Barr, 243
Barrachin, 155
Bartolozzi, 246
Basketwork, 245; moulded, 91
Bassano, 100
"Batavian" ware, 66
Battersea, 229
Bat-printing, 246, 276
de Baynal, 112
Bayreuth, 200
"Beach" china, 12
Belgian china, 211, 212
Bellevue, château de, 121
Bengraf, 195
Benjamin, 156
Bergen china, 296

INDEX

Berlin china, 187-190
Berthevin, Pierre, 213
Bevington, Timothy, 283, 285
de Beyerlé, Baron Jean Louis, 169, 170, 171
Billingsley, William, 266, 267, 273, 280-284; manner, 281; roses, 277, 281, 282
Biscuit, 15, 17, 94, 100; Bristol, 262; Sèvres, 142; Swansea, 284
Blanc de Chine, 61
Bleu du Roi, 117, 126, 131, 146, 199
"Blue and white" ware, 28, 47, 48, 51, 63, 80
Bloor, Robert, 248, 251
Boboli, Gardens, 83
"Bodiless" porcelain, 46, 53
Bohemia, materials from, 201
Boileau, M., 135, 153, 167
du Bois, brothers, 119, 120, 122; Madame, 5
Boizot, 147
Bone, ash, 20, 21, 224, 225, 235, 243, 290; china, 235, 285; paste, 23; procelain, 20, 21
Bonnin, Gousse, 295
Boston, 4, 294; *Evening Post*, 294
Böttger, Johann Friedrich, 178, 179, 180, 184
Boucher, 238; children, 211
Bouchet, 147
Bouillat, 147
"Bourbon sprig", 272
Bourdon-Desplanches, 155, 156, 157

Bourg-la-Reine china, 149, 150,
Bourgogne, Duchesse, de, 105
Bow, 34, 87, 98, 195, 197; workmen and decorators, 257
Bow china, 220-230
Bowcocke, John, 221-223
Brameld, Thomas, 285, 287
Brancas-Lauraguais, Comte de, 166
Bristol, china, 260-264; London warehouse, 261; works, 259
British Museum, 46, 60
"Brocaded" ware, 80
Brodel, Giovanni, 101
Brongniart, 88, 141, 142, 143
Broseley dragon, 269, 272
Brunswick, Duke of, 195
Brussels china, 211, 212
Buen Retiro china, 176, 177
Buontalenti, Bernardo, 83
Burlington Magazine, 236, 237
Burmah, 42
Burton, William, 17, 20, 25, 36, 41, 224; Mr., of Linton, 268
Busts, 89
Butterflies, 279
Byerly, Thomas, 279

C

Cabbage-leaf jugs, 245, 256
Cadet, 160
Caen china, 174, 175
Caffieri, 147
Cairo, 9; porcelain market, 42
Camelford, Lord, 259

INDEX

Campo, 88
Canary-yellow, Derby, 287
Canton, 10
Capo di Monte china, 95-100; 91, 176; factory, 88; figures, 277; imitations, 204
Carl Eugen, Duke of Würtemberg, 197, 198
Cartouches, 148, 209
Cassel, 200
Castle Green, 260
Caughley china, 268-271; "blue and white," 257; factory, 242; "willow pattern," 257
Cauldon, china, 291, 292; Place Works, 292
Cavendish, Lady, 229
Celadon ware, 29, 75, 80, 108; exported, 41, 42; origin of name, 42
Chabry, 147
Chaffers, Richard, 253, 254; & Co., 254
Chamberlain, Robert, 242, 243; factory, 247
Champion, Richard, 259-261, 263, 264
Chanou, 160, 161
Chantilly china, 111-114; 34, 87, 90, 91, 118, 122, 137, 235; Château de, 111; formula, 122; "Chantilly sprigs", 270
Chapelle, Jacques, 127, 128
Charles, III. King of Naples, 95, 96, 176; VII, 78; Théodore, 168, 198
Chartres, Duc de, 154

Chelsea china, 230-239; 87, 195, 197; decorators, 241; "claret-colour", 287; factory, 247; painters, 244, 245
Chelsea-Derby, china, 234; period, 238, 239, 250
Chicanneau, Dominic, 108; Geneviève, 107; Jean Baptiste, 107; Pierre, 107; M. 106
"Chicken cups," 49
Chihli, 43
China, 9; mania, 1-13; clay, 17, 18; "of china," 14; stone, 17, 18, 20
Chinaware, making of, 22-29; Oriental, 38-82; what it is, 14-21
Chinese, dragon, 257; chrysanthemums, 227; lattices, 279; *motifs*, 202, 227; porcelain, 52-54, 241; chief periods of, 38, 39, golden age of, 50; peonies, 227; shapes, 109; taste, 117
Ch'ing Dynasty, 39, 50-52; Emperors of, 40
Ching-tê Chên, 43-45, 50, 51, 53, 74, 76
Chinoiseries, 95
"Chintz" patterns, 202
Chinsi, 88
Chocolate-drinking, 2, 3
Christian, Philip, 253
Chrome green, underglaze, 146
Chün Chou yao, 41, 63
Church Gresley china, 268
Cinnabar, 63

Cirou, Ciquaire, 111, 112
"Claret-colour," Chelsea, 246, 287; claret-coloured ground, 238
Classic, devices, 95, 99, 100
Clay, "short", 22; "fat", 22
Clignancourt china, 161-163
Clodion, 147
Cloisonné, 45
Coalport, china, 271-273; China Co., 271; factory, 269
Cobalt, 28; blue, 63; Persian supply, 47
Cock & Co, 222
Coffee, W. T., 268; drinking, 2, 3
Coke, John, 266, 267
Colours, 90; coloured decoration, 24
Comb pattern, 80
Condé, Prince de, 111, 112
Contour, characteristic Chinese, 56-60; of periods, 35; flat bowl, 34; Japanese, 78
Cookworthy, William, 258, 259, 260; & Co., 261, 264
Copeland, 274; Copelands china, 273
Copenhagen china, 215-217, 257; "Copenhagen" patterns, 184, 217
Copper-red, 63
Cornflower *motif*, 148, 157, 171, 272
Cornish, coast, 10; customs gauger, 11; kaolin and felspar, 258
Cosway, 246
"Cottage china", Bristol, 262, 265
Coudray, Barbe, 107

Courtille, Fabrique de la, china, 159, 160
de Coussy, Mathieu, 8
Cox, James, 233, 234
Cozzi, china, 92; Geminiano, 93; factory, 94, 95
Crackled ware, 55, 61
Craft, T., 223
Crockery, 2
Crowther, John, 221, 223
Crusaders, 7
Cumberland, Duke of, 231
Custine, Comte de, 170, 171
Cutts, Mr., 267
Cyfflé, 170
Cyphers, 148

D

Daishoji, 81
Danish china, 215-217
Darton, 213
Davenport, china, 278, 279; John, 278
Davis, William, 240
"Dead-leaf" brown glaze, 186
Decoration, Chinese, 60-71; depending on glaze alone, 60-63; slip, 61, 63; underglaze colour, 61, 63-65; glazes of several colours, 61, 65; enamel colours over glaze, 61, 65-67; *famille noir*, 61, 65; *famille verte*, 61, 65; *famille rose*, 61, 65-67; chrysanthemum and peony, 61, 66; "Mandarin", 61-63, 64, 66; "India", 61, 64, 66;

INDEX

"Imari", 61, 66; Kakiyemon, 61, 66; reserved panel, 61, 66; "Jesuit", 61, 66, 67; "Lowestoft", 67; coral red, 61, 65; Japanese, 78, 79; *en camaïeu*, 119, 127; enamel painted, 28, 29, 50; coloured, technique, 49; monochrome, 44; polychrome, 44, 45, 90, 109; individual types, 34; methods of, 26-29; white, 26, 27; colour and gold, 27-29; underglaze colours, 29; coloured glazes, 29

Deleneur, 150

Delft, 207; decorations, 256; pottery, 2

De Moitte, 162

Derby china, 247-251, 36

Diaper patterns, 45, 67, 68, 69, 80, 81, 126, 146; lattice, 147; "partridge eye", 117, 131, 146; trellis, 147; diapered borders, 228, grounds, 67

Dietrich, 181

Dihl, 164

Dillwyn, L.W., 280, 282, 283, 285

Directoire, *motifs*, 148

Doccia china, 84-92; factory, 87; paste, 89

Dodin, 147

Dorez, Barthélemy, 110

Dragon, "Broseley", 269, 272; Chinese, 257

Dresden, china, 178-187, 34, 87, 90, 91, 93, 112, 120; occupied, 180; factory looted, 186; paste, 124, manner, 124, 272

"Dress, services", 246

"Dryander, M., 170

Duesbury, William, 223, 233, 234, 238, 247-250

Duplessis, 120, 124, 143, 147

Durnford, Clark, 255

Dutch, china, 207-211; East India merchants, 76

E

East India Companies, English, Dutch and French, 7; East India Company, 10; French East India Co., 110

"East India" flowers, 185

"Egg-shell," porcelain, 46, 53, 80

Egypt, 41; Egyptian *motifs*, 148

Ehrenreich, 213

Emblems, 67, 71, 72, 73

Embossing, 26

Empire Style, 89; "frigidities" of, 181

Enamel colours, 24, 27, 28, 29, 75, 81, 90, 95

England, 12, 13

English china, 220-292; "English pink", 28

Engraving, 26, 81

Este china, 102

Etruria, 279, 280

Etruscan, *motifs*, 148; types, 91, 92

Etterbeek, 211, 212

d'Eu, Comte, 149

European, porcelain, 19

"Export wares", Oriental, 38; export of Chinese porcelain, 50

F

Falconet, 147
Famille rose china, 51, 258, 266, 272, 276, 277; *noir*, 51; *verte*, 50, 51, 276
Faubourg, St. Antoine, 107, 160, 165; St. Denis, 155; St. Honoré, 107
Fauquez, Sieur, 173
Fawkener, Sir Everard, 231, 233, 237
Felspar, 17, 18, 20, 89; "Felspar china", Spode, 274
Fên Ting, 43
Ferdinand IV., 96
Ferrara, 102
Figures, 23, 89, 94, 236; Bow, 229; Chelsea, 249; Chinese, 56; St. Cloud, 108; Swansea, 284
Fillets, 71
Firing, 45, 46; coal, 155; china, 24; Japan, 25; processes, 23
Fischer, Moritz, 203
Fitzwilliam, Earl, 285
Flight, Thomas, 242; &Barr, 242
Florence, 11, 83, 84, 85
Flowers, modelled, 114, 122, 123, 125; flower, holders, 123; pots, 116
Fontaine, 148
Fontanieu, 160
Forget-me-nots, 148
Fournier, 172; Louis, 215, 216
Fox, Henry, 236
France, 13, 34
Francesco I., de'Medici, 83

Francis I., 8
Frankenthal, 153, 168, 193; china, 198-200
Franklin Institute, 296
Franks, Sir Wollaston, 60, 70
Frederick, Augustus, 120; the Great, 180, 187-189
French china, 103-175; porcelain, 87
Fretwork, 26, 27
Frye, Thomas, 221, 229
Fuchien, province of, 44; white ware, 27, 45, 53, 61, 90, 98, 109, 226
Fujiyama, 79
Fulda, 200
de Fulvy, M., 119, 120, 122, 125
Fürstenberg china, 195-197

G

Gentleman's Magazine, 241
Gérin, 119
German, china, 178-200; "German flowers", 185, 192, 202; porcelain, 18, 19
Gerona china, 177
Gerréault, Sieur, 132
Gessner, Solomon, 206
Gilding, 24, 95, 129, 156; Bristol, 263; Nantgarw, 282; raised, 202; restrictions, 136; secret of, 125; Sèvres, 148; Swansea, 284; Wedgwood, 279
Ginori, china, 84-92, 11, 35; family, 88; Marquis, 11; reproductions, 100

INDEX

Gioanetti, Dr., 101
Girandoles, 226
Glaser, 195
Glaze, character of, 24-26; composition characteristic Chinese, 54-56; crackled, 42, 52; coloured 42, 44, 45, 55, 81; "transmutation", 55, 62; "tear-drops", 56; vari-coloured, 55; Celadon, 62; *sang de boeuf*, 62; *Clair de lune*, 62; "dead-leaf" brown 62; *café au lait*, 62; soufflé, 62; jasper, 62; *flambé*, 62
Glazing, processes, 23-26
"Goat and bee" jugs, 230
"Gold Chinamen", 183, 218
Gombroon ware, 3, 9, 10, 105
Gorodayu Go-Shonzui, 74
Gotzkowski, 187, 190
Gouyn, Charles, 230, 231
Granby, Marquis of, 245
Gravant, M., 119, 120, 122, 125
Greek *motifs*, 148
Grellet, M., 172
Gresley, Sir Nigel, 268
Grisaille decorations, 263, 276
Grousfeldt-Diepenbrock, Count, 207
Grotesque figures, 108
Ground colours, 91, 100, 117, 131, 185, 246, 260, 276, 292; Rockingham, 286; Sèvres, 146
Groups, 89; Sèvres, 147
Guerhard, 164
Guettard, 160
Guiche, Duchesse de, 106

H

Hague, The, 207; china, 210, 211
Hancock, R., 245, 246
Hannong, family, 153, 154, 158, 200; Joseph Adam, 168, 169; Paul, 166, 167, 168, 169, 198; Pierre Antoine, 101, 155, 156, 158
Harbour scenes, 98
Hard-paste porcelain, 13, 16-19; conchoidal fracture, 16; enamel colours, on, 28
Haviland, M. Charles, 173
"Hawthorn" pattern, 63
Heath, John, 233, 247, 249
Heidegger, 206
Hellot, 120, 122, 123, 125, 126
Hemphill, Judge Joseph, 297, 299
Herbo, Dorchies, 151
Herculaneum, 98, 99, 277; Works, 254
Herend china, 203, 204
Herold, Johann G., 180, 184, 185
Hettlinger, 139
Heylyn, Edward, 221
Hewelche, 93
Hirado, 77, 78, 81
Hizen, 75, 80, 81; porcelain, 276
Höchst, china, 190-192; workmen, 206; runaway workmen, 187
Holland, House, 236, 237; Manor House, 287
Holdship, Richard, 249
Hudson, Manorial families of, 5
Huet, 156

INDEX

Huline, Thomas, 297, 298
Hunger, Christoph Conrad, 94, 98, 201, 218
Hyakken, 75

I

Imari, "brocaded" patterns, 185; decoration, 227; designs, 238, 275; Japanese, 54; patterns, 202, 250, 266; *motifs*, 114; ware, 76, 80, 112, 246
Imitative shapes, 33, 34; styles, 34
India, 41
"Indian flowers", 192, 202
Ink pots, 113
"Iron Stone Ware", Spode, 277
Italian china, 83-102

J

Jackfield, 271
Jacquemart, 62
Jacques et Jullien, 115, 116, 128, 149
Jade, 41
Japanese, birds and flowers, 202; China, 74-82; decoration, 34; designs, 275; examples, 226; influence, 238; porcelain, 34, 38, 74-82, 112
"Japan Patterns", Crown Derby, 275
Jersey Porcelain and Earthenware Co., 296
"Jewelled" Sèvres, 148
Julien, 147
Ju Yao, 41

K

Kaga, 75, 80
Kakiyemon, 75, 77; decoration, 112, 184; designs, 238; manner, 117, 227; *motifs*, 114; ware, 79
Kändler, Johann, 180, 183, 189
K'ang Hsi, reign of, 50
Kaolin, 17, 18, 20, 22, 53, 74, 75, 89
Kauffmann, Angelica, 246
Kean, Mr., 248, 251
King, of Poland, 178; William, 231
Kingston-on-Hudson, 6
Kioto, 75; china, 82
Kloster-Veilsdorf, 200
Knife handles, 113, 116
Korrodi, 206
Korzec, 219
"Kronenberg" ware, 198
Kuan yao, 41
Kühn, 181
Kühne, Chrétien, 212
Kutani, ware, 77, 78, 81, 82

L

"Lace" decoration, 189
"Lady pattern", 238
La Fontaine, fables, 171
Lalande, 160
Lallenment, 112
Lambrequins, 117
Lamoniary, M., 173
Lancret, 118
Lane Delph, china, 291, 292

INDEX

Lanfrey, François, 170, 171
Langen, Baron von, 195
Lassia, 160, 161
Lauraguais china, 166
Leaf-shaped dishes, 237
Leboeuf, Andrè-Marie, 163
Lecot, 147
Le Guay, 147
Leichner, Anton, 210
Leithner, 203
Leipzig, Easter Fair, 180
Lemaire, Sieur, 154, 165
Lemire, 170
Le Nove, china, 100, 101
Le Riche, 147
Levaux, 147
Lille, china, 110, 111
Limbach, 200
Limoges, china, 172, 173; kaolin, 174
Lisbon, china, 177
Lister, Dr. Martin, 105
Littler, William, 247, 251
Liverpool, *Advertiser*, 254; china, 253, 254; Museum, 253
Locker, Mr., 248
Locré, 159
London, auction sales, 222; warehouse, 222
"Long Elizas", 64
Longport, china, 278, 279
Longton Hall, 247; china, 251, 252
Louis XIV., 6, 9; XV., 137, 138, 144; court, 115; style, 36; XVI., 138, 140, 143, 144, 145, 151, 152; Philippe, 154, 165

Löwenfinck, A. F. von, 190
Lowestoft, china, 254-258; decoration, 265, 288; china warehouse, 255
"Lowestoft", Chinese, 52; manner, 228
Ludwigsburg, china, 197, 198
Lunéville, 170
de Luynes, Duc, 121
Lyes, J. 240

M

Macquer, 125
Madeley, china, 288-291
Madrid, china, 176, 177
Maestro Antonio, 92
Maine, Duchesse de, 128
Mainz, Archbishop of, 190
Manchu, Dynasty, 39, 50-52
"Mandarin" china, 83, 85, 228, 258, 277
Mann, Sir Horace, 11
Mansfield, 267
Marcolini, Count, 181
Maria Theresa, Empress, 201
Marie Antoinette, 139, 151, 163
Marieberg china, 213, 215
Marie-Josèphe, Dauphine, 120
Maremma, 84
Marks, Chinese, 71, 74; forged, 33; least reliable identification, 33; Japanese, 79
Marseilles, china, 172
Martaban, Gulf of, 42
Martabani, ware, 42
Mason, china, 291, 292; Miles, 291

INDEX

Massié, 172
Masso bastardo, 88
Mathieu, 120
Matsura, 81
Manbrée, 205
Max Joseph III, Elector of Bavaria, 192
Mazarine blue, 64, 238, 272
Medallions, 91, 98, 299
Medici, 8; china, 92
Mehlhorn, J. G. 215
Meissen, 179
Melchior, Johann Peter, 191, 193
Mennecy-Villeroy, 36, 91; china, 115-119, 137; flowers, 214, 228; factory, 149
Mérault, 147
Menlau, 158
Middle Colonies, 4
Mikawachi, 75
"Mild" porcelain, 18
Ming, "blue and white", 48; Dynasty, 39, 44-50; Emperors, 39, 40; period, 53
Minton china, 278; Thomas, 278
Modelled, figures, 81, 191; flowers, 89; ornament, 109
Modellers, Sèvres, 147
Mohammedan blue, 47, 48
de Mol, 208
Moncloa, china, 177
Mongol Dynasty, 39, 43, 44
Monograms, 148
Monsieur, Fabrique de, à Clignancourt, 161-163
Monte Carlo, 88
Morden College, Blackheath, 223

Morris, George Anthony, 295; Henry, 284
Mortlock, 289
"*Mosaik*" borders, 189, 192
Moulded, decoration, 245; ornament, 282; patterns, 226
Moulding, process of, 130
Moulmein, 42
Mugs, 2
Müller, Frantz, 215, 216
Munich, 193
Museum, curators, 32, 36; use of, 32
Mythological subjects, 110

N

Nabushima, china, 75, 77, 78, 80
Nadin, Mr., 268
Nagasaki, 75
Nankin, 45
Nantgarw, china, 280-282, 288, 289, 290; factory, 273
Naples, 88, 90, 95
Napoleon, 141
Nast, 165
Naudeck, 192, 193
Neo-Classic, contours, 144; influence, 36; style, 35; *motifs*, 89, 91; taste, 97; trend, 244
Neo-Grec, contour, 35; influence, 36; style, 89
New College, Oxford, 42
"New Canton", 220, 224
New England, 45
New Hall, 258, 261; china, 264-266

INDEX

New Jersey, china, 296
New York, 4, 5; china, 297
Niderviller, china, 169-171
Nieuwe Amstel, 208
de Noailles, Maréchal, 168
North Cambridge, china, 294
Nymphenburg, china, 192-194; palace, 193
Nyon, china, 205

O

"Old Japan" pattern, 184, 227, 229, 238
Oporto, china, 177
Oriental, chinaware, 10, 38-82, 241, 256; influence, 124, 237; porcelain, 19, 235, 237; shapes, 89, 108, 117, 236; decoration, 108
Orléans, china, 132, 133; Duc d', 106, 110; Fabrique du Duc d', 165
d'Osson, Marquis, 155
Oude Amstel, 208, 209, 210
Oude Loosdrecht, 208, 209
Owari, china, 75, 77
Oxford, Journal, 241

P

du Pacquier, Claude, 201, 203
Padova, 102
Pai Ting, 43
Pajon, 147
Pardoe, Thomas, 281

Paris, china, 151-153; factories, 101, 156, 290; porcelain making 103; merchants, 9
Parrot design, 277
Passau, china materials, 188, 195, 197
Peacock design, 277
Pélissier, Pierre, 110
Penn, William, 6
Pennington, Seth, 253
Pennsbury, 6
Pennsylvania Museum, 296, 297
Penthièvre, Duc de, 128
Peony design, 277
Percier, 148
Père d'Entrecolles, letters of, 54, 62
Perforations, 26, 27
Perrotin, 147
Persia, 41, 42; Persian, Gulf, 10; *motifs,*, 276; underglaze blue, 47
Peterinck, 130
Petuntse, 17, 18, 20, 53, 74, 75
Pewter, 2, 3
"Pheasant and border" pattern, 238
Philadelphia, 4, 5, 6; china, 294, 296, 297-299
Pigalle, 147
Pinxton, china, 266, 267; Manor, 266
Pithou, 147
Pitt, Thomas, of Boconnoc, 259
Plymouth, china, 258-260
Podmore, R., 240, 254
Polish, china, 219

INDEX

Polychrome, decoration, 49, 50; painting, 118
Pomatum pots, 113, 116
Pompadour, Madame de, 121, 128, 134, 135
"Pompeian", china, 99; Pompeian, manner, 157, 159; *motifs*, 91, 92, 148, 157, 159
Pompeii, 98, 99, 277
Pontchartrain, M. de, 103
Popincourt, Fabrique de la Rue, china, 165
Porcelain, "artificial", 19; body, 15, 18; casting, 23; Chinese manufacturing, 39-52; different sorts, 16; development of, 43-52; distinguishing properties, 15, 16; moulding, 23; glaze, 15; nature of, 14; test, 15; translucence, 15; whiteness, 15
Portici, china, 95; Villa Reale, 96
Portland, Duke of, 108
Portrait busts, Sèvres, 147
Porto Ferraio, 88
Portuguese china, 176, 177
Poterat, Louis, 103, 104, 106
Potter, 112
Pourcelaine de Sinant, 8
Pouyat, 173
Powder-blue, 52, 64, 227, 246
Prunus blossoms, 63, 90, 91, 109, 226, 227; sprigs, 125

Q

Queen Anne, 105; Charlotte, 268; Elizabeth, 8; Mary, 4, 10

R

Randall, Thomas Martin, 288, 289, 290, 291
Regulations, anti-polychrome, 118, 119
Reichard, 187
Reid & Co., 253
La Reine, Fabrique de, 163, 164; "Porcelaine à", 163
Reserved panels, 146
Resonance, 52
Restrictive edicts, 154
Reticulations, 131
Reverend, Charles, 103
Ribbings, moulded, 192
"Rice-flower" Ting, 43; rice-grain decoration, 27, 46, 47
Richelieu, Duc de, Memoirs, 121
Ridgway, china, 291, 292
Rims, 34
Ringler, Joseph Jacob, 192, 193, 197
Risampei, 74, 79
Robert, J. G., 172
Robillard, 205
Rockingham, china, 285-287; Marquis of, 285; "Rockingham green", 286
Rococo, contour, 35; influence, 36, 236; manner, 94, 117, 183, 192; mode, 144; period, 35; taste, 97; scrolls, 192; type, 89
Roman, *motifs*, 148; porcelain, 102
Rose, John, 269, 271
Rose du Barry, 145; *Pompadour*, 145, 272, 291
Rosset, 147

INDEX

Rouen, 108, 117; china, 103, 104, 106
Rue, de Bondy, china, 164; de Reuilly, Fabrique de la, 160, 161; Thiroux, 163, 164
Ruffinger, 159
Russian, china, 218, 219
Royal Crown Derby Porcelain Co., 248

S

Saint-Amand-les-Eaux, china, 151
Saint Cloud, china, 36, 87, 103, 105-110, 115, 118, 235; château de, 106
Saint Lazare, faubourg de, 155
Saint Petersburg, china, 218, 219
Salopian china, 253; Salopian China Warehouse, 269
San Ts'ai, colour scheme, 50
Sapphire blue, 47
Saxony, 13, 86, 93; Elector of, 120, 178; porcelain, 124
Scale blue, 246, 276
"Scattered flower" decoration, 114, 185, 228; and insect, 169
Sceaux, china, 91, 127-129, 149
Schaerbeek, 211, 212
Schoelcher, 156
Sculptors, Sèvres, 247
Sea-weed patterns, 276
Sesto, 84
Sèvres, china, 18, 19, 90, 117, 118, 119, 133-149; influence, 238; "jewelled", 148; imitations, 290; manner, 272
Shell salt cellars, 98

Shu fu yao, 43
Siam, King of, 9
Silesia, china materials, 188
Silver, 2, 3
Sioux, 147
Slip, casting, 23; luting, 23, 27; painting, 27
Smalt, 54
Soapstone, 54; body, Worcester, 243
"Soft paste" porcelain, 13, 19, 20; Chinese, 53, 54; enamel colours, on, 29; manner of fracture, 19; materials, 20; translucence, 19; whiteness, 19
Sonnenschein, 206
Soulavie, 121
South, the, 4
Southwark china, 294-296
Spanish and Portuguese china, 176, 177
Spengler, 206
Spode china, 273-278; Josiah the Elder, 273, 274; Josiah the Second, 274, 275; "Old Spode" 273, 274; "Stone China", 276, 277
Sprimont, Nicholas, 231, 233, 234, 235, 249
Statuettes, 23, 116, 123, 133, 195, 197, 201, 218; Chinese, 56
Steatite, 54
Stölzel, Samuel, 201
"Stone China", Spode, 276, 277
Strasburg, 101, 153, 198; china, 166-169; corporation, 166; factory, 167, 168; faïence, 169

INDEX

Stratford-le-Bow, 220
Strawberry Hill, 11
Swansea china, 282-285, 288, 289; factory, 273, 280; "Swansea roses", 272
Swedish china, 213-215
Swiss china, 205, 206
"Sultan of Babylon", 8
Sung, Dynasty, 39, 41-43; factories, 44; period, 52
Symbolism, in decoration, 71
Symbols, 67, 71, 72, 73

T

Table-services, 130, 131
Tankards, 2, 3
Tea, and coffee equipages, 263, 281; drinking, 2, 3, 7; equipage, 3, 7; "tea tackle", 3, 225
Teapots, types of, 35
Têhua, factory, 44, 45
Throwing, process of, 130
Ting Chou, 43; *Ting yao*, 43, 44, 46
Tokuemon, 75
Torino, 101
Torksey china, 266, 267
Tortoise-shell grounds, 146
Touque, 8
Tournay, china, 129-132, 210, 211
Trade, Persian and Indian, 50
Transfer printing, 190, 229, 245, 257, 269, 276
Translucence, 52
Treviso, china, 102
Trumbull-Prime Collection, 296

Tucker china, 297-299; Benjamin, 297; William Ellis, 297
Tunstall, 261, 264
Turner, Thomas, 268, 269
Tschirnhausen, 178, 179
"Tyger and rock" pattern, 238
Tyrolese *motifs*, 90

U

Underglaze, blue, 28, 47, 90; blue painting, origin of, 47; colours, 24, 27, 28; green, 28; red, 28, 48, 49; rose, 28

V

Valenciennes, china, 173, 174
Van Hysum, flowers, 276
Vaume, J. S. 211
Vaux, china, 158
Vegetable-shaped dishes, 237
Venice, 8; china, 92-95; Venetian *motifs*, 94
Versailles, 106, 137, 138, 139; palace of, 9
Vezzi, china, 92, 93; factory, 218
Victoria and Albert Museum, 8, 108
Vienna, 85, 86, 87, 90; china, 201-203
de Villeroy, Duc, 115
Vincennes, 87, 115, 117, 118; china, 119-127; château de, 119; factory, 141
Vincennes (Hannong) china, 153-155
Vinovo china, 101, 102
Volpato, 102

W

Walker, 282, 283; Walker, Brown, Aldred and Richman, 255
Wall, Dr. John, 240, 242
Wallace Collection, 146
Wallendorf, 200
Walpole, Horace, 11, 12
Wandhelein, Karl, 85, 86
Wan Li, three-colour scheme, 49, 50; five-colour scheme, 49, 50
Warehouse, Chelsea, 233
Warham, Archbishop, 42; Bowl, 42
Warmstry House, 240, 242
Watteau, 118, 185, 209, 238, 246
Weatherby, 221, 223
Wedgwood, Aaron, 251; cameos, 91; china, 279, 280; Josiah, 261
Weesp china, 207, 208, 209
Wegeli, Wilhelm Caspar, 187, 190
Wellington, Duke of, 177
"Wheatsheaf and pheasant", patterns, 238
"White" Ting, 43
William and Mary, 4

Williams, Sir Charles Hanbury, 236, 237
"Willow pattern", 292; Caughley, 269, 270
"Wirksworth china, 258, 287, 288
Worcester, 34, 90; china, 240-247; Cheapside Warehouse, 242 painters, 272; Worcester Royal Porcelain Company, 243; Worcester Tonkin Manufacture, 240; workmen and decorators, 257
"Worm sprig", 272
"Wreathing", 262
"*Wu Ts'ai*, Wan Li, colour scheme, 50

Y

Young, W. Weston, 280, 281
St. Yrieix, kaolin mines, 89, 143, 170
Yüan Dynasty, 39, 43, 44

Z

Zurich china, 602